ON THE ROAD TO BABADAG

ALSO BY ANDRZEJ STASIUK
in English translation

WHITE RAVEN

NINE

FADO

ON THE ROAD TO
BABADAG

Travels in the Other Europe

Andrzej Stasiuk

Translated from the Polish by Michael Kandel

Harvill Secker
LONDON

Published by Harvill Secker 2011

2 4 6 8 10 9 7 5 3 1

First published with the title *Jadąc do Babadag* in 2004
by Czarne, Wołowiec, Poland

First published in Great Britain in 2011 by
HARVILL SECKER
Random House
20 Vauxhall Bridge Road
London SW1V 2SA

www.randomhouse.co.uk

Addresses for companies within The Random House Group Limited can be found at:
www.randomhouse.co.uk/offices.htm

The Random House Group Limited Reg. No. 954009

A CIP catalogue record for this book is available from the British Library

ISBN 9781846550546

Map by Jacques Chazaud

This publication has been funded by the
Book Institute—the © POLAND Translation Program

Portions of this book have been previously published in slightly different form: "That Fear" in
The Wall in My Head, a Words without Borders Anthology, Open Letter Books, 2009; and
an excerpt from "Description of a Journey through East Hungary to Ukraine" in *Orientations,*
edited by Wendy Bracewell and Alex Drace-Francis, Central European University Press, 2009

Photo credits: Frontispiece, "Romanians in Warsaw" © Witold Krassowski / ekpictures. Page
163, "Travelling blind violinist, Abony, Hungary, 1921", Kertész, André (1894–1985) © André
Kertész — RMN, © Ministère de la culture–Médiathèque du Patrimoine, Dist. RMN

Printed and bound in the UK by
CPI Mackays, Chatham, ME5 8TD

For M.

Contents

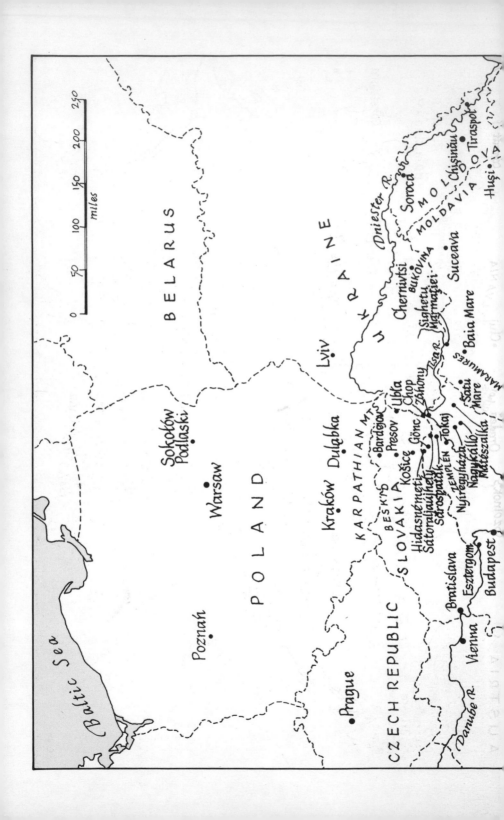

BELARUS

Baltic Sea

POLAND

Poznań

Warsaw

Sokołów
Podlaski

Kraków Dulębka

Prague

CZECH REPUBLIC

Vienna

Danube R.

Bratislava

Esztergom

Budapest

SLOVAKIA

KARPATHIAN MT.

Bardiov

Presov

BESKID

Košice

Hidasnémeti

Sátoraljaújhely

Sárospatak

ZEMPLÉN

Tokaj

Gönc

Nyíregyháza

Nagykálló

Mátészalka

UKRAINE

Lviv

Ubla

Chop

Záhony

Zsar.

MARAMURES

Satu
Mare

Baia Mare

Sighetu
Marmatiei

Bukovina

Chernivtsi

Suceava

Dniester R.

Soroca

MOLDAVIA

Chișinău

Tiraspol

Huși

miles

0   50   100   150   200   250

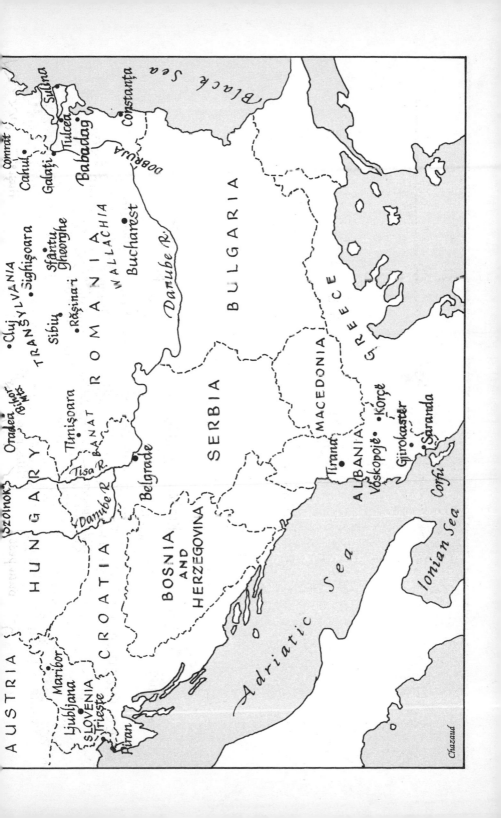

ON THE ROAD TO BABADAG

That Fear

YES, IT'S ONLY that fear, those searchings, tracings, tellings whose purpose is to hide the unreachable horizon. It's night again, and everything departs, disappears, shrouded in black sky. I am alone and must remember events, because the terror of the unending is upon me. The soul dissolves in space like a drop in the sea, and I am too much a coward to have faith in it, too old to accept its loss; I believe it is only through the visible that we can know relief, only in the body of the world that my body can find shelter. I would like to be buried in all those places where I've been before and will be again. My head among the green hills of Zemplén, my heart somewhere in Transylvania, my right hand in Chornohora, my left in Spišská Belá, my sight in Bukovina, my sense of smell in Răşinari, my thoughts perhaps in this neighbourhood . . . This is how I imagine the night when the current roars in the dark and the thaw wipes away the white stains of snow. I recall those days when I took to the road so often, pronouncing the names of far cities like spells: Paris, London, Berlin, New York, Sydney . . . places on the map for me, red or black points lost in the expanse of green and sky blue. I never asked for a pure sound. The histories that went with the cities, they were all fictions. They filled the hours and alleviated the boredom. In those distant times, every trip resembled flight. Stank of panic, desperation.

One day in the summer of '83 or '84, I reached Słubice by foot and saw Frankfurt across the river. It was late afternoon. Humid blue-grey air hung over the water. East German high-rises and factory stacks looked dismal and unreal. The sun was a dull smudge, a flame about to gutter. The other side — completely dead, still, as if after a great fire. Only the river had something human about it — decay, fish slime — but I was sure that over there the smell would be stopped. In any case I turned, and that same evening I headed back, east. Like a dog, I had sniffed an unfamiliar locale, then moved on.

I had no passport then, of course, but it never entered my head to try to get one. The connection between those two words, *freedom* and *passport*, sounded grand enough but was completely unconvincing. The nuts and bolts of *passport* didn't fit *freedom* at all. It's possible that there, outside Gorzów, my mind had fixed on the formula: There's freedom or there isn't, period. My country suited me fine, because its borders didn't concern me. I lived inside it, in the centre, and that centre went where I went. I made no demands on space and expected nothing from it. I left before dawn to catch the yellow-and-blue train to Żyrardów. It pulled out of East Station, crossed downtown, gold and silver ribbons of light unfurling in the windows. The train filled with men in worn coats. Most got off at the Ursus factory and walked towards its frozen light. Dozens, hundreds, barely visible in the dark; only at the gate did the mercury light hit them, as if they were entering a huge cathedral. I was practically alone. The next passengers got on somewhere in Milanówek, in Grodzisk, more women in the group, because Żyrardów was textiles, fabrics, tailoring, that sort of thing. Black tobacco, the sour smell of plastic lunch bags mixed with the reek of cheap perfume and soap. The night came free of the ground, and in the growing crack of the day you could see the huts of the crossing guards, who held orange caution flags; cows standing belly-deep in mist; the last, forgotten lights in houses. Żyrardów was red, all brick. I got off with everyone else. I was shiftless here, but whatever I did was in tribute to those who had to get up before the sun, for without them the world would have been no more than a play of colour or a meteorological drama. I drank strong tea in a station bar and took the train back, to go north in a day or two, or east, without apparent purpose.

One summer I was on the road seventy-two hours nonstop. I spoke with truck drivers. As they drove, their words flowed in ponderous monologue from a vast place — the result of fatigue and lack of sleep. The landscape outside the cabin window drew close, pulled away, to freeze at last, as if time had given up. Dawn at a roadside somewhere in Puck, thin clouds stretching over the gulf. Out from under the clouds slipped the bright knife edge of the rising day, and the cold smell of the sea came woven with the screech of gulls. It's entirely possible I reached the beach itself then, it's entirely possible that after a couple of hours of sleep somewhere by the road a delivery van stopped and a guy said he was driving through the country, north to south, which was far more appealing than the tedium of tide in, tide out, so I jumped on the crate and, wrapped in a blanket, dozed beneath the fluttering tarp, and my doze was visited by landscapes of the past mixed with fantasy, as if I were looking at things as an outsider. Warsaw went by as a foreign city, and I felt no tug at my heart.

Grit in my teeth: the dust raised from the floorboards. I crossed the country as one crosses an unmapped continent. Between Radom and Sandomierz, terra incognita. The sky, trees, houses, earth — all could be elsewhere. I moved through a space that had no history, nothing worth preserving. I was the first man to reach the foot of the Góry Pieprzowe, Pepper Hills, and with my presence everything began. Time began. Objects and landscapes started their aging only from the moment my eye fell on them. At Tarnobrzeg I rapped on the sheet metal of the driver's cabin; impressed by the size of a sulphur outcrop, I wanted him to stop. Giant power shovels stood at the bottom of a pit. It didn't matter where they came from. From the sky, if you like, to bite into the land, to chew their way into and through the planet and let an ocean surge up the shaft to drown everything here and turn the other side to desert. The stink of inferno rose, and I could not tear my gaze from the monstrous hole that spoke of the grave, piled corpses, the chill of hell. Nothing moved, so this could have been Sunday, assuming there was a calendar in such a place.

This sequence of images was not Poland, not a country; it was a pretext. Perhaps we become aware of our existence only when we feel on our skin the touch of a place that has no name, that connects us to the earliest time, to all the dead, to prehistory, when the mind first stood apart from the world, still unaware that it was orphaned. A hand stretches from the window of a truck, and through its fingers flows the earliest time. No, this was not Poland; it was the original loneliness. I could have been in Timbuktu or on Cape Cod. On my right, Baranów, "the pearl of the Renaissance", I must have passed it a dozen times in those days, but it never occurred to me to stop and have a look at it. Any place was good, because I could leave it without regret. It didn't even need a name. Constant expense, constant loss, waste such as the world has never seen, prodigality, shortage, no gain, no profit. The morning on the coast, Wybrzeże, the evening in a forest by the San River; men over their steins like ghosts in a village bar, apparitions frozen in mid-gesture as I watched. I remember them that way, but it could have been near Legnica, or forty kilometres north-east of Siedlec, and a year before or after in some village or other. We lit an evening fire, and in the flickering light, young guys from the village emerged; probably the first time in their lives they were seeing a stranger. We were not real to them, or they to us. They stood and stared, their enormous belt buckles gleaming in the dark: a bull's head, or crossed Colt revolvers. Finally they sat near, but the conversation smacked of hallucination. Even the wine they brought couldn't bring us down to earth. At dawn they got up and left. It's possible that a day or two later I stood for ten hours in Złoczów, Zolochiv, and no one gave me a lift. I remember a hedgerow and the stone balustrade of a little bridge, but I'm not sure about the hedgerow, it could have been elsewhere, like most of what lies in memory, things I pluck from their landscape, making my own map of them, my own fantastic geography.

One day I went to Poznań in a pickup truck. The driver shouted, "Hop on. Just watch out for the fish!" I lay among enormous plastic bags filled with water. Inside swam fish, no larger than a fingernail. Hundreds, thousands of fish. The water was ice-cold, so I had to wrap myself in a blanket. In Września the fish turned towards Gniezno, so at dawn I was alone again on the empty road. The sun had not risen yet, and it was cold. It's possible that from Poznań I went on to Wrocław. Most likely heading for Wybrzeże a day or two later, or Bieszczady. If towards Bieszczady, around Osława, in the middle of a forest,

I saw a naked man. He was standing in a river and washing himself. Seeing me, he simply turned his back. But if it was Wybrzeże, then I was at Jastrzębia Góra, and it was evening, and I walked barefoot on a forsaken beach in the direction of Karwia and saw, against the red sky, the black megaliths of Stonehenge. I had nowhere to sleep and it was as if those ruins had fallen out of the sky. Fashioned from planks, plywood, burlap. Such things happened in those days. Someone built it and left it, no doubt a television crew. I crawled through a hole into one of the vertical pillars of rock and lay down.

The Slovak Two Hundred

THE BEST MAP I have is the Slovak two hundred. It's so detailed that once it helped me out of an endless cornfield somewhere at the foot of the Zemplén Mountains. On this huge sheet, which contains the entire country, even footpaths are shown. The map is frayed and torn. On the flat image of land and little water, the void peeks through in places. I always take it with me, inconvenient as it is, requiring so much room. The thing is like a talisman, because after all I know the way to Košice, then on to Sátoraljaújhely, without it. But I take the map, interested precisely in its deterioration. It wore out first at the folds. The breaks and cracks have made a new grid, one clearer than the cartographic crosshatching in light blue. Cities and villages gradually faded from existence as the map was folded and unfolded, stuffed into the glove compartment of a car or into a backpack. Michalovce is gone, Stropkov too, and a hole of nonbeing encroaches on Uzhhorod. Soon Humenné will disappear, Vranov nad Topľou wear away, Cigánd on the Tisa crumble.

It was only a couple of years ago that I began to pay this kind of attention to maps. I used to treat them as ornaments or, maybe, anachronistic symbols that had survived in our era of hard information and full disclosure from every corner of the earth. It started with the war in the Balkans. For us, everything starts or ends with a war, so there's no surprise there. I simply wanted to know what the artillery was aiming at, what the pilots were seeing from their planes. The newspaper maps were too neat, too sterile: the name of a region and, next to the name, the stylized flash of an explosion. No rivers, terrain, topography, no indication of land or culture, just a bare name and a boom. I searched for Vojvodina, because it was nearest. War always rouses men, even when it frightens them. Red flame along the Danube — Belgrade, Batajnica, Novi Sad, Vukovar, Sombor — twenty kilometres from the Hungarian border and maybe four hundred and fifty from my house. Only a real map could tell us when to start listening for the thunder. Neither television nor newspaper can chart such a concrete thing as distance.

That may have been why the destruction in my map of Slovakia represented, for me, destruction in general. The red flames along the Danube begin to eat the paper, travel from Vojvodina, from the Banat, take hold in the Hungarian Lowlands, claim Transylvania, to spill finally to the edge of the Carpathians.

All this will vanish, go out like a lightbulb, leaving only an empty sphere that must fill with new forms, but I have no interest in them, because they will be an even more pathetic version of the everyday pretending to be sacred, of poverty gussied up as wealth, of rubbish that parades and magnifies itself, plastic that breaks first thing yet lasts practically forever, like stuff in garbage dumps, until fire consumes it, because the other elements are helpless against it. These were my thoughts as we drove through Leordina, Vişeu de Jos, Vişeu de Sus, towards the mountain pass at Prislop. Almost no cars on the road, but people had come out in the hundreds. They stood, sat, strolled, all in the dignity of their Sunday best. They emerged from their homes of wood with roof shingles like fish scales. They joined as drops join to make a rivulet, and finally spread in a broad wave to the shoulders of the road, spread across the asphalt and down to the valley. White shirts, dark skirts and jackets, hats and kerchiefs. Through the open window, the smell of mothballs, holiday, and cheap perfume. In Vişeu de Sus, there were so many people we had to come to a complete stop and wait for the crowd to part. We stopped, but our journey did not. The festive gathering enveloped us, took us against the current of time. No one sold anything or bought anything. Or at least we didn't see it. In the distance rose the dun massif of Pietrosul. Snow at the top. This was the third day of Orthodox Easter, and the occasion marked the pleasant inertia of matter. Human bodies surrendered to gravity, as if to return to the primal condition in which the spirit was not yet imprisoned, and did not struggle, did not attempt to take on any kind of feeble likeness.

After Moisei we stopped. In the desolation by the road sat four old villagers. They pointed far ahead, at something on the opposite forested slope. We understood: a monastery there. Among the trees we could make out the top of a tower. The people simply sat and looked in that direction, as if their sitting served as participation in the solemn liturgy. They urged us to go there. But we were in a hurry. We left them half reclining, motionless, watching, listening. They may have been waiting for a bell to toll, for something to move in the frozen holiday.

• • •

All this would vanish. At night on the main street in Gura Humorului, fifteen-year-old boys wanted to sell us German licence
plates. They assured us that the plates were from a BMW. All this
would be gone, it would become part of the rest of the world.
Yes, that first day in Romania the whole sorrow of the continent
weighed on me. I saw decline everywhere and could not imagine
renaissance. The attendant at the petrol station in Cimpulung
carried a gun in a holster. He appeared out of the dusk and told
us in mime that he had nothing for us. But a kilometre farther,
another station was lit up like a carnival in the ancient night.
They had everything there, but the pour spouts were stuck in
the necks of plastic cola bottles. Men came up with one or two
bottles, then went into the darkness to find their dead vehicles.

Maramureş was behind us. So was the mountain gap covered
with a hard crust of snow, and that swarthy man in the old Audi
with German plates. He opened the boot and took out a child's
motorcycle, a miniature Suzuki or Kawasaki, sat a two-year-
old kid on it, and took picture after picture. An icy wind blew
through the gap, and there was no one there but us. Nothing but
a cold, beautiful waste, the sun rolling over the marsh between
Carei and Satu Mare, and I heard the click of the camera, saw
the boy's grave face, red cheeks, then the father put the toy away,
and they continued down, west, no doubt to their home. We left
also, because on that wind-whistling height, hands turned numb
and cheeks hurt. We descended by switchbacks to the Bistriţa
valley, into darkening air.

I see now how little I remember, how everything that happened
could have happened elsewhere. No trip from the land of King
Ubu to the land of Count Dracula will hold memories you can
rely on later, as for example you can rely on Paris, Stonehenge,

or Saint Mark's Square. Sighetu Marmaţiei, more than anything, ended up unreal. We drove through it quickly, without stopping, and I can say nothing about its shape, except that it looked like a sophisticated fiction. In any case we passed it in no time, and once again green mountains rose on the horizon, and I immediately felt regret and longing. Exactly as on awakening, when we are spurred by the desire to return to the world of dreams, which relieves us of our freedom of will and gives in its place the freedom, absolute, of the unexpected. This happens in places rarely touched by the traveller's eye. Observation irons out objects and landscapes. Destruction and decline follow. The world gets used up, like an old abraded map, from being seen too much.

We drove to the Sinistra district. Everything here belonged to the mountain riflemen, to Colonel Puiu Borcan, and, when he died, to Izolda Mavrodin-Mahmudia, also holding the rank of colonel and called Coca for short. From the Baba Rotunda Pass we had a view of Pop Ivan; in the valley crawled narrow-gauge, wood-burning locomotives. The inhabitants of Sinistra wore military dog tags on their chests. Everyone who came here and stayed was given a new name. From time to time, Coca would organize an ambush atop Pop Ivan against Mustafa Mukkerman, who carried mutton by truck from somewhere in Ukraine to Thessaloniki or even Rhodos, but besides mutton in the refrigerator he sometimes carried people in heavy coats. Comrades from Poland kept Coca informed about Mukkerman's movements. He was half Turk, half German, and weighed three hundred kilograms.

Diluted denatured alcohol was used here to dry mushrooms, and it was drunk with the fermented juice of forest fruits. The frosted glass for the Sinistra prison was made by Gabriel Dunka in his workshop: he frosted a pane by putting it in a sandbox and walking on it with his bare feet for hours. He was thirty-seven and a dwarf. One rainy day he picked up a naked Elvira Spiridon in his delivery van and for the first time in his life smelled a woman's body, but loyalty triumphed over desire and he turned her in, because it was only by accident that she hadn't climbed into Mukkerman's truck.

All this supposedly took place near Sighetu Marmaţiei, but I learned about it only two years later, in Ádám Bodor's *Sinistra District*, and the story has pursued me since. Pursued me and replaced the flat space on the map. Once again, the visible pales before the narrated. Pales but does not disappear. It only loses its force, its intolerable obviousness. This is a special quality of auxiliary countries, of second-order, second-tier peoples: the ephemeral tale in different versions, the distorted mirror, magic lantern, mirage, phantom that mercifully sneaks in between what is and what ought to be. The self-irony that allows you to play with your personal fate, to mock it, parrot it, turning a defeat into heroic-comic legend and a lie into something that has the shape of salvation.

There was no water where we finally turned in for the night. The manager took a flashlight and led us down cold corridors. He explained that the pump was broken and the mechanic was three weeks now en route from Suceava or Iaşi. He explained that the man who lived in this house was a foreigner, had come from far away, and drank the local cheap vodka to cope with his loneliness, so he didn't maintain the place, but the mechanic was certain to arrive soon.

It was cold. We lay down in our clothes and turned out the light. The Romanian night entered through the window. I tried to sleep but, instead of going with the flow of time and sleep, swam upstream in my thoughts, back through that long day after we crossed the border at Petea. Black watchtowers stood on the baking plain. Soon Satu Mare began, walls peeling from age and heat, the shade of huge trees along the streets, and church cupolas in extended green vistas. Hungary was behind us, the lowland sadness of Erdőhát was behind us, and although it was equally flat across the border, I felt a definite change, the air had a different smell, and, with each kilometre, the light of the sky grew more ruthless. The distant shadow of the Carpathians on the horizon marked the limit to that blaze, framed it, and we drove on through a thick suspension of sun. Horse-drawn carts on the highway, the animals covered with sweat. Vintage automobiles carrying on their roofs pyramids of bags stuffed with wool. The dark gleaming bodies of people. A strong wind. Maybe that's why their houses looked so poor and impermanent on the great plain.

I lay in my unheated room and went over all this, just as now I am trying to remember that room and the morning when I rose and went outside to see that there had been a frost overnight and that its white was disappearing in patches of sun. People on the way to their wells with buckets looked at me, pretending that they weren't, that they were going about their business, that they were blinded by the light of the new day. Now, remembering, I see that a story could have begun exactly there. For example: "On that day, when I saw my father for the last time, because three men put him in a car and took him somewhere, on that day I touched the breast of Andrea Nopritz." Or: "On that day, Gizella Weisz set out, and everyone praised her. Even great Comrade Onaga looked deep into her eyes and said, I understand, our comrade has noble and lofty plans." On that day, that morning, the man who broke the pump might have appeared. He might have approached by the narrow village street between the wooden fences to ask what I was doing in front of his house. Swollen, with bloodshot eyes, with rumpled clothes, a kind of rustic Geoffrey Firmin leaning nonchalantly on a railing demanding to know what the hell brought me to this Pîrteştii de Jos or Pîrteştii de Sus, to the house where he lived, to observe him in this state at six thirty in the morning, as over their fences Germanized Poles were watching, and Romanianized Germans, and Polonized Ukrainians, the whole mongrel bunch from abroad, that golden dream of the followers of the cult of multiculturalism . . . A cynical monologue might have ensued, or a neurotic monologue, as buckets clattered in wells among the various morning noises appropriate to that backwater locale, the cackling of hens, the hewing of firewood, the shuffling and slapping of bovine backsides, and the 6:35 rusty passenger train to Suceava trundling through the valley. That would make a good beginning for the development of a tale, the unfolding of a fate, a trip back in time, when events shine brighter the more removed they are from today. But the man of the broken pump never approached me, and his life has remained in the realm of guesswork — that is to say, of complete freedom.

So I went up to an actual man, who was standing quietly by his fence and smoking. We started a conversation. The passenger train to Suceava was in fact trundling through the valley. The man, about sixty, stocky, in a faded twill suit, resembled most of the men I'd seen in my life. The smoke from his cigarette was blue, then grey, then gone. He talked. I listened and nodded. He said times were bad, had been better under Ceauşescu: there was justice then, equality, work, and order in the streets. I knew this tale but listened to it once again — avidly, because there is something beautiful in our travelling so far from home and seeing that so little changes. He told about the night visits of Securitate and, in the same breath, about the factories now shut. I asked him what he knew of the famous resettlement, in which seven thousand villages disappeared and their people were moved to concrete apartment blocks. Yes, he knew, had even seen the planes used to take the photographs that helped in the planning of that operation, but no price is too high to pay for justice and equality. I said nothing, for what could I say, seeing as I had come here, to this fence, as a visible sign of inequality, that I had come and would depart whenever I liked, leaving the old man in the wrecked suit holding a cheap cigarette on a rough road between two ancient houses made of wood, which had survived by some whim of history, though their inhabitants hadn't particularly wanted them to survive. I kept my mouth shut and listened to his pining for the dictatorship. Power must manifest itself in a concrete figure, and once it achieves that embodiment, it abides beyond good and evil. We are all orphaned children of some emperor or despot. I gave the man a Sobieski Super Light. The sun had now climbed above the green line of the hills, and I felt that my freedom to come and go meant shit here, was worth nothing.

We said goodbye, and I went for a bucket to draw water from a well.

It's night, rain is falling, and I am remembering all this for the hundredth time. Ádám Bodor and the Sinistra district are a transparency superimposed over an actual Maramureş and Bukovina, and to both clings the flickering and vital substance of my thoughts, my love, my fear. Sinistra won't let me sleep. On the shelf, side by side, *A History of Ukraine*, *A History of Bulgaria*, *A History of Hungary*, with many smaller books and accounts, along with the *History of Slovakia* and Eliade's *The Romanians* — but to no effect. I read them all before bed and finally drift off, but not once have I dreamt of Jan Hunyadi or Czar Ferdinand, of Vasile Nicola Ursu, called Horea, or Vlad Țepeș, of Father Hlinka or Taras Shevchenko. I dream, at most, of the enigmatic Sinistra district. Of the uniforms of non-existent armies. Of old wars in which no one truly perishes. I dream of white limestone ruins and moustached border guards, and when you cross those borders, everything changes and nothing changes. I dream of banknotes with the portraits of heroes on one side and romantic windswept crags on the other. I dream of coins too. And of cigarette packs for cigarettes I never smoked. And of petrol stations on plains, all of them like the one in that suburb of the Slovenské Nové Mesto, and of Red Bull with the inscription *špeciálne vyvinutý pre obdobie zvýšenej psychickej alebo fyzyckej námahy*, "developed especially for periods of increased mental and physical exertion". I dream of mouldering watchtowers in wastes and cyclists taking their rusted bikes over hill after hill to places whose names can be said in at least three languages, and I dream of horse harnesses and people and food and hybrid landscapes and all the rest.

Yes, the rain falls on all these places, on Maramureș, on my dreams, on Sinistra, on Spišské Podhradie on that day, Friday, July 21, when we stopped at the muddy parking lot beside the Morgečanka. A one-floor building ran along the only street. We took a narrow pavement and came upon a yellow synagogue. Its facade was crowned by four spherical tin cupolas. The vaulted windows were all black and dead, as if they had been taken from a nineteenth-century factory. In the span between the place of worship and the houses you could see hills and the distant towers of Spišská Kapitula. On a slope above the town shone the white ruins of a castle, so large and bright they resembled a kind of atmospheric caprice, an angular stacking of cumuli or a mirage imported from the sky of a land that had long ceased to exist. A car went by, another, then stillness. The grey rear of a Škoda vanished in the green shade of trees, but it was really vanishing in time. Taking a tunnel dug into immobility. The road cut through the town as through a mountain, a foreign territory that graciously allowed such passage. From the low house at the turn, a dark, squat woman came out, tossed soapy water on the asphalt, and scrubbed away all trace of the vehicles.

A few steps on, I saw through a low open window the interior of a large room. Someone had begun work and stopped. A fresh brick wall across the centre. A TV on, somewhere in the back: blue flickering in the dimness. By the new wall, a billiard table. Several balls stopped in mid-play. It was too dark for me to see their colours. The smell of wet plaster and mildew. Beyond the wall, beyond the dark and the burble of the television, you could hear men's voices raised. Then I saw them, in a gap between the houses. They were arguing over an upturned wagon. One was turning a spoked wheel, another was gesturing, shaking his head: the thing was garbage, worthless, they had to start over. The men were dark, stocky, animated, as if their bodies did not feel the inertia around them, as if they inhabited another, weightless space. That was definitely it. They lived in the old Jewish quarter, at the edge of a Slovak town, at the foot of a Hungarian castle, so in order to exist and not disappear, they had had to create their own rules, their own special theory of relativity, and a gravity that would keep them on the surface of the earth and not let them fall into the interstellar void, into the vacuum of oblivion.

We went back to our car and drove on. The squat woman again came out of her house with her bowl of suds. The Morgečanka flowed below us on the right. On the left rose the ridge of Drevenik. Outside the town, on the slope, on terraces carved along the slope, stood their homes. Not the homes of others, not ancient homes, homes inherited, but their very own. Like children's drawings, so simple, small, and fragile. Like ideas only just forming. Fashioned of barely stripped pine logs, more poles than logs, not thicker than a man's arm, and with gable roofs all tarred. They were so modest, the most you could do in them was sit and wait as time elapsed between one event and the next. They leaned against each other, piled and climbing like a pueblo of wood. From the thin chimneys curled resinous smoke. The jumble of yards, rummage, the vivid conglomeration of stuff seemingly useless and exhausted covered the ground like post-industrial vegetation. It could have been the day in which they appeared or the day in which they departed. Below, along the shaded road, children played. The grown-ups stood and talked of grown-up matters, perhaps about the foreigners who passed through every now and then. Here everything belonged to these people. I had no idea that a space could be so unequivocally and unconditionally owned without doing it injury. A little farther on, quite alone, stood a girl in a red dress. Very pretty, she was looking to one side, in a direction in which not a thing was happening. I saw her for a moment; then, in the rear-view mirror, the red flame went out.

Răşinari

"INFESTED WITH LICE and placid, we should seek the company of animals, squat beside them for a thousand years, breathe the air of the stable not the laboratory, die from disease not medicine, keep within the borders of our wild and sink mildly into it."

All day, it blew from the south. Under the sky's blue glaze, the dry light etched black outlines on objects. On such days, the world is as delineated as a cut-out. Look too long in one place and you could go blind. The air carries a dazzle we are unaccustomed to here. The African, Mediterranean light flows over the Carpathian range and descends on the village. The landscape is stripped, transparent. In the leafless branches you can see abandoned nests. High up, along the edge of a meadow burned to bronze, a herd of cattle. Then they have vanished in the woods, where it's still, dark, and where green brambles spread. The animals retreat a few thousand years, leave our company, return to themselves, until in a day or two someone finds them and drives them home.

"We should seek the company of animals, squat beside them." I read this in July. In August, I went to see the village where Emil Cioran was born. Never able to accept that an idea is an abstract thing, I had to go to Răşinari. Across the Gorgons, across the Ukrainian and Romanian Bukovina, past Cluj and Sibiu, I reached the southern border of Transylvania. Right after the last houses of the village, the Carpathians began. Literally. The way was flat, then immediately you climbed by cattle path, stopping to catch your breath every several steps. To the north, in a grey mist, lay Transylvania. The steep, warmed meadows above Răşinari smelled of cow dung. It hadn't rained for many days, and the earth exuded its accumulated odours.

A few days later we witnessed the evening return from the pastures. Along the road from Păltiniş, in the red rays of the sun, came hundreds of cows and goats. Over the herds rose heat and stink. Grizzled, wide-horned cows led the way. People stood in the open gates of the paddocks and waited. All this took place in silence, without yelling, without pushing. The animals separated themselves from the herd and entered their pens. They disappeared in the twilight of shaded yards, and the carved stable doors closed after them in a very civilized way. Enormous buffalo shone like black metal. Two steps of theirs equalled a cow's three. They were monsters, demons. The wet, quilled muzzles brought to mind some distant, sensual mythology. In a jerky trot, the goats came last. Mottled and animated, both. Goat reek hung over the herd. The asphalt shone from cow slobber.

This was Răşinari, the town in which Emil Cioran was born and spent his first ten years. The sun fell vertically on the paved little streets, on the pastel houses, on the red husk of the roofs, and brought out the oldest smells. At first I didn't know what was hanging in the air, penetrating the walls, the bodies of passersby, and the chassis of old vehicles. Only after a couple of days did I realize that it was the mix of animal effluvia. From locked yards came pig shit; the soil between the cobblestones had collected a century of horse piss; wisps of the stable rose from innumerable harnesses; from the fields came the choking air of pasture, from the gutters the cesspool seep of barns and sties; and one day in the river I saw entrails floating. The current was carrying the opalescent, flickering red in the direction of Sibiu. From the mountains the wind brought the sharp, acrid smell of pens—a mélange of trampled herbs, sticky, fat fleece, and dried green balls of excrement like stones. And occasionally a thread of hickory smoke in the air, a whiff of fried onions, a puff of petrol fume.

"It would have been better for me had I never left this village. I'll never forget the day my parents put me on the cart that took me to the lyceum in town. That was the end of my beautiful dream, the destruction of my world."

Now a tram goes from Rășinari to Sibiu. The line loops at the edge of the village. You sit on the steps between the bar and the cobbler. In the bar they sell vodka that tastes of yeast; it's thirty-six per cent and cheap. Before the tram arrives, several men down a glass or two. Like that Gypsy we kept meeting for a few days in different places. Once he was waiting for a bus to Păltiniș; another time he was hanging around the station in Sibiu. A black felt hat on his head, a folded scythe and handle in his hands, an old knapsack on his back. It was August, haymaking time, and it's possible he was simply looking for work but couldn't find any or didn't want to, so he killed time, waiting for it all to pass, to end, so he could go back to wherever he came from.

Mornings and evenings we went to the pub on Nicolae Bălcescu Road. You enter down a few steps. Inside, the flies flit and the men sit. We drank coffee and brandy. You could take the same steps to the barber, where there was an antique barber's chair. The place was open late, to ten, eleven, and someone was always in the chair. We also drank beer, Ursus or Silva. From the street came the steady clop of horses. Sometimes, in the dark, you saw sparks from a horseshoe. Every drawn cart had a licence plate. The shops worked late into the night. We purchased salami, wine, bread, paprika, watermelon. When the sun set, the shops glowed like warm caves. Our pockets were full of thousand-lei banknotes with Mihai Eminescu on them and hundred-lei coins with Mihai the Brave on them.

"Now, at this moment, I should feel myself a European, a man of the West. But none of that; in my declining years, after a life in which I saw many nations and read many books, I reached the conclusion that the one who is right is the Romanian peasant. Who believes in nothing, who thinks that man is lost, can do nothing, that history will crush him. This ideology of the victim is my idea as well, my philosophy of history."

One evening we went down the mountain to the village. Rășinari lay in a valley filled to the brim with heat. I felt its animal proximity. The village gave off a golden blaze, but in the tangle of its side streets there was almost no light at all. The blinds, which during the day kept out the sun, now sealed the feeble light inside the homes. That's how it used to be, I thought. People didn't make unnecessary things; they wasted neither fire nor food.

Excess was the duty and privilege of kings. In the square before the Church of Saint Paraskeva, a pack of children had gathered. In the dark, the gleam of chrome from their bicycles. Eighty years ago, little Emil spent the last of his vacation in the shadow of this very shrine. It was August then too, evening, and the boys teased the girls. There just weren't as many bicycles then, and the smell of Hungarian rule still hung in the air, and a few people kept using the name Resinar or Städterdorf. He would be leaving the next day and would never return.

Today, across from my house, four men gather wood. They pull to the forest edge stumps of spruce, stump by stump. When they have three or four, they load them onto a cart. They work like animals — slowly, monotonously, performing the same movements and gestures performed one hundred, two hundred years ago. The downhill road is long and steep. They use stakes to stop the cart. Even braked, the wheels slide on the wet clay. Wrapped in their torn quilted jackets and cloaks, the men seem fashioned from the earth. It's raining. Among the few things that distinguish them from their fathers and forefathers are a chainsaw (Swedish) and disposable lighters. Well, and the cart is on tyres. All the rest has remained unchanged for two hundred, three hundred years. Their smell, effort, groans, existence follow a form that has endured since unrecorded time. These men are as primeval as the two bay horses in harness. Around them spreads a present as old as the world. At dusk, they finish and leave, their clothes steaming like the backs of the animals.

I went out on the veranda to look south again. A truly November dark there, but I was looking back, to last August, and my sight stretched across Bardejov, Sárospatak, Nagykálló, the Bihor

Mountains, Sibiu, to reach Rășinari on that day at three in the afternoon, when we descended, the black-blue clouds thickening behind us. We went down and down, finally to that mercilessly beshitted field on which stood and lay dozens of red, grey, and spotted cows. Below the field the village began. The first houses were makeshift, scattered, resembling more a camp than a settlement. Over the road and river rose a cliff with young birches; they clung to the vertical rock with the aid of some miracle. Several dozen metres over our heads, a solitary man felled saplings with an axe. Then he tied them together in a knot and let them fall. These sliding bundles knocked stones loose, and the rattling plummet echoed through the valley. At the bottom, women and children waited to pull all this across the river and pile it into wheelbarrows. They were in no hurry. Along the road lay blankets, a campfire, a mangled doll. Their home was a few dozen metres away, yet they had set up another shelter here. Near the fire lay the remains of a meal, plastic bottles, mugs, other things, but we didn't want to pry. One clump of saplings caught halfway down the cliff, and the man slowly lowered himself to free it.

Rain began to fall after we were back inside. I sat at an open window in the attic, listening to the patter on the roof and on the leaves of the grapevine that filled the yard below. The pale mountains in the south darkened like a soaked fabric. A herd of white goats took cover in a thicket. I reflected that he would now be eighty-nine and could be sitting where I sat. This house, after all, belonged to his family. Our host was Petru Cioran. He had Emil's books on his shelf, though I doubt that he ever opened them. Anyway, they were in French and English. He and his wife showed us washed-out photographs: This is Emil when he was eight, and this is Relu, his younger brother. The stocky fifty-year-old man was proud, but every day he ran his store. He got up early, put crates in the van, drove to town for merchandise. At breakfast, we had a shot of slivovitz. It smelled like moonshine, was as strong as pure alcohol, and went well with smoked pork, goat cheese, and paprika.

So Emil could have been sitting here instead of me, could have been watching the rain wet the sacks of cement piled on the platform of the van parked in the street. The pavement shines, the smoke from the chimneys disappears in the grey haze, the water in the gutters swells and gathers trash, and he has returned, as if he never left, and is merely an old man alone with his thoughts. He no longer has the strength to walk in the mountains, nor the wish to chat with the shepherds. He looks, he listens. Philosophy gradually assumes physical shape. It enters his body and destroys it. Paris and travelling were a waste. Without them, things would have gone on a little longer, and boredom would have taken a less sophisticated form. From the kitchen on the ground floor comes the smell of heated fat and the voices of the women. The grapevines gleam and rustle in the rain. Then, from the east, dusk arrives, and the men assemble in the shed by the store. After the long day, they will be tired and dirty. They'll want a bottle of yeast vodka. The woman selling it will give them a thick glass, and they'll finish off the bottle in fifteen minutes. He will hear their talk, which becomes louder and faster, and smell the smell of their bodies through the foliage. The first man will give off tar, the second smoke, the third goats in a stable at the threshold of spring, when the animals begin to reek of urine, musk, and rut. The third will get drunk the quickest, and his friends will hold him up, prop him against a wall, with no interruption in the talk. A pack of Carpati cigarettes will be empty in an hour, and by then they will be drinking yellow beer from green bottles. The gold-grey light from the store's open door mixes with their hot breath, with the stuffy night, making their shapes light, transparent, cleansed of dirt and weariness. Then a couple enters: he swarthy, with a thin moustache, in a plaid jacket, gallant, graceful, boots shining and black trousers pressed, aglow and fluent; she a bit confused, occupied, as if deciding something important. The woman will smile timidly and adjust her peroxide hair. He will entertain her, hop about, brag, at the same time buy things — chocolate, vodka, beer — and stuff it all in a plastic bag, keeping up the nuptial dance throughout. They drink one beer on the premises, standing and gazing at each other. She from a glass, he from the bottle. Then they leave, arms round each other, into the dark, and her high heels tap the pavement.

So let's assume he heard it all and smelled the perfume through the foliage. The night filled the room in the attic, and he could recall his life without obstacle, because insomnia, just as many years ago in Sibiu, has again taken the place of eternity for him. On Brazilor Avenue and Father Bratu Avenue and Episcopei Avenue and Andrei Saguna Avenue and Ilarie Mitrea Avenue, the animals sleep. In the dim, close barns the cows lie and chew as they sleep. The horses stand with lowered heads at their empty cribs. As it ought to have been and as in fact it is. The heat departs from him forever and over Răşinari joins the heat of the livestock. Then it lifts into the black sky above the Carpathians and flows towards the cold stars like a vision of the soul, a vision he couldn't stand, because it kept him awake.

Three months later I was driving, at dusk, through the village Rozpucie at the feet of Słonne Góry, Brine Mountains. The cows were returning from the meadows and taking up the full width of the road. I had to brake, then come to a complete stop. They parted before the car like a lazy reddish wave. In the frosty air, steam puffed from their nostrils. Warm, swollen, indifferent, the animals stared straight ahead, into the distance, because neither objects nor landscape held meaning for them. They simply looked through everything. In Rozpucie too I felt the enormity and continuity of the world around me. At that same hour, in that same dying light, cattle were coming home: from Kiev, say, to Split, from my Rozpucie to Skopje, and the same in Stara Zagora. Scenery and architecture may change, and the breed, and the curve of horn or the colour of mane, but the picture remains untouched: between two rows of houses moved a herd of sated cattle. They were accompanied by women in kerchiefs and worn boots, or by children. No isolated island of industrialization, no sleepless metropolis, no spiderweb of roads or railroad lines, could block out this image as old as the world. The human joined with the bestial to wait out the night together.

There will be no miracle, I thought, putting the car in first gear. In the rear-view mirror I saw swaying behinds. The tails hung unmoving, because there were no flies now. All this will have to perish in order to survive, if only in rudimentary form. The "worst and smallest" nations live with their animals, and would like to be saved with them. They would like to be respected with their livestock, because they have little else. The dark-blue abyss of a bovine eye is a mirror in which we see ourselves as animate flesh, yet flesh vouchsafed a certain grace.

At the highway I turned left. I wanted to get free of the hairpin turns on the main summit of Brine Mountains before the sun went down. It was empty and cold. Not a soul on the road. In Tyrawa, mist blended with chimney smoke. Here the evening persisted with a will, but after five minutes the sky suddenly cracked and out poured a brilliant red. I left the car at a miserable roadside parking area and walked to the edge of the drop. The highway to Sanok—grey as ashes. In Załuż, the first lights coming on: weak, barely visible, like pinpricks. The fog in the valley obscured the houses and farms, as if no one were there. On the other hand, the Carpathians were on fire. The western wound stretched across the horizon. The entire south was freshly cut meat, a dazzling slaughterhouse.

I recalled the trip from Cluj to Sighişoara. We went by train. In our compartment sat a Japanese collector of folk costumes and his Romanian interpreter. After Apahida, the grassy plain began. I had never seen earth so naked. Gentle hills in a row in the distance. When the train climbed a little higher, you saw that beyond the horizon was another, and still another. The treeless, uninhabited expanse was a pale, desiccated yellow, the colour of something waiting for a tremendous blaze, a single match. Nothing there. On occasion a far building flicked by, a cottage with a pigsty, a hayrick, then again a vastness of air and folded earth. Small flocks of sheep appeared. With them, always, a solitary man no larger than a pin. Under the burned sky, on the baked land, they seemed lost in a blinding afterlife. Going from somewhere to somewhere else. In the brittle grass lived only flies, birds, and lizards. The earth gave off heat and dust.

Now it's a wet, snowless December, and the weather maps say December is in that place too. Like a sheet heavy with water, the sky hangs over Erdély, and the hills are covered with mud and rotting grass instead of dust, and I would like to be there and repeat my summer route, this time getting off at Boju-Catun with ten Romanian words in my head and five Hungarian. I don't remember the station, it was so small and hopeless. Possibly it is nothing more than a metal sign by the rails. But I would like to be there on December 14, with no plan in mind, because the future has not been of concern to me for a long time now and I am drawn increasingly to places that tell of a beginning or else where sadness has the power of fate. In a word, screw where we're headed, I'm interested only in where we came from. So ten words in Romanian, five in Hungarian, the Boju-Catun station, and, let's say, a million lei in small bills, to see the void between heaven and earth through which black buffalo wade. Five hundred kilometres to Vienna, 800 to Munich, 1,800 to Brussels, all of it more or less, approximately, as the crow flies. But the air cracks somewhere en route, parts like tectonic plates separating continents. Yes, a little money, good shoes, something for the rain, Bihor palinka in a plastic bottle, and I'll be fine, because I'm haunted by the vision of those hills; they gleam through all the landscapes I've seen since, because somewhere between Valea Florilor and Ploscoş I believed again that man was fashioned out of clay. Nothing else could have happened in that land, and man grieves only because his making cannot be repeated, ever.

"My country! At all cost I desired to connect with it — but there was nothing to connect with. Neither in its present nor in its past did I find anything genuine . . . My mad lover's rage had no object, you could say, because my country crumbled under the force of my gaze. I wished it were as powerful, immoderate, and wild as an evil power, a doom to shake the world, but it was small, modest, and without the qualities that make destiny." So wrote Emil Cioran in 1949, returning in his mind to his adventure in the Iron Guard.

The cows have disappeared into the woods. They moo in the December dimness. Romania Mare, Greater Serbia, Poland from sea to sea . . . The incredibly stupid fictions of those countries. A hopeless yearning for what never was, for what can never be, and an adolescent sulk over what is. Last year in Stará L'ubovňa, at the foot of a castle, I overheard the jabber of a Polish tour group. The leader was a forty-year-old moron in Gore-Tex and sunglasses. He knocked at the gate of the museum, which was closed at that hour. Finally he kicked the gate and told those assembled, "It should be ours again, or Hungarian. Then there would be some order!"

Indeed. In this part of the world, everything should be other than it is. The discovery of maps came here too early, or too late.

I drink strong coffee and think constantly about Emil Cioran's broken heart in the 1930s. About his insanity, his Romanian Dostoyevskianism. "Codreanu was in reality a Slav, a kind of Ukrainian hetman," he would say after forty years. Ah, these cruel thoughts. First they devastate the world like a fire or earthquake, and when everything has been consumed and dashed into tiny pieces of shit, when there is nothing around them but desert, wilderness, and the abyss before Creation, they throw away their self-won freedom and submit to a passionate faith in things that are hopeless and causes that are lost. Exactly as if trying to redeem doubt with disinterested love. The loneliness of a liberated mind is as great as the sky over Transylvania. Such a mind wanders like cattle in search of shade or a watering place.

In the end, however, he did return to Rǎşinari. Before the house in which he was born stands his bust. The house is the colour of a faded rose. The wall facing the street has two windows with shutters. The facade is done with a cornice and pilasters. The bust itself is on a low pedestal, Cioran's face rendered realistically and unskilfully. A folk artist might have done it, imitating refined art. The work is "small, modest, and without qualities" aside from its resemblance to the original, but it suits this village square. Every day, herds of cows and sheep pass it, leaving behind their warmth and smell. Neither the wide world nor Paris left any mark on that face. It is sad and tired. Such men sit in the pub next to the barber and in the store-shed under the grapevine. Everything looks as if someone here had made his dream come true, granted his final wish.

"Acel blestemat, acel splendid Răşinari."

Our Leader

But that's what it's like: any moment you take the wrong turn, stumble, get lost — geography's no help — and forget the objective eye. Nothing is as it first appears; splinters of meaning lurk everywhere, and your mind catches on them like pants on barbed wire. You can't simply write, for example, that we crossed the border at Siret at night on foot, and the Romanian guards, who kept in check the entire passageway and five buses carrying dozens of tons of contraband, let us through with a gruff but friendly laugh. On the other side, there was only the night. We waited for something to come from Ukraine and take us, but nothing came, no old Lada, no Dacia. It's strange finding yourself in a foreign land when the only scenery is the dark. Off to a side, crawling shadows beyond the glass, so we went in their direction, because at that hour a man is like a moth, drawn to any light. In the border tavern, two guys sat at a small table playing a game resembling dominoes. We ordered coffee. The bartender made it in a saucepan on a hotplate. It was good, strong. Hearing us speak Polish, he tried too, but we understood only *babka* ("grandmother") and *Wrocław*. We asked about the bus or whatever, but he spread his arms and said something like "dimineaţă tîrg in Suceava". In that blue, breath-humid light I drank Bihor palinka for the first time. It was worse than any Hungarian brandy, but it warmed, and I wanted something more than coffee since this fellow had a grandmother in Wrocław.

We went back to the road, but nothing had changed. A glow above the border; the darkness to the south, like India ink drying. An hour before dawn, cars began to assemble in front of the tavern. They stopped and waited for those buses that had been imprisoned between barriers; they were waiting for merchandise. A Dacia arrived, its tail scraping the asphalt. Four men inside. The driver got out and said, "Suceava zece dolar." He grabbed our knapsacks, threw them on the roof of the car, and tried tying them down. I asked him how the hell he thought this could work, pointing at the guys packed inside. He smiled and patted his knees: we'd fit somehow, one on top of the other. He was in a wonderful mood, and you could smell the drink on him. M. shouted no, she didn't care to end up a statistic without seeing even a little of verdant Bukovina. So we untied the cords and pulled our stuff down. The driver made a sad face and said, "Cinci dolar." M. replied, "Eu nu merg"; then we were alone in the cold wind blowing from Chernivtsi.

When the sky had turned to dark blue, a red Passat Kombi drove up and a man said, "Cincisprezece dolar," and we didn't object, because this conveyance was empty, spacious, and warm. *Cincisprezece* is not much for fifty kilometres after a sleepless night. We took off like a bat out of hell. Ahead of us, mist. The man chattered, mixing Romanian, Russian, and German. He attempted Polish. He had done Europe, including Warsaw. He said he would take us, then come back here, because the buses with the goods would be let through eventually, and the wheeling and dealing would start up just past the barriers. They always let the buses in, and he would fill his Passat to the top with bicycle wheels, tyres, boxes of laundry detergent, chocolate bars, earflap hats in the middle of summer because they were cheaper now, and all the other riches of the Ukrainian land. He would take us, then return, and go back again to Suceava, to the big market not far from a factory that stank of sulphuric acid, a field covered with tented booths to the horizon. He went on and on, and in his headlights now and then we saw the gleaming eyes of horses pulling unseen wagons with sleeping drivers. He talked, but I kept dozing off. T. turned and remarked, "Look at that steering wheel." Again we passed a mysterious vehicle, and the man made a full half-turn of the wheel before the car responded. Our speedometer was broken, but I was certain he had the accelerator to the floor. So I opened my eyes and listened to the map of Europe: Berlin, Frankfurt, Kiev, Budapest, Vienna . . .

Suceava was a shadow in ultramarine. We tore across a viaduct. The main station was under repair, so we went to Gara Suceava Nord, wanting to continue south, without stopping, along the Siret River and turn west only around Adjud, leave Moldova, and get to Transylvania. That was our plan. To keep going and sleep on the trains, which would all come at our convenience and take us where we wanted to go.

Gara Suceava Nord was as big as a mountainside and dark. Like entering a cave. The yellow light barely dispersed the gloom. We made our way through a crowd. A crowd at four in the morning is a curious thing: a meeting in a madhouse. Those who stood or moved had their eyes open but seemed asleep, under a spell, the effect of that insomniac light, which trickled out from who knows where. It could have come from the ceiling, from the walls, or maybe from people's bodies. Not enough of it, in any case, for us to believe in the reality of all these tableaux vivants, in fitful slow motion, in the belly of the station. Someone here wasn't real: either we or they.

At any rate, there were no trains heading south at that hour, and we didn't have the strength to wait. We went outside. Taxis in a row, their drivers chatting and smoking. Mainly Dacias, and two ancient Mercedes. Instead of going by rail, I thought we could take a car across the Petru Vodă Pass, the Bicaz Gorge, the Bicaz and Bucin Passes, in this way crossing the main ridge of the Carpathians to reach at last the heart of Transylvania. But the keepers of meters went wide-eyed when they heard "Tîrgu Mureş", and they shook their heads when they heard "Sighişoara". It was only three hundred kilometres, we said, but they opened their arms and kicked the tyres of their automobiles, because they didn't believe that any of them could climb so high and return in one piece. Only one, who drove an old green boxy Mercedes, put his hands in his pockets, spat, and said, "Două sute dolar." We realized then that they took us for lunatics.

A young, slender boy said he would drive us to a hotel, so we could sleep. Like children, we let ourselves be packed into a red Dacia. We were powerless. Hotel Socim, we said. He didn't advise that. But we were stupidly stubborn, thinking the kid wanted to fleece us. He smiled, as if to say, "Lord Jesus has forsaken you," but he helped us with our bags and drove us into the dawning city. He took what was on the meter, no more, and promised that if we phoned, he would come for us.

And what an awakening that was on Jean Bart Street 24 . . . The ceiling so low, it was hard to sit on the bed. To be safe, I didn't get up, only listened to one big truck after another right at the window. They passed by like a train, without pause. You couldn't close the window, either, because it was an oven inside. An oven at the window too. The room had only the bed and a dresser. I was afraid to open it. Odd noises came from the corridor. I was afraid to go out. But I finally did, in search of a toilet. From a window in the corridor I saw laundry on a line, an apartment building, sheds, a white horse grazing. In the bathroom, a cleaning woman yelped with fright at the sight of me, overturning a bucket of dirty water. It didn't matter, because there was a wooden grating on the floor, as in barracks and prisons. The bathroom was cool, quiet.

We slept no more than three hours. It was just as stifling in the street as it was inside. Dust hung in the still air. Toddlers sitting in the shade of concrete stairs watched us pass. From a bar on the corner came the smell of food. We had sour tripe soup, with a roll and hot green paprika, which made us break into a sweat. We phoned, and the driver actually came for us. Again he was all energy and happy to help. We asked him if he had slept. He said no. He looked at the door of Hotel Socim but was tactful and said nothing. We told him we needed to buy train tickets, to change money, to be in Cluj that evening. To everything he said, "No problem." He put our bags in the boot, but it wouldn't close, so he tied it with wire, and we were off, leaving Jean Bart Street 24 forever. In fact everything for him was no problem. He found an exchange office that gave the best rate. At the window counter, he took the wad of bills from me and carefully counted them; only then did we leave. At the Romanian Orbis, the line had been there two hours and was hardly moving. The computer screen at the cashier's desk was blank. When someone reserved a seat, the woman phoned all the stations and made the reservation. We didn't want to wait. Our train would leave in half an hour, and it didn't matter to us whether we boarded with or without a ticket, as long as we left baking Suceava. Our taxi driver, however, said something like "Take it easy" in Romanian and stood at the head of the line, delivering a speech to the people there. Ten minutes later we were rushing through the city, our pockets full of small brown-and-green tickets in antique cardboard. Everyone honked at us, and we honked at everyone. The red Dacia took the turns like a fire engine. Our new friend drove with one hand, looking for music on the radio with the other. We were at the Gara de Nord five minutes before departure. We wanted to run to make the train, but he said the trip was long and we had nothing to eat or drink. The line at the station kiosk was long, almost half that for the tickets, but he entered the glass stand, asked us through the window how many beers we wanted, mineral water, and what on our sandwiches, as he hugged and kissed the girl working in a white cap behind the counter. That's how it was, I'm not making this up. The girl took our money, gave us change, and we were at the platform on the dot, with just time enough to say goodbye and shake hands. The kid took what was on the meter, no more.

So we travelled south-west: Gura Humorului, Cîmpulung Moldovenesc, Vatra Dornei, in the heart of green Bukovina, among the mountains. I remember nothing in particular of that trip, so I must invent it from scratch. A heavyset man in our compartment took up a seat and a half and didn't like us. He was about sixty, well fed, and no doubt remembered better days, when there was order in his country and foreign riff-raff didn't wander in at will and drink Ursus beer on trains. At any rate he made that sort of face. Now I reconstruct: his grey suit and the purple shirt he removed before Vatra Dornei. The light-blue towel he hung around his neck. He went to the toilet in a white undershirt, his arms flabby and hairless. Anyway, I have to make up these details because something must have happened that long day before the evening in Cluj, where it poured as it is pouring now. I have to invent, because days cannot sink into a past filled only with landscape, with inert, unchanging matter that finally shakes us from our corporeality, brushes off and away all these little incidents, faces, existences that last no longer than a glimpse. So the old man returned and dozed, though we had hoped he would wash before he returned, not before bedtime. Perhaps one travels for the purpose of preserving facts, keeping alive their brief, flickering light.

In Cluj it poured. In front of a pizza parlour by the station, guys in leather jackets did some business while their girls gossiped. And as happens everywhere, two grabbed a third by the arms and dragged him into the dark. The station in Cluj: again a crowd, dim yellow light, the stink of bodies and cigarettes. We had to get our tickets stamped for the next day. A boy spotted us in the crush, saw that we were not local, standing there like calves, unsure where to go. He took the old-fashioned cardboard from us, and in five minutes the stamping was done. He said, "Drum bun," and disappeared in the crowd like a guardian angel in worn Adidas.

The next morning, Horea Street gleamed in the sun. The synagogue, not far from the bridge on the Şomes, had four towers topped with gilded cupolas. It resembled the one in the Gypsy quarter of Spišské Podhradie but was larger. For lunch we had the usual, *ciorba de burta*, Romanian tripe soup, with a roll and paprika. Somewhere in the vicinity, Hungarian lords had burned Gheorghe Doja at the stake, then quartered his remains and hung them on the gates of Buda, Pest, Alba Iulia, and Oradea. Szeged got the head. The typical end, this, of "peasant kings".

Even when an army of tens of thousands stands behind them and the pope gives his blessing for a final albeit failed crusade against the Turks. I sat at a pub on the street named after Doja, drank coffee, and in a couple of hours would be looking, from the windows of a train, at the grassy waste of Transylvania, where five hundred years ago Doja's peasant divisions marched. In the compartment of the train was that Japanese man who collected women's folk costumes. According to T., he put them on in front of a mirror in his home in Tokyo or Kyoto.

His tour guide had said that Ceaușescu united the Romanian people, making everyone equally guilty, and anyone claiming not to have taken part in it was lying. But I gazed at the scorched hills and tried to picture the divisions of light cavalry, dark moving points on the horizon appearing and disappearing with the rhythm of the hills. I tried to imagine this death dealing procession of beggars. For the first and last time as free people they measured their land. In clothes and weapons taken from their masters, on horses taken from their masters, they marched to Cluj, to Timișoara, to fall at last in defeat under the July sun. Fifty thousand cut down, hanged, left to the birds and thrown to the dogs. Ravens drawn from the Carpathians, the Hungarian Lowlands, from Moldavia and Wallachia. The heat hastens decay, erases the traces. Nothing is left of these rebel poor. Doja was burned on a mock throne with a mock sceptre in his hand. So writes Sándor Petőfi.

On the train I looked out of the window and imagined the tattered and ecstatic army of shepherds, swineherds, peasants who attempted, if only for a moment, to grasp for themselves the life of their masters — that is, to be free, to seize the wealth of others, and to rule by force. A few months earlier, I had sought out the grave of Jakub Szela in Bukovina. I asked here and there, my excuse for travelling to the end of the world. Some said he lay in Clit; others, near the Ukrainian border, in Vicşani.

I believed them both. I even began to think that the Austrians dealt with him somewhat as the Hungarian lords had dealt with Doja: dismembering the memory of him, a memory that at any moment might prove dangerous. Finally Szela, according to Ludwik Dębicki, "pretended to be a mystic and sectarian in a peasant's cloak". Of all possible places of concealment I liked Vicşani best, unlikely as it was: lost among fields, far from everything, godforsaken. Beyond it, nothing, nothing in any direction. The great expanse of treeless land, which nevertheless someone tilled here and there, was a breathtaking contradiction of the pathetic little village where the only machine I saw was one bicycle. Our automobile here was a monstrosity, a challenge. In this piece of upland between Rădăuţi and Suceava, small horse-drawn carts moved among endless folded fields. The black earth, newly ploughed, joined the sky, and those tiny figures — thin, veined horses — were practically invisible in their insignificance. If they stopped moving, there would no longer be a reason for their existence. A whim: to set little toys in a vast landscape, to enjoy the helplessness of figurines out of a Christmas crèche.

The village smelled of manure and spring. Orchards bloomed behind fences. The cooperative store was located in a brick building. A peasant clad in black told us they had beer there. We found a girl with keys at the farm next door. She opened it for us. We asked about Szela, said to have been buried around there, but she didn't know, didn't even seem to know the name, though she was Polish. A few small tables, and a peculiar jumble, as if someone had been building sets for a film. The interior a greygreen. Wooden boxes on the floor, the sort once used to transport siphons for seltzer, except they were filled with litre-and-a-half bottles of wine. Two kinds of beer, two kinds of cigarettes, ashtrays full of butts as if after a reception. Propaganda posters on the wall, and a window that opened to a yard in which pink piglets wandered. That was it. Yet these few objects, pieces of furniture, and commodities together created an extraordinary chaos, as if things had been tossed here in the middle of their use, dropped, as if in this very spot the energy of the world had run out. We drank a beer each.

The girl was silent but finally said she would take us to the old cemetery outside the village; maybe Szela was there. But only clumps of thorny plants were there — no gravestones, crosses, or markers. A pity, I thought, for him to have to lie here — and someday be resurrected here, of all places. Little imagination was needed to see him enter the cooperative store: it would come as no surprise, because immobility, sorrow, and abandonment do not change in time or space. It must have been the same in the tavern of the Jew Semek in Siedliska on February 20, 1846. Snow lay on the fields; it was cold and dim inside, full of the stink of heated, unwashed bodies. "Get to work, boys, and hurry, for time passes." Szela wore his black cassock, held in his hand the sabre taken at Bogusze and tapped the ground with it like a walking stick. In the courtyard, blood seeped into the snow. You could smell the vodka from broken kegs. The Austrians had made him king of the peasants for twenty-four hours, and the day was drawing to a close. "Get to work, boys, and hurry, for time passes." The cursed blood of the lords seeping into the snow, the taken sabre, the peasants with ducats clinking in their pockets, but the dimness and the stink were unalleviated. The village elder Breinl told him in Tarnów, "The Archduke Ferdinand is number one, but in Galicia you are second in command." Some say Szela planned to take the ten-year-old Zosia Boguszówna for his wife. Peasant blood would mix with noble blood and give rise to a race that would inherit the reborn land. It's possible that he had no faith in his strength, that the blueprint for a new world would repeat the gestures of the lords in an empty, abstract reality that puts up no resistance.

So he could rise from the grave and enter the cooperative store in Vicşani, and it would be as if he had never died, since no doubt there was little difference between that store and the tavern of the Jew Semek. He could simply start again after a hundred and fifty years, though without the Austrian blessing. So I reflected, standing in the noon sun. Having travelled several hundred kilometres, I had the right to these thoughts. In addition, I came from his native region. I looked in the direction of Moldova and wondered whose blood he would want to shed today, and with whose blood he would want to mix his own. The flies flew heavy and slow in the cooperative store. On the shelf were two kinds of cigarettes, the cheapest. No aristocracy nearby, yet the air inside had the same stuffy, impoverished taste. I thought: You sit here, Szela, drinking Ursus or Silva, and there's no one for you to go after. If you try, the world will part before you like a phantom, and your hands will clutch emptiness. You'll accomplish shit here. The most you could do is go to Suceava and like a post-industrial Luddite smash a sky-blue ATM. Nowadays you can't become another person through the simple transfer of goods or objects. Killing won't let you enter your victim's body and life. Wealth has become an elusive thing; it floats in the air, materializing now and then — here, there. Whereas poverty, abandonment, and ruin are concrete, tangible, and thus it will always be. All the treasures of the world are now the property of no one in particular, and no plunder will exalt you, no violence ennoble you. Left to you is only the ATM in Suceava as a physical emanation of the remote, all-powerful evil that will never permit the last to be first.

In this way I spoke to the spirit of Jakub Szela on the edge of Europe among the lanes of Vicşani. I was filled with left-wing sentiments but had no regard whatever for revolutionary fire. A kilometre on, in an open field by the road, sat a man reading a newspaper. Nothing as far as the eye could see, yet he hardly looked up at our car. We drove south, to the village of Clit, to check another possible resting place. Which made sense, because Clit lay a few kilometres from Solca. The Austrians sent Szela to Solca when it was all over. At an intersection after Rădăuţi stood a Romanian cop. He stood smack in the middle of the intersection. At the sight of our car, he turned his back pointedly and looked off into the distance. A friendly gesture, probably, pretending not to notice us, because we were a provocation.

In Clit, people spoke an odd tongue. Like Ukrainian, but I understood only every fifth word. I asked a woman in a kerchief if this was a Ukrainian village. *My Ruskie*, she replied: We are Russians. We asked about Szela, if she had heard such a name here or in the area. She shook her head, then said she would take us to the oldest man in the village. The road was dry and dusty. The wooden houses had white-and-green walls and shutters. On the ground lay pink and white petals from flowering apple trees. In the distance, the gleam of a pond. Geese walked in that direction, unattended. A man in faded jeans emerged from the shadows and dust. He didn't look so very old. He pondered awhile, asked that the name be repeated, then asked us himself, directly, if this Szela person . . . was that one of our "father leaders"? "Perhaps, in a way," we answered evasively. He finally gave up and said there was someone here, not old but worldly, just got back from Germany, who might be able to help. The old man called him out of a roadside bar. This person was about forty and dressed in overalls with a sewn-on Esso patch. P. remarked that Esso was practically Shell, so we might be close. We spoke in Russian, Ukrainian, German, and Polish, but it turned out that all they could do for us was show us where the cemetery was. They took us there, wished us luck, a pleasant trip, good health, and left us in the cool of the trees. The old man went down the hill slowly and carefully. Occasionally the younger man took his arm. They didn't have to accompany us; they could have pointed to the hill from a distance; but in that part of the world, looking for someone's grave is far more important than the usual tourism, and people treat it with respect. By entering their cemetery, apparently we became their guests.

Yes. Szela could have been lying in Clit. From the hill we had a view of a white, cupolaed Orthodox church and a neo-Gothic Catholic church. His native Smarzowa was also in the Pogórze range, though the valleys there were narrower and the peaks covered with forest. Here everything was naked, whether tilled or grassy. On the horizon, a ribbon of blue heat. There was no trace of our "father leader".

Nor could there be a trace, because as you travel, history constantly turns into legend. Too much is happening and in too big a space. No one can remember it all, let alone write it down. You can't devote attention to events that come out of nowhere and whose purpose and sense remain unclear to the end. No one will wrap things into a whole, cobble a finished tale. Neglect is the essence of this region. History, deeds, consequences, ideas, and plans dissolve into the landscape, into something considerably older and vaster than all the striving. Time gets the better of memory. Nothing can be remembered with certainty, because actions do not line up according to the principle of cause and effect. A long narrative about the spirit of the times in this place seems a project as pathetic as it is pretentious, like a novel written from the point of view of God. Paroxysm and tedium rule here in turn, and that is why this region is so human. "One of your father leaders?" Why not? I thought. In a sense, both ours and yours. Ultimately, in Szela was embodied the desire for violent change, a rejection of one's fate that at the same time suddenly turns into acceptance of what that fate brings.

Description of a Journey through East Hungary to Ukraine

I'LL NEVER FORGET the sky when at dusk we left Nagykálló for Mátészalka. The entire train a single carriage. In addition, it was an express, and we had to make seat reservations. The heavy woman at the ticket window smiled and did a few broad sitting motions in her chair to show us what a seat reservation was.

Hungarian train tickets are pretty, resembling small banknotes. The young Gypsies going to Szerencs made accordions out of them, decks of cards, fans. In the Gypsies' ears were gold rings. But that happened two days earlier.

Now, a crest of crimson feathers unfurled in the west. A hand of fire poised above the plain, and below, in the cornfields and orchards, a blue dark had begun to float. We drank aszú from the bottle and sat with our backs to the front of the train, so the west, in a flood of blazing blood, was before us, and we could see the night slowly lifting from the earth, climbing, turning colder, until finally all was extinguished and the lights went on in the little red carriage of our train.

Less than half an hour had passed, and already we were reminiscing about Nagykálló: the bright warmth of the afternoon as we walked downtown between yellow houses. How we found an enormous church. How musicians sat on the bench by the entrance. One of them raised a gleaming trombone in greeting. I ventured into the vestibule, wanting to see what a Hungarian church looked like, but there was a crowd, a young couple standing up front, and at the altar a pastor. No organ, no chasubles, only the Word at its plainest, as it was in the beginning and shall be at the end, instead of all these wonders made by human hand for human consolation. Then the procession exited, slow, stately, and the three musicians waiting in their white shirts — the trombonist, the accordionist, the guitarist — who seemed so trifling, almost frivolous, practically Catholic, played a subdued piece, and the crowd moved in a cortège towards the marketplace.

We had gone to Nagykálló because, according to our guidebook, "at the end of a long and creepily empty square" stood a psychiatric hospital. Which might be, I thought, some kind of physically manifested metaphor, a metaphor for Eastern Europe. My imagination evoked a large dusty space surrounded by crumbling buildings. Divisions in various uniforms file through the square from time to time, but they stay no longer than needed for the ravage and rapine. They ride off, and the hot dust of the plain immediately hides the horsemen. From the windows of the hospital, the insane follow them with their eyes and pine, because in these eastern regions power, violence, and madness have forever lived in concubinage and sometimes in a completely legal union.

But no, nothing of the sort: this square was not a waste. It was shaded, cool. Before the hospital door, several madmen in dressing gowns smoked cigarettes. The atmosphere was, more than anything, that of a sanatorium, so the heated imagination of the tourist could take a breather.

So anyway, we were drinking aszú and travelling east. Actually, we were fleeing the west, fleeing hopeless Budapest, where in the worst gussied-up dive on Rákóczi Street a shot of pear brandy cost three times what it did in Nagykálló, and the coffee even more. Fleeing the rain as well, because the sky had opened up on the Danube, on Gellért Hill, on the bridges, on everything. But it was August 20, Saint Stephen's Day, therefore even with the downpour parachutists jumped from vintage An-24s, trailing ribbons of smoke in the national colours: green, red, and white. Around Parliament the police stood and made sure no one got too close. The rain fell in buckets on the big limos too, nature being a democrat. On Zoltán Street near the covered market, we had to step back, because the pavement filled with roller skaters, five hundred strong, raising their arms and reciting. They looked like a foreign horde bent on conquest. M. said, "That's what cities are becoming. To survive, you'll have to belong to something like that. As it used to be. Loners won't have a prayer." "Unless," I replied, "you're someone like Snake in *Escape from New York*." Cars couldn't move in the jam. At a bus stop, two black men conversed in Hungarian. The water gurgled in our pockets and shoes. Sirens howled, horns honked, the glare of the city doubled, tripled, and we were ghosts now, having lost confidence in our existence. On Dohány Street, opposite the Great Synagogue, I found the small pub in which, a year before, a producer from Israel told me how a lion had eaten the hand of its trainer, a mishap that sank the film project, because no one in his right mind would do a comedy with a man-eating lion in the lead. The pub was now packed; between the walls papered with gazettes from the days of Franz Josef, it was so bad that mothers had to hold their children in their laps, the children dozing from the smoke and hot breaths. The weary barmaid knew what I wanted, reading my face, and over the heads of the customers she passed us two pear brandies and two coffees. We sat outside under a leaky umbrella, rain pattering in the cups and glasses.

When we took Rákóczi Street to the station at last, we saw a tremendous assembly on its steps. Black-market money changers were there, cabbies, young ladies, railroad employees, smooth operators, vendors—in a word, everyone: all looking into the deep night. We too turned to look. In the leaden sky over the Danube burst a thousand purple sparks, a myriad scarlet spiders and golden stars. The reports from the explosions, muffled by the rain and distance, reached us with delay, which made the spectacle doubly unreal. Celadon and bile, turquoise and violet, sapphire and silver, emerald and crystal—fictional, ephemeral gems that died instantly in the rain and did nothing to lift the darkness. As if old Austro-Hungary were making yet another effort to give a sign from the beyond. The wet night was a maniacal ballroom full of glistening black mirrors, spectral chandeliers, trick candelabra and sconces. The Turks on the street brandished long knives to cut meat for kebabs. A German who had lost his way, pulling a suitcase on wheels, muttered, "Scheisse, scheisse." And, wrapped in blankets, a Gypsy couple slept in a tunnel walkway beneath the street. A black hat lay beside his head; beside hers, a carefully folded, flower-patterned scarf.

We got on the train to Nyíregyháza, that being the farthest point east, and it would run until morning. Which was fine: we had to sleep somewhere. South and east, our plan. Somewhere near

Hatvan the conductor appeared. I tried explaining that we didn't have tickets. He was over six feet, all smiles, and repeated, "Kein Problem." Then, with the aid of a piece of paper and a pen, he told us not to worry, we could stay on, he would return, maybe at Füzesabony or Tiszafüred, and sell us the tickets then, so they would be cheaper. He vanished, then reappeared in half an hour, apologetically, saying that it had to be now, there was someone on board more important than he who might come through and check. With elaborate flourishes he wrote us a receipt. We also had some aszú with us but no corkscrew. Seeing the long-necked bottle, the conductor threw up his hands helplessly, but then disappeared and reappeared with a curious tool for locking compartments and punching ticket holes. We tried it, but the tool was too short, the cork came less than halfway out. Tremendous disappointment on the conductor's face. Again he disappeared, and all we could hear was the echo of his strides in the empty corridor. He returned in a few minutes, beaming, and pulled at my sleeve. The man is so invested in this Tokay, I thought; a pity that the bottle's only half a litre. He explained excitedly, pulling me to the john, pointing at the toilet-paper peg, which was thin, long enough, strong enough. We pushed the cork in. With a sigh of relief, I handed him the bottle. "Drink, brother," I said in Polish. He stood at attention and with solemnity pointed to his uniform, cap, all his officialdom, then clapped me on the shoulder and said something that must have meant "To your health". He appeared again at dawn. He was half asleep and repeated, "Nyíregyháza, Nyíregyháza." He made sure we hadn't forgotten anything on the train, then waved from the window.

It was that way everywhere. That's how it was at Hidasnémeti at the border station half an hour from Košice, where we got off on a hot platform and the sun rolled in the west like a cut-off rooster's head trailing a ribbon of red. Nothing, as far as the eye could see. The black railway wires vanished in the vastness of burned fields and blowing wind. About the station, guards in Slovak and Hungarian uniforms milling. The borders at the edge of old Europe must have looked like this: emptiness, wind, and garrisons, where you wait for something, for the enemy perhaps, and when the years pass and the enemy doesn't show, you put a bullet through your head out of boredom. A man on a rusty bicycle approached, but I knew only one Hungarian word — the name of a town, Gönc — so I repeated it over and over, until he finally squatted and wrote the departure time with his finger in the sand. He touched my backpack to tell me that the train would be red, raised a finger to tell me it would have only one carriage. He smelled of wine, beer, and cigarettes. He took off on his bicycle but returned in two hours to make sure we boarded the red carriage at the station.

It was that way also at Gönc, where in the middle of the night a Gypsy with a gold earring led us down dark lanes between vegetable plots and barking dogs, for several kilometres because he couldn't understand our request, and we followed till we reached a noisy pub where a man sat at a table: the only person in the neighbourhood who spoke English. It was he who informed us, finally, that the local pension was closed, the hostess having passed away three days ago. But not to worry, he added, and put us in his Lada, and we went barrelling up a hundred hairpin switchbacks deep into the Zemplén Hills. Now and then, in the distance and below, mercury lights flashed from the Slovak side, and over Vel'ka Ida rose a ghoulish industrial glow. But here, on the road to Telkibánya, was nothing but green forest, spruce. Gabor drove us to a hotel stuck in the mountains.

Nothing in Telkibánya, a village that hadn't changed in a hundred years. Wide, scattered houses under fruit trees. The walls a sulphurous, bilious yellow, the wood carving deep brown, the door frames sculpted, the shutters and verandas enduring in perfect symbiosis with the heavy, Baroque abundance of the gardens. The metaphor of settling and taking root appeared to have taken shape here in an ideal way. Not one new house, yet also not one old house in need of repair or renovation. Although we were the only foreigners, we drew no stares. From the stop, in the course of the day, four buses departed. Time melted in the sunlight; around noon, it grew still. In the inn, men sat from the morning on and without haste sipped their palinka and beer in turn. The bartender immediately knew I was a Slav and said, pouring, "*dobre*" and "*na zdorovye*". It was one of those places where you feel the need to stay but have no reason to. Everything exactly as it should be and no one raising a voice or making an unnecessarily abrupt movement. On a slope above the village, the white of a cemetery. From windows of homes, the smell of stewing onions. In market stalls, mounds of melons, paprikas. A woman emerged from a cellar with a glass jug filled with wine. But we left Telkibánya eventually, because nothing ends a utopia quicker than the desire to hold on to it.

The return trip to Gönc ran through forests and limitless fields of sunflowers. The driver of the white delivery van talked nonstop and didn't mind at all that we couldn't understand him. We too talked. He listened with care and answered in his own tongue. In Gönc he pulled up in front of the Hussite House, but we were less interested in museums, more in the old women sitting in front of the houses on the main street. Like lizards in the sun. Their black clothes stored the afternoon heat, and their eyes gazed on the world without motion and without surprise, because they had seen everything. The women sat in groups of three, four, and in utter silence observed the passage of time.

A shiny Škoda Octavia drove up, with Slovak plates, and a family got out. They looked around with uncertainty, and the father, like a brood hen, pushed them together and cast suspicious glances to either side, because — as everyone knows — Slovaks and Hungarians hold mutual grievances. This time it probably had to do not with history but with intuition, instinct, because those newcomers were white and plump as raised dough, round as loaves of bread, dressed up in tourist smartness — shorts, knee-high socks, pocket flaps — while the main street in Gönc was swarthy, dark-haired, and sinewy-nimble even in the quiet of siesta. This was the sort of thing we wanted to see, not the Hussite House with its "curious wooden bed that pulls out like a drawer", as the guidebook said. What happened on the main street in Gönc was more interesting than what had become mere history. It drew us, because life is made of bits of the present that stay in the mind. The world itself, really, is made of that.

The Slovaks drove off, and I went into a liquor store, because it was August 18, the hundred-and-sixty-ninth anniversary of the birth of Franz Josef, and I was determined to celebrate it. When I was again seated on the low wall before the store, there appeared beside me a bearded man in a herringbone coat and nothing under it. Without a word he produced from an inside pocket an enamel mug and lifted it towards me. How could I refuse him, and on this day, the birthday of His Highness? Here I was, travelling through his country, and he granted audiences even to simple peasants and made no distinction between Serb and Slovak, between Pole and Romanian. So I took out the flask of pear brandy I had just purchased and shared it with my fellow man. He drank in silence and pointed at my pack of Kossuths. I gave him a cigarette. Some citizen came by and in the international language of gestures gave me to understand that I was dealing with a lunatic. I reflected that in the empire lunatics too had their place, and I refilled the mug. We drank to the health of Franz Josef. I told my new friend that I had always been partial to sovereigns and caesars, that I particularly missed them in these threadbare times, because democracy cannot satisfy the thirst for the aesthetic and mythic, and so people feel abandoned. My friend nodded emphatically and held out his mug. I poured and told him that the idea of democracy contains a fundamental contradiction, because true power cannot, by its nature, be immanent; it would in that case resemble the most ordinary anarchy, though without all the entertainments and pleasures of anarchy. Power must come from without; only then can we embrace it and revolt against it. "Igen," said my new friend, nodding. A small crowd had gathered around us and was listening to the discussion. People also nodded and said, "Igen, igen." Then my friend proposed that we arm-wrestle. He won twice; I won twice. The crowd kibitzed and cheered. When it was all over, men came up to me, clapped me on the back, and said, "Franz Josef, Franz Josef."

South of Gönc, the plain began. Fields of corn to the blue horizon. The green-gold sea licked the Zemplén foothills and returned in a wave of warm air. On the roads in the fields stood old private automobiles with trailers loaded with the first harvest. The sun shone from straight above, making our shadows no larger than a dog at heel. The roads joined, crossed, separated — from the sky it must have looked like the board of a gigantic game. Ignorant of the rules, we took the wrong turn. That is, we had been making wrong turns from the start, the whole point of our trip, but this time we went in circles. Everywhere — hot wind and the rustle of leaves baked dry. One cornstalk is like another, so we were in a labyrinth. It took us three hours to get out. In a straight line, we must have gone three kilometres.

In Göncruszka the pavements were violet from the plums. A swarm of wasps over the fruit, and not a soul in sight. We walked through a village. No sound from any yard. The windows all shuttered. Only Gypsies — they were having a fiesta instead of a siesta, drinking beer in the full sun before a roadside pub. An old Gypsy woman with the face of Ella Fitzgerald was telling her man to stand up. She had her hands on her hips and spoke in a voice that climbed to a scream, but he sat, answered her calmly, indifferently, punctuating his words with light gestures of his right hand. Apparently a scene that the couple had been repeating, with no variation, for God knows how many years. The woman stamped the ground, raising dust.

We walked on, beyond the village. The posts along the road were light blue, and each had painted on it a white infinity sign. Fifty metres apart, they went evenly up and down the hills, and we thought maybe they were a hallucination from the fierce heat, but when the Slovak van finally picked us up, they didn't vanish, they continued flickering past the window until Vilmány, where we got out to look for a railway station among the sunflowers. The station was simply one pair of rails and a patch of beaten earth — no board, no building, no sign or semaphore; we found it only because some people were gathered there, a couple of kids stretched out on dry grass and resigned, with an almost empty bottle of mineral water and a small backpack. There was no roof or tree to provide shade, but to the west lay a vast landscape that shimmered in lilac. The long ridges were indistinct in the heat, but you could make out the church spires in Hernádcéce, Fáj, Garadna, Novajidrány, Vizsoly, and who knows, the hot air may have carried apparitions from Miskolc and Eger all the way here to the Hornád valley. Anything was possible that day. Budapest itself could have sailed in, floating over our heads, and we wouldn't have been surprised.

But it was a train, not the capital, that appeared. Ella Fitzgerald sat in the middle with three children. Evidently she had been unable to persuade her husband. We moved slowly. There is no better kind of rail travel in a foreign land than the local, second-class kind. People get on, get off, and perform their life in so unhurried a manner that it begins to resemble our own. Everything becomes familiar. Guys returning from work smell exactly like those who get on at the Żerań station in Warsaw and are bound for Nasielsk. A mother accompanying her sixteen-year-old daughter to the train hands her a plastic bag of sweets. The girl gives her mother a perfunctory kiss, is a little sullen, gets on, and when the train moves, the mother waves with a helpless smile, but her child is already elsewhere in her thoughts and doesn't notice. That might have been in Boldogkőváralja . . . No, it definitely was, because there was a medieval castle on a hill to the left. The girl wore faded jeans and black boots with silver buckles. The conductor came and asked the Gypsy woman for something but got a flood of words, so he threw up a hand and passed. One could open a window, one could smoke and in lazy anticipation think of what would happen in an hour, in half an hour, and wonder, for example, if that dressed-up blonde with the red fingernails was going to Szerencs or would get off at some more backwater spot. Forty kilometres an hour at a steady clip lets you come to an understanding with space, lets you control it without causing it any injury.

The station at Szerencs smelled of chocolate, because right next door was the biggest chocolate factory in Hungary. Drinking beer, palinka, and coffee, we considered our next move. The timetable simply held too many possibilities, and for the moment intuition was dumb. To be able to go everywhere means not going anywhere. We decided to do nothing and let the world do. And we were right: after an hour, an empty bus pulled up, practically to our outdoor table at the summer pub, with the sign TOKAJ.

I woke up early in the morning and stepped out on the balcony. The red roofs had darkened from the night rain. The street pavement shone, steamed. The town was still. You could hear drops falling from leaf to leaf in the garden below. Only the storks made a racket. One by one they flew up from the Tisza and settled on their chimneys. I must have counted five nests. The birds clattered, raising echoes, then smoothed their feathers and returned to the river somewhere among ancient poplars. Tokaj lay motionless, glittering like fish scales. I stood in that preternatural silence, smoked a cigarette, and thought that all mornings of the world should be like this: we wake in absolute peace, in a foreign city that has no people in it, and everything around us is a continuation of sleep. Before the pastel gates of the houses, wrought-iron signs swayed in the breeze: ZIMMER FREI . . . SZOBA KIADÓ . . . ZIMMER FREI . . . In the east, a violet lid of cloud hung heavily, let through a few rays, sank. It was all so beautiful, I wondered if I had died. To check, I returned to my room. M. was still asleep, so everything was okay, because we had never figured that we would go together, arguing instead who would outlive whom.

Don't assume there will be something to eat at eight in the

morning in Tokaj. At the glassed-in pub on Kossuth Street, you can drink coffee after coffee and watch the rain fall in the empty square. Curious thoughts enter your head. For instance, should you follow the lead of that couple at the next table, who ordered two 300 ml glasses of aszú, or ask yourself quietly a question in the vein of "What am I doing here anyway?" — the fundamental mantra if not prayer of every traveller? For it is precisely on a trip, in the morning, in a strange city, before the second cup of coffee has begun to work, that you experience most palpably the oddness of your banal existence. Travel is no more than a relatively healthy form of narcotic, after all. Have another cup, wait for the rain to let up a bit, and walk to the river, the green and twisting Tisza, and your imagination will speak to you as unmistakably as a growling stomach. Because the water that poured at your feet here was on Montenegro a few days ago and will join the Danube near Novi Sad a few days from now. That's the way of it: geography orders space but muddles the head, and a man would rather be a fish than mentally straddle north and south, east and west.

Persistently, if indirectly, we tended east. Somewhat in the style of Švejk's peregrination to České Budejovice. From Tokaj we ran to escape the rain, only to have the sky open on us in Budapest. From Budapest we ran to escape the crowds, chaos, and homelessness, only to find ourselves, at four in the morning, escorted off the train by an over-six-foot conductor, in the unknown yet sizable city of Nyíregyháza. Four in the morning is an hour when you either sit and weep or keep going. At the platform just then, an antique narrow-gauge pulled in, so we didn't hesitate. In the carriage was a genuine coal stove, its pipe going right through the ceiling. We rocked the whole way to Sóstófürdő, because our pretty green choo-choo ended there. Sóstófürdő still slept. A health resort at five a.m. is an uncommon sight. Between the trees gleamed the saucer of a salt lake. An old-fashioned water tower; huge umbrellas with the inscription *John Bull Pub*; an exquisite hotel, in the Swiss style yet standing here on the eastern border of the Great Hungarian Plain. Limos agleam in the morning sun; villas reminiscent of Chinese socialist realism; blocked signs that said no longer ZIMMER FREI but WOLNE POKOJE, "rooms available" in Polish; and no movement or sound other than the chirp of birds at dawn. Except a dog out of nowhere sniffed at us and continued on its way. A spa without people always seems like a stage set. We found a pension on a sandy lane. A woman in an apron swept the steps. We said we wanted to sleep, nothing more. She told us, in an English German, that we could sleep until five in the afternoon, because a disco started then.

We woke to the sound of our native tongue. Before the pension, three guys in baggy shorts urged their girlfriend, "Andżelika, fucking take it!" "You have to pose," replied Andżelika, trying to get the swaying group in her lens. "We're all standing here, take it!" the guys pleaded, steadying one another. Our trip had become a little too Polish.

We took our leave of Sóstófürdő with a modest lunch. In the square where the pub was, a wild show advertising Sprite. Gangsta rap over loudspeakers while Hungarian kids on skateboards slalomed in and out of giant green bottles, imagining themselves black brothers. At a table nearby, the father of a family called to the waiter in Polish, "*Kotlet schabowy z frytkami!* Veal cutlet with fries! Veal cutlet, dummy!" No matter how much the man raised his voice, however, the Hungarian dummy didn't understand a word. It was time to go. I couldn't find Kossuths in any kiosk or shop. I had become dependent on them, flattened and twenty-five to a pack. Those orange packs mark the divide between provincial and urban: they are a provincial attempt at urban. You can get them in any village or Zemplén town cut to the human scale, but not in Tokaj, and no way in Budapest.

And that, more or less, was our trip. Instead of following the path of Lajos Kossuth, we took the route of cheapest possible tobacco. Lajos Kossuth endures in the names of streets, squares, and boulevards, but those cigarettes in orange packs vanish along with the world that smokes them, just as the obscure country inns in which I felt so much at home vanish. I thought of my Europe as a place where, no matter what the distance covered and despite the borders and changing languages, a person feels he is merely going, say, from Gorlice to Sanok. Thus I reflected on the last decent myth or illusion to be applied like a bandage to the wounds and abrasions of homelessness in this ever more orphaned world. My thoughts were sentimental, yet I indulged in them on the road between Nagykálló and Mátészalka under the purple western sky. The purple I imagined as the glow from burning Vienna, which was treating its provinces and peripheries to one last spectacle, sacrificing in a gigantic auto-da-fé its spit-and-polish shops, Graben display windows, archetypal burghers walking their dogs in the morning, memories and deep sadness blowing like the wind between the Hofburg Palace and Maria Theresa Square. At most only the Café Havelka would be spared, and a night sausage stand on St Stephen's Square. Thus I reflected between Nagykálló and Mátészalka, trying to stage a heroic, impressive end for a world dying naturally, of simple old age.

• • •

"This route is known for robbery. Even the customs officers on the Ukrainian side will extort money from travellers or confiscate possessions that they want." So says the guidebook. Obviously that's the route we immediately chose. Not that there was another way to get from Hungary to Ukraine.

Waiting for the border train at the station in Záhony, we took all the necessary precautions. First we hid, at the bottom of the backpack, the possession that they would want: a fifteen-year-old Praktica camera. Then we prepared ourselves for extortion, stuffing in various pockets bills of all the currencies we carried. A dollar here, two there, ten in another place in case a higher bribe was needed. Also Slovak crowns, forints, even Romanian lei, because who knew what those guys would want? For courage, we drank the last of our pear brandy, brushing aside the unpleasant thought that it might be our last in this life.

The train pulled in: all of two carriages, plus the locomotive. In the first carriage, young men and women loaded merchandise — washers, refrigerators, stoves, tyres, halves and quarters of automobiles, and miscellaneous items of daily use. The second carriage was for us and a hundred other travellers. Besides our Polish, people spoke Hungarian, Ukrainian, Russian, Romany, and Romanian. A woman sitting opposite us had only her passport and a five-litre bottle of oil. The Hungarians checked our papers as the train crossed the border bridge over the Tisza. Then something happened in the passageway between the two carriages. One skinhead kid hit another skinhead kid. The girls got into it, and so much was going on, you couldn't see a thing. Someone must have lost the fight, because one of the girls came to our compartment and asked for a bottle of water, for reviving the injured party. It seemed a completely internal disagreement, so we were calm and admired the scenery. A Ukrainian guard appeared with a customs officer. He nonchalantly looked at the passports and stamped them with no interest. Feverishly I tried to remember which pockets held which bills. Fear had driven it all out of my head, so there was a chance I might pull out, like an utter fool, a fifty. The border folk were approaching; in a panic I clutched five hundred Romanian lei in my hand—that is, enough to buy a box of matches in Bucharest. The guard finally came to us, and I handed him our passports. He barely looked at them, slipped them in his pocket, and said in Ukrainian, "See me at the station in Chop."

At the station in Chop, the unloading took time. Washers, refrigerators, halves and quarters of cars were lifted and passed over people's heads. The two skinheads, in perfect amity, carried a television set together. We saw our guard in the crowd. He gestured for us with a tired look. We followed him, and now I remembered where I had hidden the hundred dollars. He led us, like convicts, through the hall for arrivals. Now and then he nodded at someone. We passed the customs table, the passport window, pushed through the crowd, and were suddenly on the other side. Then our cicerone gave us our stamped passports and said, "I didn't want you to have to stand in those lines. You have hryvnias?" "Only dollars," I blurted, idiot that I was. He looked around the hall and waved over a short guy who held a plastic bag. The guy approached. The guard said, "Exchange money for them, but at a decent rate." The bag was full of hryvnias in bundles tied with rubber bands. The guard asked us if we needed anything else, wished us a pleasant trip, and we were again alone.

Baia Mare

ANYWAY, I SAW Baia Mare in the rays of the sun sinking westward on the Great Hungarian Plain. Remnants of rain still hung in the air, and a rainbow rose over the valley of the Lăpuş River. Damp golden dust billowed up from the plain, the road, the bridge, pastures, from the white clouds of trees in bloom, from the world: the whole province of Maramureş. Light like that occurs only after a storm, when space fills with electricity. It's possible, however, that this light emanated from deep within the earth, from hidden veins of mountain ore. Baia Mare, Nagybánya, the Great Mine, lodes of gold, a Transylvanian El Dorado 250 kilometres from my home — these were my thoughts as I crossed the Lăpuş. To the north, Ignis Mountain, still in shade, its peaks a wet dark blue. The storm preceded us and now was moving along the Black Tisa above Chornohora and Świdowiec.

I saw Baia Mare from a distance, not wanting to drive into the town. Ahead, a bypass to Sighetu and Cluj wove through industrial suburbs. There was not one car or person in sight.

The flat field was choked with rusting metal, pieces of concrete, abandoned plastic. Landfill smouldered sleepily, reeking. The sun shone on red-brown construction beams, on the broken windows of factories, on gutted warehouses, on lifeless cranes, on corroded steel, and on eroded brick. Pylons, silos, cranes, and chimneys cast long black shadows. As far as the eye could see, a tangle of wires in the sky, a web of rails on the ground. Mounds of black sludge — some kind of chemical waste — gave way to mounds of containers: polymer, cardboard, glass. Tin cans, rubber hoses, radioactive mud, cyanides from gold mines, lead and zinc, rags and nylon, acids and bases, asphalt, ponds of oil, soot, smoke, the final decadence of industry, all under a bright sky.

Among these ruins and dumps, cows grazed on patches of maltreated grass. In the shadow of a giant steel chimney trotted a flock of sheep. In Baia Mare, time circled. Animals walked between inert machines. These seemingly frail, soft, and defence-less creatures had endured since the beginning of the world and now were quietly triumphant. It was the same in Oradea: cows sunning themselves at railroad junctions, and the train carriages off on the sidings had the reddish brown colour of the animals but were cold, dead, spent. It was the same outside Satu Mare, where sheep wandered down the centre of Route 19, and in Suceava, where a white horse grazed in the heart of town, and again in Oradea, where horses, in a maze of rails and bypasses, among endless hangars and rolling trucks — bays, piebalds, greys, dapples — cropped on the toxic grass. It looked as if they had fed there forever.

A few days later in the Banat, Valiu told us about the first Romanian locomotive. It was built in the town of Reşiţa in the year 1872, and the people wanted to show it to the emperor in

Vienna, because the Universal Exhibition was fast approaching. Unfortunately there were as yet no train tracks in that region. So they hitched the steam engine to twelve pairs of oxen and pulled it towards the Danube, towards the Iron Gates, the port at Turnu-Severin or Orşova, in any case a good hundred kilometres across the green Banat Mountains. The heated bodies of the animals, gleaming with sweat, must have resembled steam engines themselves. Straps, chains, wooden yokes on necks, mud, squeaking, curses, the valley filled with the stink of golden piss mixed with the odours of people and beasts. Over the harnesses, flies swarmed to feed on cuts and scrapes. The black, oiled machine moved slowly, with dignity, and its red abdomen shone so bright that the Serbian and Romanian villagers it passed stood dazzled, made the sign of the cross, spat on the ground in disgust, fear, awe. They had never seen such a thing before and were convinced that the world was coming to an end. The riveted demon proceeded through the countryside to the crack of whips, and the wheels of the platform that carried the monster sliced the earth so deep, the marks would never heal. Fires were lit at the night bivouacs, soldiers stood guard, and the drivers drank themselves senseless, because their hearts were uneasy. Flames flickered in the dark-blue eyes of the oxen.

How long did this expedition take? Valiu, who knew everything about the Banat, didn't recall. Two weeks? Three? At the riverbank, the drivers unhitched the animals, received their pay, and with relief returned to the deep valley forest.

Yes, my Europe is full of animals. The huge muddy swine on the road between Tiszaörs and Nagyiván, the dogs in the beer gardens of Bucharest, the buffalo in Răşinari, the horses set loose in Chornohora. I wake at five in the morning and hear the clank of sheep bells. Rain falls, and the mooing of cows is muffled, flattened, echoless. Once I asked a woman why there were so many cows on her farm if no one bought milk. "What do you mean, why?" she replied, puzzled. "We have to keep something, don't we?" It simply didn't occur to her that one could, you know, cut the ancient bond between beast and human being. "What are we if we don't have animals?" That was more or less the sense of her answer: fear of the loneliness of our species. Animals are our link to the rest of the world. We care for and eat our ancestors.

You can see this clearly here, as clearly as in Baia Mare, in the rubble of the industrial world, which lasted no more than a century, and even if someone rebuilds it, it will carry the seeds of its own destruction. Machines are zombies. They live on our lust after objects, on our greed, on our thirst for immortality. They live only as long as they are needed. We look away, and immediately they begin to fall apart, wither, and shake like vampires deprived of blood. Only a few reach a graceful old age. That ferry in Tiszatardos, for example: the creaking wooden platform, propelled by a small diesel engine, slowly and reluctantly crossing the green Tisa. Willows and poplars on both shores. No superstructure but a tin shack where pear brandy and strong coffee were served. The heat bringing the stink of fish and muck up from the river bottom. At one end of the run, a herd of black-and-white cattle belly-deep in the water. The honey sun slowing all motion and sound. In its light, the old boat like a dried leaf blown in from some remote autumn. The engineer as hoary as the boat. For the thousandth time gazing at the scenery, at the verdant mirror of the river. The diesel whirred, smelled of petroleum, blended into the picture. I could not conceive of its absence here. When the chill of autumn came, the old man could warm himself beside it. During longer stops, when no customers waited on either shore, he must have tended to it, inspected it, wiped its dun chassis to make sure there was no fuel or oil leak. I think that both were lonely in that unending journey, which brought them neither close to nor far from anything. They were on a pendulum across the current of time.

The day after, I had to be in Baia Mare, which once was called Nagybánya. I had to sniff out that incessant *once*, which, where I live, is the present, because tomorrow never arrives; it remains in distant countries. Our tomorrow is seduced by their allure, bribed, or possibly just tired. Whatever is to come never gets here; it gets used up en route, flickers out like the light from a lantern too far away. A perpetual decline reigns here, and children are born exhausted. In the slanting light of late autumn, the gestures and bodies of people are more expressive the less meaning they have. Men stand on street corners staring at the emptiness of the day. They spit on the pavement and smoke cigarettes. That's the present. That's how it is in the town of Sabinov, in the town of Gorlice, Gönc, Caransebeş, in the whole region between the Black Sea and the Baltic. They stand and count the cigarettes in the packs and the change in their pockets. Time, approaching from afar, is like the air that someone else has already breathed.

Țara Secuilor, Székelyföld, Szeklerland

MEANWHILE I PIECED my old map back together with tape. It had torn and cracked from being constantly folded and unfolded in the wind, across my knees, on the hood of the car. I bought it long ago in Miercurea-Ciuc, 150 kilometres to the east. No maps are for sale here, though the land between Sachsenbach, Magyarcserged, and Roșia de Secaș is like an illustration out of the oldest geography book: treeless undulation. The hills collapsing under their own weight, the enormous sky bearing down. In this limitless monotony of ground, the flocks of sheep are nearly invisible. The animals are the colour of sunburned grass.

It's an oven every time I come here. I consult my map and notice that on the field path from Cergău two men are pushing bicycles. They mount when they reach asphalt and ride along a desolate hollow. They roll like black pebbles on the edge between sky and bleached grass. Soon I can make out the fluttering of their open jackets. When the road sinks a little, they don't need to pedal. The first passes me and takes a hairpin turn down towards Rothkirch. The second brakes, approaches, stands. He is tattered and dirty. The clothes and old-fashioned bicycle are both coming apart. Of what he says, I understand only *foc* and *fuma*, so I take out my lighter as he digs in his pockets and finds a pack of Carpati. I light his cigarette; he inhales, thanks me, and takes off again on his squeaking bicycle, whose rust has eaten the grease in every mechanical part. The cloud of smoke and the body odour he leaves behind dissipate in the air, which in turn fills with ubiquitous sheep dung and trampled herbs. The wind again lifts his black jacket, then the man is gone forever. I consult the map and try to determine if he is headed towards Székásveresegyháza, Tău, or Ohaba, villages that resemble muddy turtle shells lying in a depression. Seen from above: the walls a dusty, dingy bile-yellow, the roofs covered with bronze scales.

It's the same at Spring, a ground-floor town. The houses run like walls along either side of the road. Squat and heavy houses, whose canopied gateways lead to cramped yards, but that's just my guess, because the gates are all shut and seem permanently locked, in fear of the vastness above the bare hills.

Desertum — that's what this region was called when King Bela III brought settlers from Flanders and from the Rhine and Moselle regions. In those days, a distance of 1,500 kilometres meant for the common man that he would not have the strength to return. Clumsy carts on huge wheels, yoked oxen across the Brabant, up the Rhine. Through Moguntia, the narrow valleys of the Black Forest, with cattle blatting-bellowing all about, in mud, then near Freiburg they had to find the thin thread of the Danube, then endure rain at stops between Augsburg and Ratisbon, campfires made from wet logs, the smoke blackening earthen pots, the continent tilting gently to the east, but what suffices for the flow of a river is small comfort for people who are mired and dread a future that mingles with and is mistaken for open space.

I stopped at Şpring, for coffee. But it easily could have been in Gergeschdorf. The pub had iron chairs and tables. A hot and filthy place. Two men sat in a corner, reeking of sheep, looking as if they had emerged from a primeval time: black, thickset, with beard and matted hair tangled into one. Beside them, a dilapidated pinball machine. They had obviously just left their animals: the trousers at the knees gleamed with the grease that covers wool. Despite the heat they wore sweaters and cloaks. They drank their Ciuc beer without a word, staring, to each side, at the room, which must have been too small for them, confining, so they drank gulp after gulp, to get back outside as soon as possible.

The bartender had a white, puffy face. I spoke a few words in Romanian, but he only took my money, gave me change, and returned to his dreary kingdom of a couple of bottles of Bihor palinka, Carpati cigarettes, and capped, potbellied flasks of wine cheaper than Coke or Fanta. There was also an enamel pot and a percolator covered with charred brown — a veteran of hundreds of boiled coffees.

I took my coffee and sat by the window to gaze out at the Transylvanian swelter. The two men now had produced, from somewhere, 1.5-litre plastic jugs and were waiting at the counter for them to be filled with beer. Then I saw them walking down the baked street, their silhouettes as dark as their shadows, their movements quick, minimal, efficient, like those of animals.

No one else entered. The guy behind the bar killed time with the help of little activities that invariably slowed and stopped.

Pale and massive, he absorbed time like a sponge. Moved something, wiped something, adjusted something, but the future never came. His ancestors arrived here eight hundred years ago on carts drawn by oxen. They built cities, villages, and fortified churches on hilltops. They established hospitals and homes for the elderly. They chose their own priests and judges. They answered to the king alone and were exempt from paying taxes. They only had to provide the Royal Hungarian Army with five hundred mounted soldiers. They brought with them, in their heads, images of their homes and shrines left along the Rhine, to re-create them here in the same shape and proportions. A Gothic of brick and stone thus materialized among the hills of this desert. Clocks on four-sided towers were wound and began marking the hours, which before had passed in an uninterrupted flow.

Nothing happening outside the window. From over the dry hills the heat came, floated in through the open door, filled the interior, all the crap and clutter, dirt, notched glasses, greasy steins, cloudy bottles, cadaverous plastic. The heat settled in stifling waves on the broken furniture, pressed against the walls, against the flyspecked panes, swept this entire dumping ground of remnants pretending to be useful, resolutely playing out a comedy of survival. The Transylvanian desert entered the pub in Gergeschdorf and made itself at home.

I took my cup to the counter. The man didn't even look up. Only when I said, "Danke, auf wiedersehen," did he look, as if seeing me for the first time. He tried to do something with his heavy face, but I was no longer there.

That same day I drove to Roşia, a village forty kilometres south-east. I wanted to see the place where the pastor lived who wrote books and was a prison chaplain. He wasn't at home, had gone to Budapest. Or that's what the man said who opened the church for me. Inside, it was cramped and bare. Cushions on the benches. In that space of stone, all the fittings were random and flimsy, as if somebody had attempted to put furniture in an ancient cave. From the motto on the black pennant, I could recall only " . . . so will ich dir die Krone des Lebens geben". Six-armed candelabra, red tapers. The pews held no more than a dozen people. I had read that the parishioners were mostly Gypsies. The smell of sacred antiquity had permeated the walls, and now the walls exuded it, but as a feeble, reproachful scent, attenuated by many years of damp and cold, as in the house of old people whom no one ever visits. Or in a dollhouse long outgrown by its owner. Afterwards, I went to the edge of the village, to look at the Oltu valley. On the northern slopes of the Negoiu and Moldoveanu lay snow. A swarthy family in a small cart rattled down a yellow stone road, and the children yelled at me in greeting: "Buna ziua! Buna ziua!"

On the way back to my car, I noticed the little shop. A few steps up to the entrance; inside, room enough only to stand and turn round. A narrow counter divided the tiny area in two. Over it, a few shelves on the wall. The merchandise was like that in other shops in this Romanian province: a bit of this and that, everything faded and humble. The jars, bags, bottles looked as if they had been there forever and would stay to the end, until a time of some graceful evaporation. But the pity of this insignificance, this reminder of the necessities — sugar, rice, matches, Carpati cigarettes — created in that dark and close interior an aura of the heroic. Everything was in order, tidy without compromise. The shelves were lined with clean paper, the various objects placed at distances from each other measured precisely.

A world that was gone, passed on, yet it would take with it to the grave its considered and purposeful style.

From a narrow door leading to a supply room, a little old woman emerged. I didn't need anything but asked for something to drink. She moved like a wizened ghost: slow, noiseless, careful not to disturb the still of the shop. She smiled and said she had to go down to the basement, which served as her icebox. She returned with a cool bottle of some kind of juice. She gave me my change slowly, counting the money with great care.

I went out and sat on the steps. The late afternoon smelled of manure and resignation. From the high walls round the houses no sound reached me. The burning shadow of eternal siesta filled the lanes and weakened time in the village of Roşia. No doubt there were clocks in the homes, but their hands turned to no purpose.

The next day I was in Iacobeni, forty kilometres to the northeast. Unable to extricate myself from the Siebenbürgen labyrinth. Leaving Hortobágyfalva, I ended up on the Härwesdorf turnpike. I drove into Alţina, drove out of Alzen. What began as Agnita ended up Szentágota. Everything took much longer than any calculation of kilometres and hours would have indicated. Travelling through a multiplied land, I went twice, three times as slowly.

Iacobeni was empty. In the centre of a big square grew several old trees. A grassy parade ground was rimmed by buildings close together. Most of the houses looked abandoned. The rest of the village too gave that appearance. The sun was at its zenith, so possibly everyone was asleep, yet no one could have been that tired, to leave both square and houses to their own devices.

Overgrown, crumbling, tilted, full of cracks, returning to the soil. Paint fell from boards, plaster from walls. Unsupervised, matter was collapsing under its own weight. I stood in the shade of a tree.

Then, out of nowhere, five kids. The oldest could have been ten. They were incredibly alive in that dead afternoon landscape. As if the sun gave them strength. They surrounded me in a circle and one after the other tried to start a conversation, in several languages at once: Romanian, German, an indeterminate Slavic tongue — Russian? Slovak? — inserting the occasional English word and, who knows, Hungarian. At the centre of this verbal vortex, I could only laugh. At last I understood: they wanted to show the ignorant wanderer their village — that is, Saxon curiosities in the form of ruins of a fortified church. I clearly wasn't the first or last. I went with them but had not the least interest in venerable monuments. I watched these young Gypsies. The whole village belonged to them. Most likely they hadn't been born here. Their parents occupied homes of Germans who had returned to the old country. Everything here was in Gypsy possession now. This village of several hundred years had become an encampment. What had seemed immutable was now temporary, practically non-existent. The kids showed me a medieval church that they hadn't built, gave me pears from roadside trees that they hadn't planted, and spoke in languages that were not their own. They arrived two hundred years or more after the Saxons, and no one had invited them. They did not bring with them, in their heads, images of a homeland, pictures of residences or shrines that they could reproduce. Their memory held no history, only tales and fables — forms that by our criteria belong to children and are not worth preserving. As for artefacts, they had only those that would disappear with them and leave no trace.

They showed me the house in which the local priest or pastor lived. They called him *pater*. Through the closed and grated gate, not much could be seen: a cared-for yard, a grapevine shielding the house, and something like a pool. In comparison with the rest of the village, it seemed absurd. I rang, but no one appeared. I asked if the priest was all right: "Bun pater?" They shook their heads: "Nu bun, nu . . ."

I considered this decaying village, the trash in the centre of the square, the rectory and pool all fearfully gated and locked, and decided that it was the Gypsies' victory. Since the year 1322, when Europe first noted their presence on the Peloponnesian peninsula, they had not changed. Europe brought into being nations, kingdoms, empires, and governments, which rose and fell. Focused on progress, expansion, growth, it could not imagine that life might be lived outside time, outside history. Meanwhile the Gypsies with a sardonic smile regarded the paroxysms of our civilization, and if they took anything for themselves, it was the rubbish, the garbage, the ruined homes, and alms. As if all the rest were of no value.

Now Saxon Iacobeni had fallen to them. Among the walls that had absorbed centuries of effort, thrift, tradition, and all such virtues that maintain the continuity of civilization, they simply set up camp, exactly as one sets up camp in an open field, as if no one had been there before them.

We left the locked rectory in peace. The kids pulled me down various lanes. Chattering nonstop, singing, whirling about me, until finally our procession à la Breughel reached a shop, because that had been their purpose all along. It was completely unlike the one in Roşia: a dark cubbyhole sort of depot-shack. Black-market stuff, soap, jam, everything in jumbled heaps and piles, thrown here and forgotten, covered with dust and waiting for a buyer to take pity. I bought several bottles of some kind of carbonated beverage, a bag of sweets, and we went outside. I gave it all to them, and in an instant they had divided the booty according to a complex system but one that followed the basic principle that the strongest and oldest get the most. Engaged in eating and stuffing into pockets, they no longer paid attention to me. They returned to their world, and I stayed in mine. That's how it had to be, how it had been since 1322.

On my old taped map the place-names are in Romanian, Hungarian, and German. Țara Secuilor, Székelyföld, Szeklerland. No one thought to write them also in Romany. I think that the Gypsies themselves are the least interested in this. Their geography is mobile and elusive. It very likely will outlast ours.

The Country in Which
the War Began

AT 5:30 IN THE MORNING it was still completely dark. I went out to Prešernovo Nabrežje, Prešeren Quay, and turned right, north-west. The water was black-blue and smooth. In the light of the streetlamps, the beach stones gleamed after yesterday's rain. I had travelled here to see the western edge of Slavic Europe.

From the narrow inlets between the stones came the stink of cat piss. The lighthouse beacon at the promontory delivered its last flashes into the night; in half an hour it would go off. At its base, a solitary red Renault was parked. It looked run-down; you could see the lighthouse keepers here didn't have it so good. Passing it, I reached the other side of the peninsula. The sea was heavier here, louder, more in motion. A few dozen metres from the shore, the water merged with the dark, yet I saw, in the distance, white clouds. Brighter there.

The waterfront stopped, but I went on, hopping from stone to stone. To the right, a vertical cliff of slate. Someone had put up the sign that you proceeded at your own risk.

I came for only three days and was ready for anything. Less

than twenty kilometres to the north-east lay Trieste; Venice was eighty to the west. The only thought that entered my head: the air there is just as cold and damp. From the port, the putter of diesel engines. Soon I saw the first fishing boat, small and indistinct on the dark mirror of the water. The motor died. The man at the stern sat as if waiting for the dawn to begin in earnest.

Correction: those were not clouds. An hour later I stood in the courtyard of the Saint George Cathedral and from that height could see the bay, the white peaks of the Julian Alps, and, who knows, maybe even Triglav itself. Because what are a hundred kilometres on a morning like this, when the sun shines as bright as on an afternoon in July and objects cast shadows as dark as night? The mountains burned red, orange, dimmed to violet, then dun, as the light slid down the ridges and valleys. This crystal air rendered distance null and void. The fishing boats seemed to float in the bay, only to become stuck, in an hour, in half an hour, in foothills. I had to leave the vista; it was too unreal.

Bells ringing at Saint Steven, Saint Francis, and the Immaculate Mother of God. The red rooftops of the homes arranged in an intricate mosaic. From the chimneys, vertical columns of sky-blue smoke. The smell of resin and incense, logs burning in stoves. No doubt an illusion, but I could have sworn there was also a whiff of ground and steamed coffee. Among the geometry of the tiled surfaces, the green daubs of gardens. Not one scrap of free space in this town; nothing wild, nothing abandoned or in disrepair, no space simply as space. That's why there were so few dogs here, despite those occasional containers with a picture of Fido taking a dump. This was a town of cats. Looking down, I saw them coming out of their nooks and crannies to find a warm patch of sun. Dozens of toms and tabbies in a hundred different colours and shades. Singly, in pairs, chasing down, sidling up to, courting, ignoring, tails lifted as they tensely patrolled the perimeter of their territory, gambolling, enjoying a morning stretch. They were small, medium, and as large as an ordinary dog. In thirty minutes in one spot I counted fifty cats. They rubbed against chimneys, licked themselves, jumped from their place and back to it. A veritable feline kingdom. It was the only movement I could observe from the high walls of Saint George. All to the accompaniment of the bells of the Immaculate Mother of God.

It is good to come to a country you know practically nothing about. Your thoughts grow still, useless. Everything must be rebuilt. In a country you know nothing about, there is no reference point. You struggle to associate colours, smells, dim memories. You live a little like a child, or an animal. Objects and events may bring things to mind, but in the end they remain no more than what they are in fact. They begin only when we experience them, vanish when others follow. So they truly have no significance. They are made of that primal substance that touches our senses but is too light, too evanescent, to teach us anything.

When I returned to the waterfront, the day was well under way. The pubs were open, the cars were manoeuvring on the narrow boulevard, guys in overalls were skilfully hoisting buckets on scaffolds, garbage men were removing furniture that had been put out but looked perfectly fine, women in high heels were stepping round what was left of puddles, and stewed onions filled the air. A man in a sweater, old boots, and track pants went to the water's edge and cast his spinning rod. After the fifth or sixth cast, he reeled in a fish. He struck it against a stone slab and disappeared with his stunned prize down a small street. Children with backpacks walked to school, and pairs of elderly ladies took their strolls in mincing steps. At the port marina, fishermen in wool caps worked on their boats. One of them threw fish guts on the shore. A black cat immediately appeared. A moment later, a dog ran up, but the cat sent it packing. Under the arcades of the open market facing the port stood young men with tired faces, traditionally waiting for the day to bring an opportunity or surprise.

All this in blinding sun along the land's very edge. The interior of the town was dark, humid, labyrinthine. The houses grew one out of the other, leaned on one another, parted to a width of outstretched arms, and the dirty little cobblestone streets took paths in a way that bordered on the perverse. A hair separated neighbour from neighbour. Sometimes a door opened directly on the street, and you could see a neat row of boots, clothes on hangers, a mirror a person had quickly consulted before leaving. Wandering through the centre of town, even when there was no one around, was like wandering through an invisible crowd. Voices on the other side of walls, conversations, tables placed under lit lamps, the smell of food, the sound of water in bathrooms, arguments, gestures, the entire intimacy of life in reach of your eyes, ears, nose. The town was one big house, a thousand rooms connected by cold, dark corridors — or a comfortable prison where each inmate could engage in his favourite activity. Piran: a monastery for the laity.

Such cities were possible, I thought, only by the sea or in the desert. In a locked landscape, the inhabitants might go mad. Here, only a few dozen steps were needed to take you off the human termitarium, this creation half architectural, half geological, to where limitless sea and air began, bounded only by the indistinct line of the horizon.

At eight in the morning I sipped coffee and watched the white ferry leave Pula for Venice. The waitress wiped the raindrops off my table. From a pub wafted *Buena Vista Social Club*. A little dog ran inside, lifted its leg to the leg of a chair, pissed, calmly departed. It was dim within, all wood, like an old ship, but I preferred to sit outside and see the air brighten. The delivery vans busy around the marina. The masts of yachts moving like uncertain needles on dials. A couple of old women chatting in Italian. More and more cats. They warmed themselves on the boulders along the beach. A quiet, unreal place, this, resembling no other, bringing to mind nothing but the abstract idea of harmony. Eight in the morning, sun, coffee, a white ferry, and Cuban music: an eclectic dream come to life.

Except I was here to see the country in which the last Balkan war began. It lasted ten days and claimed sixty-six lives. It's possible that the Yugoslav army departed in such haste because the Serbs felt that they were in a truly foreign land. Having no graves here, no memories, they confronted their deprivation. The invading of small, peripheral peoples is by necessity a provincial matter. You acquire territory that in some way reminds you of home, of the village you grew up in. Foreignness is a problem for the conqueror: it undermines his identity. Tiny Slovenia turned out to be too big for Greater Serbia. What could the Serbs do in this tidy, well-ordered land like some Hapsburg dream of the empire's mission to civilize? War must have a common language, some shared meaning, and bloody deeds are like all deeds, in that they cannot exist in a vacuum.

"I do not wish to defend the Balkan peoples, but neither do I wish to ignore their merits. The love of devastation, of internal disorder, the world like a brothel in flames, the sardonic view of cataclysms both past and future, the sourness, the sweet

inactivity of those who cannot sleep or those who murder . . .
They alone, the primitives of Europe, give Europe the fillip she
needs, but she invariably considers it the ultimate humiliation.
Because if the South-east were nothing but an abomination, why
should she feel, abandoning it and turning to these lands, as if
she were falling — however magnificent the fall — into desert?"

At 8:15 I sat over my empty cup and ruminated on these words
of Emil Cioran. And tried to situate the south-east and the
Balkans.

I took home promotional material from some roadside inn near
the Croatian border. The colourful brochure contained, in addition to ads for pubs, hotels, and camping grounds, a small map
of Europe. Spain had its Madrid, France its Paris, Switzerland
Zurich, Austria Vienna, and so on. But to the east and south of
Prague and Budapest lay a terra incognita: countries without
capitals, and some countries weren't even there. No Slovakia.
Moldova, Ukraine, and Belarus all evaporated in the dried-up
sea of old empire. Yet the map was quite new, because the borders
of the post-Yugoslav nations were clearly marked. The only city
that had been preserved in the enigmatic south-east was Athens,
apparently old enough to assume the role of fossil. Sofia, Bucharest, Belgrade, Warsaw, and Bratislava were gone, swallowed by a
primordial void that one could point to but not name or describe.
Which made sense, because what could come from that region
other than inchoateness and weather reports? Names organized
nothing, having no fixed, established, verifiable meaning.

It was late afternoon when I crossed the border at Hodoš.
The winter light gave objects an extra sharpness. The customs

officer asked me how many dinars I had, though for more than ten years now purchases had been made only in tolars. He took a second look in my boot, said "Hvala", then I was driving between the rotten yellow hills of Prekmurje. At that time of the year, you always see more, because the bare landscape collects what has been dropped by human beings and reveals the vulnerability of matter left to itself. This time, however, nothing of the sort: the country seemed completely finished, done with care, polished. I could find no cracks in the scenery that imagination might slip into. Nothing here recalled the places from which I had come. Everything was second-hand yet at the same time respectably new. As far as the eye could see, no sign of decay or growth or ostentation. Sturdy grey walls, gabled roofs, dead gardens, and vineyards left for the winter in the best condition — you took it all in at a glance, but nothing claimed your attention. This country was made in imitation of the perfect country. Stuck in the corner of Europe, between Germanic Austria, Romance Italy, Finno-Ugric Hungary, and Slavic Croatia, it endured by mimicking a universal ideal. As I was getting ready to come here, my acquaintances said, "Go, it's one of the prettiest spots on the Continent." Immediately pleasing to the eye. Nothing superfluous anywhere. Quiet villages lay at the bottom of valleys. White churches on hilltops stood watch over such good fortune. In the towns, a Hapsburg Baroque drew refined shapes against a dark sky. Murska Sobota, Ljutomir, Ptuj, Majsperk, Rogatec, Rogaška Slatina. I couldn't stop, constantly feeling that there would be a sudden reversal, that the land — for my benefit alone — would do a salto mortale, but no, it remained on good terms with itself. I was a barbarian from the unwashed, unfinished east. There was no contrast here, no chaos, no trap to put my wits to the test. Accustomed to discontinuity, to losing the thread, to plot twists dreamlike and in bad taste, I could not deal with a space arranged in so irrevocable a way.

I slept in Prelasko. The inn was empty. At the bar sat two locals. Not particularly different from our locals who worked on a slightly better class of farm. They drank Laško beer and some kind of clear liquor in turn. Smoked cigarettes, conversed in low voices. Wore dirty clothes, looked like beggars. Unshaven, rumpled, and evidently not worried about the day's division between work and rest. They were the kind who could get into bed as they were. They had another round, but I saw no change in them. They drank calmly, as if performing a duty. In their words and gestures, not a trace of the impatience so common where I came from. They were stolid and solemn in their drinking, without inebriation or male neurosis. Both drank "internally". The peace and melancholy of their conversation didn't go at all with the four or five fifties they drank in the course of an hour or hour and a half. Not to mention all the beer. Finally they rose, shuffled in their rubber boots, and left, and the innkeeper didn't even come out from behind the bar to see if the right money had been left on the table. I was alone with my wine. The boss got into a black Mercedes with double exhaust pipes and took off. I went out to the driveway to look at the Slovenian night. Frost had settled on last year's grass. The round moon silvered the long mountain ridge. In the distance, a lone dog was barking.

"He sensed and at the same time knew: this is the home of devils, depressed and morose . . . Here among the alpine valleys and a little farther, on the plains of Panonia. They are in the wind, in the air; you cannot hide from them. In the lakes and among the hills, in the roots of trees, in the fens, among the rocky cliffs. They are in the village taverns and on the city streets empty on a Sunday. They are in children, men, old men . . . Everyone here is steeped in death. Death in the likeness of a lovely landscape, autumnal and cold, vernal and warm. In the autumn, Gothic; in the spring, Baroque. They are strewn, as the churches are, throughout the country; as thick as gravestones — which the people here love to decorate with flowers, candles, angels . . . On Sunday afternoons, when foreigners and immigrants wander the abandoned streets, surprised at the emptiness — on Sunday afternoons it does not seem out of place that a man will open a window on the fourth floor, where every window is shuttered, and throw himself out with a rope around his neck."

The next day I drove across Kočevski Rog, a stretch of mountains to the south, near the border with Croatia. For thirty-five kilometres I saw no other car. The gravel road ran through a forest and climbed the main peak, Visoki Rog. I was on snowy, icy switchbacks, doing no more than thirty kph. Not a soul. This was one of the most beautiful roads I had ever seen. The sun a golden mist floating among the fir trees. Snow melting in the warmth, and sometimes, when I stopped, I could hear, in the stillness of the high forest, the whisper of a thousand drops joining to make a stream. Light and shadow intermingled endlessly, and though it was a bright day, everything seemed submerged in green water. The southern side of the peak steamed. I saw birds I couldn't name. This was neither Gothic nor Baroque. Kočevski Rog suggested an architecture that would never come to pass, because the simplicity of its beauty would throw into question the whole point of an imagination.

In the dark valleys lay 10,000 bodies. I was driving through the largest unmarked cemetery in Slovenia. In the summer of 1945, Tito's Communists murdered in this place, without a trial or witnesses, prisoners who had been handed over to them by armies of the Allies. These were partisans who had fought on the wrong side — the Croatian Home Guard, the Slovenian White Guard. Tito didn't brook competition. It's possible that the wolves, lynxes, and bears — more numerous then, definitely, than today — took care of the burial. Later the Marshal came here to hunt. Who knows, it might have occurred to him that he was killing the souls of traitors living on in the bodies of the animals.

At nine I left the blue coast and walked to Tartinijev Square to see some fifteenth-century Venetian Gothic architecture and the memorial to Tartini. He stood on a pedestal, in a wig, with a violin in his lowered hand, most likely bowing to the audience. I would have preferred to feel like a tourist but felt instead like a spy doing cursory reconnaissance. I could touch things but had no idea what they meant to those for whom they had been made. I remembered the golden light at Kočevski Rog and couldn't shake the thought that there were places, whole cities, whole countries, whose form and content defied description. Because if communism elsewhere was simply a crime, then here, in this land, it must have seemed a marriage of horror and imbecility. An idea conceived in empty heads fearing empty space was applied in a land that had ruled out the possibility of change. Marshal Tito in a white uniform among palm trees on a promenade in nearby Portorož must have seemed an African chieftain. Communism, after all, had been the fruit of long, hopeless winters, when people began to go mad from boredom and from the fear of the self. It made sense, if it made sense at all, only on a flat, featureless plain where nothing happened and therefore anything could happen.

Small countries should be allowed to cut history class. They should be like islands off to the side of the main current of progress. That was my thought two days later, on the highway to Ljubljana. Near Postojna it suddenly turned cold and foggy. I considered this fairy-tale, utopian variant as I passed Croatian trucks. Small countries should be protected as childhood is protected. The citizens of hypertrophied powers should visit them to learn sense. A wasted effort, no doubt, but why not give people a chance to reflect on the many other ways to look at this best of all possible worlds? The existence of small countries of moderate temperament is simply a challenge to common ideas on such subjects as expansion, might, size, mission, and all those other collective axioms. As for me, I've always wanted to live in a smaller country — never, God forbid, in a larger one. It is much more difficult for negligibility to turn into a caricature of itself than for greatness to do so. And in any case it does less harm to its surroundings.

The Slovenian writer Edvard Kocbek, in his *Parisian Notebook*, wrote:

"Our history is not marked by great passions; its poverty does not permit the assumption of any weighty mission. We can rely on no original declaration of faith, no communal character. The nature of our country is convex rather than concave; it has no true centre of gravity, which would indicate a geographic as well as moral centre. For this reason we lack thinkers of centripetal energy, souls who bear witness to our identity, souls of a crystallized fate . . . We never regarded our national borders as a test of quality, as trustworthy passage, as solution or inspiration — or as temptation, shame, and an opportunity for smuggling."

So again, that lack, that unfulfilment, that sigh for a life elsewhere. Greatness does not apply here. For sure something similar has been written by a Romanian from Romania's twenty million, by a Pole from Poland's forty million.

I circled Ljubljana's congested downtown area, looking for a place to park. On Congress Square I managed to squeeze in between a Land Rover and a BMW. On an ice rink with lanterns and music, children and an old man with a grey moustache were skating. It was Viennese-ish, except more cheerful. I heard laughter, a loud conversation on the street, and saw girls dressed in a way that was at once careless and refined. My first time here, yet I felt I knew this city. It was alive, charming. It gave the impression that it was exactly where it ought to be, not thinking about its destiny, not asking itself hard questions. Quite possibly it was utterly indifferent to, did not pine one bit for, the rest of the world. Mist shrouded the spires of the churches. At a bar not far from the fish market, I ate a sandwich and drank a small beer.

At night somewhere outside Maribor, I was stopped by the police for doing eighty in a residential area. They were in black leather and polite. I asked what would happen if I didn't pay. They told me that they would take my passport, let me go, and wait at the station for me to appear with the money. Twice as much as I would pay on the spot. They didn't look bribable. They gave me a pretty receipt with ornamental stamps, took practically everything that I had in their currency, and wished me a pleasant trip.

To get even, I decided to spend the night in Hungary.

Shqiperia

AT FIVE THIRTY in the morning in Korçë in front of the Grand Hotel, several men were already standing. In the course of the day, more came. Particularly on the wide street that led to the fairgrounds. But they also stood in front of the post office and in the shaded lane by the newspaper kiosk. By the afternoon there was a whole crowd of them. All guys. In twos and threes or by themselves, engaged in conversation or staring into space. Sometimes they took a step or two forward, then back, but the movement had no direction, it was a short break in the absence of motion. A few held bundles of Albanian bills in their hands and tried to exchange these for euros or dollars. But most just stood, smoking long, thin Karelia cigarettes, at almost three-quarters of a dollar a pack. They seemed to be waiting for something, an important piece of news, an announcement, an event, but no news came, and at each dawn they assembled again, the crowd growing as the hours passed, thinning a bit at siesta time, but in the afternoon the street was packed, the crowd swaying yet never really moving in the heat. Women appeared from time to time, secretly, sideways, barely visible. They carried bags, packages, but were ignored by the male herd. The men stayed in place, awaiting some change, staring at the vast emptiness of time, sentenced to their own stationary presence. I had seen the same thing in Tirana, at Skanderbeg Square, and in Gjirokastër, on the main street that ran from the mosque on the hill to the town. In Saranda, at six thirty in the morning, at the Lili Hotel, I went down for breakfast and found the bar filled with men. They sat over morning coffee and little glasses of raki, immersed in cigarette smoke — fifteen, maybe twenty men. They watched the street, and sometimes one spoke to another, but evidently the day had no surprises in store for them. Prisoners of the day from its beginning, they had nowhere to go; wherever they went, it was in the shackles of nothing to do.

Around Patos the land began to flatten. The mountains were now at our back. To the Adriatic it was a dozen kilometres, and the horizon to the left took on a grey-blue colour. It was hot and stuffy in the bus. People tossed cans of cola and beer out of the windows.

On the outskirts of Fier, on either side of the road were abandoned cars, mostly Mercedes and Audis, in various stages of decay. The cars were ten, fifteen, twenty years old, and there were hundreds of them, in smaller or larger groups. Near Dur-rës, the hundreds became thousands in the beating heat, on the bare ground, among clumps of burned grass. Some were nude, stripped, their metal pulled off, revealing the whole pornography of axle, undercarriage, transmission, brake drum, rusted remains; others still had parts of their chassis, baked dull, and stood staunchly on bald, wrinkled tyres. Through this endless field of bodies wandered blackened men with blowtorches, there to cut off sheets of metal still in good health. White streams of sparks brighter than the sun. A butchering of the unalive. Other men waited to receive the needed parts. The rest of the cars, lying about, had taken root in the ground: the broken bones of connecting rods, crooked pistons, blind headlights, crushed radiators, fenders eaten through, petrol cans full of holes, gutted oil filters, gearboxes with their insides strewn. Gangrene in hoses, cancer in floorboards, syphilis in gaskets, and the cataracts of shattered windows. The suburb of Durrës was a great field hospital for automotive Germany, a hospital in which only amputation was performed.

Durrës is a port, so these thousands of bodies must have come here by ship. I remember photographs of the famous Albanian exodus of 1992: people hanging over the sides like desperate bunches of grapes, from the quarterdeck, from the rigging, and fishing boats, ferries, and barges all covered with living human tape, as if the whole nation wished to flee from itself, to go as far as possible, beyond the sea, to the other side of the Adriatic, Italy, the wide world, which seemed salvation, being an unimaginable, fairy-tale opposite of their cursed land. Now from that wide world came flotillas laden with scrap, junk, internal combustion corpses.

When the highway turned towards Tirana, the bunkers began. Grey concrete skulls, jutting a metre above the ground, gazed with eyes that were black vertical slits. They looked like corpses buried standing. Each with room to accommodate a machine-gun crew. Scattered across low, flat hills, they overlooked the lifeless automobile junkyards. Junkyard and bunker both indestructible. Astrit said that in the whole country, most likely, there was not one mill in operation in order to melt down all this German metal. Nor enough dynamite to level these 600,000 bunkers built to hold off an invasion by the entire world.

An hour and a half by boat from Corfu. Half an hour by hydrofoil. The building at the Greek port is long and squat. Italian, English, and German tourists sit on piled luggage or drag day packs on wheels. The crowd pushes at the edge, divides into separate streams, forms lines at the gangplanks leading to the ferries, some of which look like seven-storey department stores. Tour buses bring all of Europe. Heaps of carry-ons with keypad locks await baggage handlers. Five guys in black leather tend their burdened Hondas and Kawasakis. At the quay stands the three-mast *Von Humboldt,* the colour of dark vegetation. Also a mahogany yacht with a British flag. On board, young men in white trousers hurrying. Glittering snakes of automobiles slowly slide into the deep holds. In the sky, you can see the white bodies of Boeings and DCs descending to land. Couples take their last snapshots in the Greek light.

We didn't have to ask where the ship to Saranda was. The crowd of people waiting there was still, pressed at the gangplank. They had boxes, cartons, circles of green garden hoses, those plastic bags in red-and-blue checks familiar in Europe and throughout the world, packages wrapped in foil, ordinary duffels, plastic bags with store names long since rubbed off, and they all seemed weary, but their weariness was not yesterday's or last month's. It was significantly older.

A Greek border guard in a white shirt and dark glasses took passports from a wooden box and called out names: Illyet . . . Freng . . . Myslim . . . Hajji . . . Bedri . . . The people grabbed their things and ran onto the feeble ship. The border guard handed the passports to a stocky civilian. It was as if a shadow had fallen on them, as if they stood under an unseen cloud, while the rest of the port — the vacationing crowd, the tanned arms of the women, the gold rings, sandals, and backpacks — was bathed in a light straight out of Kodak.

A small Amstel on board cost two euros. We sailed along the strait, the land remaining in sight. The mountain shore on our right was treeless. The burned ridge looked as if the sun had always stood at the zenith above it: eternal south, rock as old as the world, flaking from the heat.

Then I saw Saranda. It began suddenly, without warning. On the bare slopes, the skeletons of houses appeared. From a distance you'd think there had been a fire, but these buildings were unfinished. Darker than the mountains but as mineral, as if baked in a great oven and stripped by fire of everything that might suggest a home. Deep in the bay, the city thickened a little, gleamed with glass, turned green, but we sailed on, to reach the shore. A rusted crane stood in a cement square. Over a grey barrack fluttered the two-headed Albanian eagle and the blue flag of the EU. Inside were a desk and two chairs. A woman in a uniform told us to pay twenty-five euros, took thirty, gave us a receipt, and said with a smile that she had no change. On the hill above the port stood apartment blocks of rust-red concrete. But for the clothes drying on lines and the satellite dishes, they looked abandoned.

Yes, everyone should come here. At least those who make use of the name *Europe*. It should be an initiation ceremony, because Albania is the unconscious of the continent. Yes, the European id, the fear that at night haunts slumbering Paris, London, and Frankfurt am Main. Albania is the dark well into which those who believe that everything has been settled once and for all should peer.

"Welcome in bloody country," Fatos said, in English, when we met at the Café Opera in Skanderbeg Square in Tirana. I was drinking beer and wondering if something as cosmopolitan as a blessing honoured national boundaries. If the Greek border guards sent it back at the road to Kakavilë, if the Italians did not permit it to be taken on board the ferries to Bari and Brindisi. In the square, in the shade beneath trees, dozens of men were exchanging money: 136 leks for a dollar. In the crowd of these black marketeers I saw several radio cars. The cops as well as the money changers and the rest of Albania smoked thin Karelias that summer, at a hundred leks a pack. In the square, an air of in-different symbiosis. Everyone was connected by a time that had to be waited through. Seconds and minutes grew, swelled, and burst open, but there was nothing inside.

I asked Fatos if the exchange was legal. "Of course not," he said.

"And the police?"

"They're just here to keep the peace," was his reply.

It was still dark at five thirty in Korçë. Men sat in the bar near the bus station, drinking their morning coffee and their raki in small tumblers. They boil the coffee with a handheld coil right in the cup. The raki is drunk at dawn, because it dispels sleep even better than coffee. But you have only one: raki isn't a drink, it's a custom. Then an old Mercedes bus pulled up. It slowly filled with people. The driver handed out plastic bags. The first horse-drawn carts of produce began gathering for the market. When the sky had turned an unquestionable grey, we set off, south. Two cops, standing at the front, wore antique Soviet TT-33 pistols with worn stars on the butts. It was only ten kilometres to the Greek border, but the names of the places we passed sounded Slavic: Kamenicc, Vidice, Selenice, Borove . . .

When we got on the first switchback road, I understood the reason for the plastic bags. A fat woman wearing a lot of gold and holding a battery-run fan began to groan, and her family got up to help. They took the pocket fan from her hand, and she began vomiting into the bag. Another woman did the same, and another. Then it was the children's turn. This sickness, Astrit told us later, afflicted only women and children. The men travelled without the side effect, but they took part in the general excitement of the misfortune — the whole bus did, offering words of comfort, making comments, and throwing the used bags, passed from hand to hand, out of the window. The driver immediately distributed new ones.

At Ersekë the mountains grew more powerful. We climbed to 1,700 metres: second gear, first, and the constant corkscrew at cliff's edge without a barrier. I saw no houses, paths, or animals. Yellow burned grass covering the domed peaks, white scree, and for an hour and a half not a sign of human habitation. I counted the bunkers. I stopped counting at the fifty-seventh. They were everywhere, as far as the eye could see. Skulls of cement stuck on slopes in places no vehicle had a chance of reaching. Maybe the cement and steel had been transported by mule and donkey, or maybe it had all been carried in on shoulders, I don't know. Grey concrete toads, sometimes singly, sometimes in twos and threes, guarded the imagined passes and gorges; they intersected lines of anticipated attack, awaited the offensive, the invasion, and their black, empty stares took in the whole horizon. They gave the impression of something that would endure to the end of time. Older than the mountains, indifferent to geology and erosion. I kept reminding myself of their number: 600,000. In each, let's say, you had two soldiers manning a machine gun or holding sub-machine guns — that is, 1,200,000 people, which meant about half the population of the country. During the artillery tests, goats were locked in them. The holes for shooting resembled oversize sunglasses. In this empty landscape, where a car might appear once in an hour, I couldn't shake the feeling that I was being watched.

A stop in Leskovik, near a small bar, where coffee, raki, and hard-boiled eggs were served. A man approached our table but didn't sit. He only needed the tabletop. He rolled the egg on it to crack the shell under his palm. It took him a long time, because he would lose track, watching us — maybe seeing and listening to foreigners for the first time in his life. The shell had cracked, the white was visible, but he kept watching, without a word.

There were bunkers too in Leskovik, but much larger. They resembled concrete yurts with double doors of steel. Among them, donkeys grazed. The animals were the same colour as the shelters, and the stony field was the same colour, too, and so were the mountain slopes framing the scene. After the town, we entered the shade of the Nemerçke range. I had never seen such mountains. They seemed moulded out of ash. The timberline stopped as if cut, and then there was only a barren, vertical massif, which from this distance appeared to be floating, detached, impermanent. There was nothing there but nakedness. The truncated summit of Papingut looked like a pile of dust, a dump that reached the sky. This dust, this dirt, must have sifted from somewhere above, from space, from the farthest corners of the universe.

Albania, see, is ancient. Its beauty brings to mind species and epochs that are long extinct and have left behind no likenesses. The landscape endures yet is constantly disintegrating, as if the sky and air were tearing at it with their fingers. Hence the cracks, ravines, fissures, and the persistent weight of matter that wishes to be left alone, to be rid of its shapes, to rest, and to return to the time when there were no forms.

Gjirokastër is a town of white stone. The roofs of the houses are covered with black tiles that once were white too. The windows of the pension Hajji Kotoni directly face the minaret. Several times a day from the high tower, the loudspeakers come on, and the metal voice of the muezzin fills the streets, the alleyways, and the whole valley of the Drinos River. Next to the mosque is the Greek consulate. A crowd has been standing there since morning: dozens of women and men waiting for a visa. On television is a kilometre-long line of Albanian cars at the border in Kakavilë. For a few days now the Greeks have been letting no one in. They say that the computer system is down. The Albanians say it's intentional: Let the Albanians learn their place, let them stand and ask for Greek work and the Greek euro, let them know it's the Greeks who grant it. But, the Albanians say, without us their vineyards will grow wild, their olive groves too, as ours have, because we must leave them and go to Greece, because that's where the work is and the money. Greeks don't know how to work, say the Albanians. They despise us, but without us they couldn't drink wine, because they have grown fat and lazy.

I sip a black Albanian Fernet and look down on the hometown of Enver Hoxha. In the early afternoon the streets empty, and the crowd before the consulate disappears. The sun, directly overhead, sweeps the shadows from the narrowest alleys. It becomes so still, it's as if everyone has left, abandoning the town to its fate, to the predation of time and the heat. From the mountains, wolves will come down and breed with the dogs; the vineyards will pry apart the stone walls; the hundred-year-old Mercedes will pine for their chauffeurs and die; the Turkish fortress on the hill will fall into itself; the wind will fill the rooms of the Sopoti Hotel with sand; rust will eat into the Muslim loud-speakers; the raki will burn through the screw tops of the bottles in the Festivali Bar; the discarded packs of hundred-lek notes with Fanem Noli on them will all turn into oxygen; and finally the grey carapace of the mountains will cover everything.

So I drank black Fernet and tried to imagine a country that one day everyone would leave. They would abandon their land to the mercy of time, which would break open the envelope of the hours and months and in pure form enter what remained of cities, to dissolve them, turn them into primal air and minerals. For time, here, was the most important element. As persistent and heavy as a giant ox, it filled the river valleys, crushing the mountain peaks from Shkoder to Saranda, from Korçë to Dur-rës. It was in time's gut that these men lived who appeared on street corners and squares. Possibly they saw its coming death and knew fear, because the final throes of the beast in whose belly they waded would mean, for them, isolation: if the beast died, they could never meet again. They would be carried away by the separate little streams of minutes and days, streams that were only a pathetic human imitation of the original current, whose power brought to mind the power of no motion. They would have to live off the carrion of eternity, whose taste is pre-cisely that of freedom.

On the beach in Saranda, people moved the trash to make a place for themselves. They pushed aside the plastic bottles, cartons, cans, those emptied wonders of civilization, the shopping bags of Boss, Marlboro, and Tesco, to clear patches of sand on which entire families could spread out. The wind carried the transparent tatters landward and draped them on the trees. It blew from the west. Never in my life had I seen such a mess and the calm with which people lived in it and added to it constantly. The patches of cleared sand were the size only of a mattress or a little larger, allowing a group to sit. There was something elegant and contemptuous in their gestures as they discarded used things, a kind of lordliness of consumption and a theatre of indifference towards whatever didn't give instant gratification. The wind blew from the west both literally and figuratively, yet it brought nothing of value. Perhaps those things of value, which no doubt were there in the West, simply couldn't be transported and lost their worth en route, spoiling, decomposing. But perhaps they would have been of no use to the people here in any case.

The first day, as we walked from the port, Genci latched on to us. He was about thirty, wore sandals (no socks) and filthy black shorts. On his back he carried a kid several years old. In fluent English he asked us where we were from and if we needed a room. We certainly needed one, after a night of no sleep. He led us among apartment blocks that were a few storeys high and coming apart: stench, gutters choked with rubble and rotten trash, piles of stones, indestructible plastic, a kind of Balkan morning after. Tanned children looked at us with curiosity. We hadn't the strength to get rid of this well-wishing character. Genci gave a shout, and an old woman appeared, all in black. We followed her. She unlocked a gate that enclosed a patio on the ground floor of one of the blocks, then unlocked the front door. It was cool inside and absurdly clean. The two-room apartment gleamed. The terracotta floor gleamed, the refrigerator, the bathroom, the television set, the large fan. There was even a shine and smell of cleanliness on the bedding. As if no one had ever lived here, just cleaned and cleaned. "She's a widow," Genci told us, "so you have to pay her twenty-five dollars a night."

We met Genci a few more times after that. He talked non-stop and was always promising us something. He said he knew the writer Ismail Kadare, that Kadare was now in Albania and Genci could arrange a meeting. He offered us an air-conditioned apartment in downtown Tirana for ten dollars. He told us about his conversion to Protestantism; about his wife, who worked for the Soros Foundation; with pride about his father, who during the Hoxha regime was a security guard. One day, when we were discussing Europe in general, he asked if there had been communism in Poland.

From the pier promenade in Saranda you can see the misty shore of Corfu. You can sit at a coffeehouse table in the shifting shade of a palm tree and watch the passenger ferries move through the smooth water of the strait and vanish in the open sea. It's very possible that the international tourists look at the Albanian shore as they might look at the shore of, say, Liberia or Guinea. They may even hold binoculars. The seven-storey floating hotels sparkle in the sun and are gone. A touch of safari in this, and mirage.

I drank Greek retsina and tried to imagine this place twenty years ago. Tried to imagine the country cut off from the rest of the world like an island in some godforsaken part of the ocean. A country that had about 160 enemies (let's say that at the time there were that many nations on the political map). Danger lurked to the east and to the west. Capitalism lurked, communism lurked in its degenerate Soviet and Chinese forms, African monarchies lurked, and the technocratic regimes of South-east Asia, and Greenland lurked and the island Republic of Cape Verde, and there lurked the cosmos debauched by the Americans and the Soviets. Enver Hoxha, leaving Tirana, locks the television station and takes the key with him, so no one in his absence will let in a Greek, Italian, or Yugoslav programme. In Saranda today, it's late afternoon, except that there are not all these hastily assembled concrete bars and hotels. People sit on the seashore and look at passing ships that belong to the enemy. The huge semi-transparent homes sail on to their destruction, because they belong to a world over which hangs a heavy curse. Dusk falls. That world has no meaning, no form, it is a kind of anti-world, or anti-reality ruined by a fundamental lie.

Three hundred and twenty kilometres at the longest place, 140 at the widest. Which comes to about 28,000 square kilometres of absolute truth and complete isolation. In 1948, Yugoslavia was the renegade; in 1961, it was the Soviets; in 1978, China. Betrayal hems in Albania on every side. Village teachers set slogans in stone on the hilltops. "Vigilance, Vigilance, Vigilance." "The Most Dangerous Enemy Is the One You Forget." "Think, Work, and Live like a Revolutionary." Carelessness or error may bring the accusation of treason. Three hundred and twenty are sentenced for carelessness, 140 for error, and there is no chance of escape, because the rest of the world does not exist.

The slogans in stone are best seen from above, from the sky. They were a challenge to the cosmos. Apparently the goal was maximum: to convert not China, not the Soviets, but the entire universe.

One day we set out from Korçë to Voskopojë. We wanted to see what was once the largest city in the European part of the Ottoman Empire, 30,000 homes built so close together "that a goat could walk from one end to the other on the rooftops", and 22 houses of worship. We wanted to see the place where the caravan trails intersected from Poland, Hungary, Saxony, Constanța, Venice, Constantinople, and where 280 years ago the first printing press was established in the Balkans.

To get there, we hired a small delivery van. It was driven by Jani, and his buddy kept trying to start a conversation. He knew a few Slavic words. His "lady comrade" was Slovak. They met in an olive plantation in Greece. We went up and up a road full of potholes. For thirty kilometres there was no crossroad, only a donkey path now and then coming down the mountain. The men gave us cigarettes and showed us their signet rings in the form of a lion's head.

Voskopojë was all ground-floor. It didn't seem constructed at all, just slapped together with stones. Some of the houses sank under their own weight, and it wasn't the result of neglect or age but of the material used — simply, nothing larger or higher could be assembled with that sifting stuff. This was more geology than architecture. As if one day the earth parted and gave to the world its rendition of human building. And now the falling walls, dribbling facades, cracked clay trickling from joints, split roofs, and the wood of the gates and fences splintered by the heat, with the help of erosion and gravity, were doing their best to return to the bosom of the earth.

Jani and his buddy waited for us in the bar, which was a single small stone room with a Greek woman, over fifty, at the counter. She listed for us all the churches that once stood here. She served us cheese, paprika, bread, and raki. She didn't want money; she wanted to talk, to tell. It didn't bother her that we all had to guess at what we were saying to one another. Others came, to look at us and shake our hands. Jani and his colleague drank one Albanian brandy after another and chased them down with Tirana beer. We wanted to stay longer but were afraid for our guides, who measured time in shots of liquor. People came out of the bar to stand and watch us leave. The men talked and talked. We were in a cornfield; people tore off golden ears and stuffed them in our pockets. Now it was downhill all the way, and we coasted in neutral to save petrol. Jani put on monotonous, trancelike music, some kind of Turkish techno, and he and his buddy started dancing in their seats. They pitched and twisted as if they were riding camels. Jani let go of the steering wheel and raised his arms in fluid circles. Sometimes they turned to make sure we were having fun too. Then, to the dull desert rhythm, they began to yell, "Ben Laden! Ben Laden!" and with such swaying, with open windows letting in the hot air and dust, we reached Korçë. But that wasn't the end of it, because we absolutely had to visit a shop belonging to a friend of Jani, and of course we had to drink beer. We sat on benches among herbs, tomato plants, and the buzzing of flies, and Jani explained to us that the owner was a police officer but had decided to start his own business. The black-haired man smiled shyly, gave us cigarettes and hard red apples. The fiancé of the Slovak woman slept, his head between two white round cheeses.

Of the old fortress in Krujë, all that remained was a stone tower, a few walls, and an outline of foundations. The rest was reconstructed in 1982 by Pranvera Hoxha, daughter of Enver. She was an architect and had power, and this was how she imagined medieval Albania. It was here that in 1443 Skanderbeg hung the flag with the black two-headed eagle and declared the country's independence. He challenged Turkey, before which all Christian Europe trembled in those days. Callistus III spoke of him as "Christ's athlete", though George Kastrioti in his youth had converted to Islam, hence the name Skander. He lost, of course, and Albania had to wait until 1913 for its independence. All this, the whole tale of many centuries, with the flags, likenesses of heroes, statesmen, documents, and a copy of Skanderbeg's helmet, could be found in the building of Enver's daughter. At the entrance, guarded by a soldier with a Kalashnikov, stood a line.

We walked back, down a long, narrow street of ancient homes. There were about a dozen, and in each the old times were sold, thousands of objects, tens of thousands. In chaos and dimness, put in piles, set in stacks, hung in bundles, the entire past of Albania was gathered here. Carved chests, heavy dark tables, narghiles, curved knives, necklaces of silver coins, hand-sewn dresses permeated with age and decay, dioramas of Istanbul and Mecca, pieces of harness, mountaineer shoes desiccated and flaking, oriental filigree, sabres, wood furniture, bone utensils, objects made of horn, divans, blackened iron pots — a kind of dusty supermarket of a culture, all worn smooth by the touch of generations, not the least bit fake, only recently pulled from the dark and given a wipe for sale. We stopped at each treasure den in turn, but the variety of stuff and its barbaric splendour pushed us away. At one point, the power went out. The sellers led us deep into a black maze and with flashlights showed us items. A golden circle jumped from object to object, from one fragment of the past to the next. Out of the grey murk, a gleam, the shred of an outfit, an ornament, the metallic blink of jewelery, and it was like trying to learn about a world you couldn't completely believe in. Part museum, part flea market, part archive-storehouse. The helpless beam of light, wandering lost, turned it into a metaphor for Albania. In one of the shops, on an archaic ottoman, lay the owner. His boots upright beside him as he slept.

In practically every antique store there was a corner where the latest history was piled in a heap. Paper, mainly, likenesses of Enver; tomes and albums in which the leader posed against the background of his accomplishments: Enver before the multitude, Enver before a new housing development, Enver before a tilled field or a factory. Besides paper there were medals and ribbons with the obligatory red star. Only these things were left, and were for sale. I don't know if anyone was buying them. For an album about the life of Hoxha, one merchant wanted thirty dollars. He gave the price and wasn't interested in bargaining. He repeated his "thirty" and finally, impatient, turned his back. "Albanians don't bargain," Astrit told me later. "Particularly with a foreigner. They think all foreigners have more money than they do, and if you try to pay less, it's an injustice."

There were bunkers here too. Everywhere, in every shop — dozens, hundreds of miniature bunkers in white stone. They could serve as ashtrays, paperweights, knick-knacks. A souvenir of Albania when you left.

Albania is loneliness. I recall a late afternoon in Korçë. The market, a relic of Ottoman days, was empty now. All the antique Mercedes had left, as well as the horse-drawn two-wheel carts. A woman had swept the square of its litter. That day the sky was grey, and when the crowd dispersed and the colourful riot of commodities disappeared, the grey flowed down and filled the empty place. The abandoned market was inert, as if no one had ever come by. Then, in the farthest corner of the square, I saw three men. They were squatting round a tiny grated fire and roasting ears of corn. You could hardly see them against the grey wall. The gathering dusk erased their profile. You could see only the flame, a red, uncertain flicker in the wind.

One day Astrit and I were talking about emigration routes in Europe, the never-ending westward flow from east and south, the guest-working nomads from Poland, Ukraine, Belarus, Bulgaria, Romania, the indigent coming to make conquest of the land of the Germans, French, Anglo-Saxons, and all the rest, to find employment in Cape Saint Vincent, Cape Passero, and the fish-processing plants of Iceland. I told Astrit about Poles and Ukrainians at German construction sites and farms; I sang the old ballad of how hard it is for the worse off to live in a better-lit place. All to balance somehow his Albanian tale. When I finished, he said, "It's not the same. You don't know what it means to be an Albanian in Europe." We changed the subject.

"These remain from '97," Rigels said. It was in Gjirokastër, and I had asked him about the ruined ground floors of some of the buildings. No doors, no display windows, only huge holes at the base filled with rubbish, bits of furniture, stones. In the spring of 1997, the financial pyramid collapsed. The government of Salieri Berisha maintained to the end that everything was under control, and in a way it supported the activity of these fictional institutions. Tempted by the geometric rise of wealth, people sold everything they had — homes, apartments — took loans, and put the money in accounts so it would shoot up like the mercury in a thermometer when you run a fever. Tens of thousands of Albanians lost everything. "So what happened then?" I asked Rigels. "The shops, the little bars, belonged to the government?" He smiled. "No, they belonged to those who had something. The ones who robbed, who destroyed, they had nothing. It was revenge taken for the possession of anything."

I tried to imagine. We were sitting in a pleasant bar in the bowels of an old fortress overlooking the city. We drank white wine. Rigels greeted acquaintances. Nearby, teenage boys were drinking beer and talking about girls, and I tried to picture how five years ago kids their age had drilled the air with Kalashnikov rounds in a moment of joy because justice and truth were finally theirs. A few, from windows, shot neighbours they had never liked. I pictured this reckless revolution of people who had been robbed blind. Revolt in Gjirokastër and Vlora, in the south, while Berisha was north. The geographic divide so strong historically, it spelled civil war. The president in the north ordered the armouries opened, in the hope that his compatriots would launch a crusade to crush the rebellious south.

"But it soon became apparent that the north-south civil war was not going to happen. Anarchy took its place. The Albanians — some of them — followed orders; others followed their old dream of getting a rifle; some, fearing the future or just copying others, broke into the armouries and took whatever they could put their hands on, mines and radioactive material included. Later they shot into the air — in celebration, joy, terror, or simply to try out their new weapons. Armed people went to the prisons and released 1,500 prisoners, 700 of whom had been convicted for murder. On that day [March 10, 1997], more than 200 died, mainly from the bullets shot into the air, and thousands were wounded. Marauding thieves began their work, and no one knew whether these were Berisha people or just bandits. It got to the point that railroad tracks were taken apart, so that the individual rails could be sold as scrap in Montenegro."

I can't help seeing a resemblance between the slogans in stone and the suicidal shooting into the air. Both gestures are absurd, yet in a way they constitute a challenge to reality. The citizens of the collapsed government, having been chained by Hoxha's totalitarian vision and having embraced anarchy, behaved as if the world would perish with them. At the same time, Enver was as confident of his immortality as the rebellious mob. Both he and they lived entirely in the present. Hoxha probably believed that everything depended on his will, so no limits existed for him. The men shooting into the air felt that nothing depended on them, therefore they could do anything.

"Shqiperia" is "Albania". Even its true name, in a sense, means isolation, because outside the Balkans hardly anyone knows it. For two weeks I listened to Albanian spoken in the street, on buses, on the radio, and I don't think I heard once the word *Albania*. It was always *Shqiperia, Shqiptar, shqiperise* . . .

The word comes from the verb *shqiptoj,* which is simply "to talk", "to speak". In a tongue that no one else understands.

Moldova

Tɪɪs ᴄᴏᴜɴᴛʀʏ ɪꜱ 300 kilometres at its longest and 130 at its widest. The entry at Leuşeni is all grey concrete and deserted. A woman in a uniform takes your passport and disappears for fifteen minutes. Only Moldovans and Romanians cross here, and probably not one of them comes for pleasure. After that, to the right, is a village on a slope. Several houses atilt; the rest have fallen. The earth sank and took a few dozen farms with it. On an untouched scrap of ground is a church outlined against the sky. The hills are long, low, green. In an occasional valley you can see a village, which at a distance resembles a camp: the houses all the same size, shape, and colour, and all topped with the same asbestos tile. They look like tents of bleached canvas. Nothing stands apart; they are all of them together. Then you have nothing until the next village. Endless green, a grey blotch of cramped habitations, more green, more green, and again a clump of cement squares kept in place by an invisible perimeter.

The average salary here: twenty-five dollars. A dollar is about thirteen Moldovan lei. Moldovan bills are small and faded.

Stephen the Great is on every one of them, with some official landmark on the back, a church or monastery. In Moldova there are 130 official landmarks. The list fits on one nine-by-twelve-inch page of the Moldovan atlas I bought in Chişinău. Half go back only to the nineteenth and twentieth centuries. The bills are generally threadbare. I spent not a little time wondering how the ATMs dealt with them. The machines gave me stacks of crumpled, limp, greasy, torn banknotes, but the sum was always correct. Until then I had thought that an ATM could count new bills only, or nearly new — or at least those that were still a little crisp. There are also coins, though few people use them. The fifty-bani piece is quite pretty: small, a matte gold colour, with clumps of grapes on the back, in a lame attempt to convey prosperity. The cheapest cigarettes, Astras, cost two lei; the most expensive, Marlboros, sixteen.

You go to Cahul from the Sud-Vest Bus Station. It's at the edge of Chişinău, where the white apartment buildings end and the monotony of the hills begins. Under a metal overhang waits a solitary bus. The south is churchmouse-poor. The world ends there, and the best a person can do is move to Romanian Galaţi.

Moldova is like an inland island. In order to get anywhere, the country recently obtained from Ukraine five hundred metres of Danube shoreline not far from Giurgiuleşti at the very south. But the big trucks still must grind through Ukraine and Poland to get to the Berlin and Frankfurt of their dreams. On the bus to Cahul, the passengers are all friendly. They share fruit. In exchange, they are glad for a slug of Ukrainian beer, Chernihiv, in a litre plastic bottle. They ask about everything and tell about themselves. They cannot fathom why someone would travel to Cahul or any other place. "But we have nothing there," they say.

On the day the Lord God distributed the earth to the human

race, the Moldovan overslept. When he woke, it was too late. "And what about me, Lord?" he asked sadly. God looked down upon the sleepy, pitiful Moldovan and tried to think, but nothing came to Him. The earth had been divided up, and, being Lord God, He couldn't go back on His decisions, let alone start transplanting populations. Finally He waved a hand and said, "Too bad. Come on, then, you can stay with me in Paradise." So goes the legend.

When you travel to Cahul or any other place here, the legend rings true. The monotony suggests eternity. Continual green, continual fecundity, the land undulating, the horizon rising and falling, showing us only what we expect, as if not wishing to cause us the least unpleasantness. Grapes, sunflowers, corn, a few animals, grapes, sunflowers, corn, cows and sheep, on occasion a garden, and rows of nut trees always on either side of the road. No free space in this scenery, no sudden disjunction, and the imagination, encountering no ambush, soon dozes. Most likely events took place here a hundred, two hundred, three hundred years ago, but they left no trace. Life seeps into the soil, disperses into the air, burns calmly and evenly, as if confident that it will never burn out.

The stop in Cimişlia was the sort of place that is impossible to recall. Some kind of nothingness that for a moment attempted to be a bus station. A concrete apron open to the whistling wind at one end and closed off by a building at the other. Greyness, dust, and heat. The beer tap at the bar was a rubber hose wrapped with wire. Farther inside, everything was thrown together, layered haphazardly, by whim. Part dwelling, part rubbish heap; a dark, narrow, low area full of welded iron struts, pieces of sheet metal, laminated panels, all discarded from the start, to get the ruining over with early. The despair of objects despised. People sat, ate, drank, and waited, yet seemed naked, exposed to the wounding edges of all the junk.

A cart waiting at an intersection, hitched to a donkey. Nothing in the vicinity. It was only farther on and lower, where the cornfield ended, that the cement village appeared, grey. A woman got off the bus, pulling a cage thing on two wheels. A small bag was attached to it. Cage and bag were both home-made. A girl was waiting for her. They hugged, as if after a long separation. Then they climbed onto the cart. The two bigger, together, than the entire vehicle. The brown donkey made for the village. It seemed a game, because woman and girl hardly fitted on what looked like something stolen from a child's merry-go-round.

What to say about Cahul? From there it's a couple of kilometres to the Romanian border, and then you're off to Galați, by the Danube. On the main street in Cahul you felt the proximity of the border. Cars passed with a rumble, and in the pubs the melancholy kings of life warmed themselves in the air. They ordered Moldovan cognac, drank it by the glass, but their faces didn't move. They were able only to move their mouths, that was it; the rest was permanently frozen. They adjusted their gold chains and made sure people were looking. They even kept their cars running, so everyone would know that they had plenty of petrol. Cahul at first glance: a hick town on the border, the nervous indolence of two-bit confidence men driving in circles to kill time.

In a park by a white church, a guy was renting out go-carts. He sat behind a desk in the shade of a tree and, using an hourglass, kept track of the time per ride. After him, the city imperceptibly became village. The trees were now taller than the houses. Goats cropped the grass at the foot of a partisan memorial, its cement heroes with big scars across their faces. In a nearby shop, a yellow light burned, though it was in the middle of the day. Three men entered, and a woman behind the counter poured vodka for them into shot glasses. A pub, I realized.

In the square before the hotel, dogs chewed at themselves all night. And howled. At dawn, carriages began assembling with merchandise. It was a bazaar. Train cars without wheels served as stores. An insanely varied spectacle from my sixth floor. Everything sparkling and shimmering in the sun: foil, plastic, cellophane, glass, metal. Pickles, tomatoes, watermelons I went down and saw that here was everything a person needed to live. Belts, golden corn, pickling jars, barrels for marinating. The music went in a loop. Women sat motionless over their wares, hands folded in laps, as if at home or on a bench by the front gate. I saw little gesturing, a lot of simple waiting.

The owner of a light-blue Renault refused my twenty euros. He said the roads were awful and the car would be destroyed. He wanted thirty, not including the petrol. He was in light blue too, dapper. Next in the line, a Zhiguli. So old, I don't remember the colour. The driver was big, fat, and unpleasant to look at. He said he'd take us, and his name was Misha. He was about fifty. We left Cahul. The road went up through rolling hills, vineyards, cornfields. The villages began suddenly and stopped as if cut off with a knife. Times were bad now, Misha told me. He brought up Stalin, though he was too young to remember him. Stalin was worth bringing up: he shot thieves. The problem with Moldova today, in Misha's opinion, was thievery. The whole country had been stolen from the ordinary people. In the Soviet days, when everything was communal and didn't belong to anyone, theft was not a problem. Like everything else, it was communal:

everybody stole, and nobody lost. Now only the richest stole, and they made sure the poor couldn't, by inventing property. Property was an invention against ordinary people, who owned nothing. That was Misha, in Russian.

I wanted to go to Comrat, the capital of Gagauzia. It's not completely known who the Gagauz people are. In Moldova, they number 20,000. Their language is Turkic, their faith Orthodox Christianity, and they came to the Comrat area from Dobruja, when Russia annexed Moldova in 1812 and called it Bessarabia to erase the past. They could be Bulgarized Turks or Turkified Bulgars; no one is sure. And practically no one knows that they exist. So I went to Comrat, on roads as empty as landing strips.

It's hard to describe Comrat, because it's so easy to overlook. You ride through a city you can barely see. There are homes, streets, but they are all sketched in, a stopgap not thought through, the sadness of matter only half materialized, lacking the conviction to take full shape. A monument to Lenin had gold paint slapped on. A funeral procession went down the main street, its open coffin on a pickup truck. Beside the coffin, on a chair, sat an old woman in black. It was hot. Flies circled above the face of the deceased. The woman brushed them away with a green branch: a slow, tedious motion. Peculiar, these mourners walking in silence through the din of the everyday, between booths selling bread and vegetables, among bicycles, cars, and carts. Pushing their way against the current of life.

Before the Gagauzia Museum stood a statue in honour of the heroes of the war in Afghanistan. A kid with a rifle was painted silver. I thought I'd try the museum, and it seemed that the group inside was waiting just for me. A woman tour guide, accompanied by two other women, took a wood pointer and began to speak about the great migration of people from the heart of Asia.

She tapped the map, and it turned out that the Gagauz were Turks after all, who instead of occupying the southern coast of the Black Sea strayed north. We proceeded from room to room, in chronological sequence. An old man appeared through a side door and told us he was a member of the Union of Sculptors of Gagauzia. He was born in 1935, in the village of Świątkowa Wielka, not far from where I live. His name: Andrej Kopcza.

Misha kept getting lost. Fifty kilometres from his neighbourhood, and his sense of direction left him. I showed him the map. He wouldn't trust roads he had never been on. They might be on the map, but he refused to believe in their existence. "Only Turks live there, so what's the point?" "Nothing but Bulgars there . . ." He wouldn't get out of the car, refused coffee, said no to lunch. It was beyond him how someone could waste time and money like this, why someone would come here. What kind of destination was the village Albota de Sus? Or Sofievca? Misha stayed in the car and looked at the grey post-Soviet pocks and scars spread throughout the green landscape, and I looked at him, and our minds were mutually impenetrable. He pined for what had been and despised what was left. "I am Soviet man," he declared that morning. But how could anything other than this be left, if there had been nothing other than this in the first place? The poverty and misery of objects created ad hoc could do only what they had been created to do: eat away at reality. The whole region seemed abandoned. A tractor and cart on the empty road, a man tossing out fresh-cut greens with a pitchfork, a few clumps at each turn. Charity or some kind of payment?

We were in Baurci at dusk. Misha took his money and drove off. In Baurci there are only Gagauz. We looked for Elena. We had met her two days earlier on a bus to Cahul. She had red hair and a shy, beautiful smile. She said she worked in Istanbul but was coming home now to see her children. She invited us, so here we were, trying to locate her in a village of 10,000 situated on low hills in the middle of a treeless plateau. "That's the one who had two husbands, and the second was a Turk," the villagers told us. We finally found her house. It stood in a long row of similar houses. The entrance was through a small, shady courtyard covered with creeping vines. Elena smiled again. She was surrounded by children. Her father came out. We were all embarrassed. "This is how we live," she said a few times. She wanted to show us everything at once. We went to the garden, inspected the vegetables, the grapes, here's the cabbage, tomatoes, cucumbers, we repeating after her, because we had come from afar and might not know what these things were. We inspected a gaunt roan calf tethered by a short chain to a dunghill. Pigs sat somewhere in the dark: we could smell them. Everything compact, close together. "They didn't give us much land," Elena said.

We slept in the biggest room. It was filled with knick-knacks, in glass, plastic, porcelain, metal; figurines, ornaments, souvenirs, weavings, innocent nonsense — pale ballerinas, cheap watches, crystal balls — art with no pretension, a museum of neat stuff, oriental splendour, an orgy of beauty, trinkets, and dreams, a vision made flesh. It reminded me of the rooms of my country aunts and grandmothers, but those could not compare with this room in Baurci.

In the morning we inspected the village. Everyone came along: Elena, her children, her father, sister, brother-in-law Ilya, who knew the world, having served in the army in East Germany and built houses in Moscow. On the facade of the House of Culture, a folk-socialist mosaic. On a two-metre pedestal, a concrete bust of Lenin. "The best man, he," Elena said in Russian, smiling her smile. I understood then that they had nothing else here, that the memory of Baurci began sixty, seventy years ago; before that there was a blank. A donkey pulled the wagon; a child held the reins. Inside the cavernous House of Culture, the rumble of spiritless music. We found the source: an eighteen-year-old, pasty girl making gestures learned from television. The music issued from a tape, and she sang in a mechanical voice, lost in her sad and restless dance. For breakfast that morning we had a local dish: cooked pig skin. "Someday a movie theatre comes," Elena said. Under a tree sat an old woman dressed in black. Beside her was a sack of sunflower seeds, and on a branch hung a rusty scale. The woman sat quietly, hands folded in her lap. On the tin gates leading out were images of the Olympics in Moscow: a stylized skyscraper topped with a red star.

Baurci was the true end of the Revolution. That's what it looked like. Nothing remained that could be used or that had any value — seventy years not worth shit. A caricature monument to a criminal before an empty building in which rumbled a desperate imitation of music from the rotten West. Only the donkey's harness made sense, had substance. I'll be frank: I was at a loss. People, you would think, know what is good for them, and their longing hearts cannot lie. Something didn't fit here, was not in key. I felt I was an intruder, an imbecile in a world I couldn't parse.

There was only one new building in Baurci, but it was large, perhaps even larger than the House of Culture. Beige walls, huge windows, a red roof. Simplicity, functionality, and overall a kind of bright challenge to the weary village. One sees something like that brightness in American films, say, when a young couple gets married. "Protestants," Elena said. I asked about the size of the congregation, but she didn't know. She said only that the converts "did no work and got a lot of money from somewhere".

Inside, gleaming pine pews, a pine altar, Ikea-like. Later I saw the house of one of the congregants; it didn't differ from the others, except for the Japanese off-road vehicle, a few years old, in the front. "He drives to Chişinău," Elena said, and it sounded like a reproach.

We too went to the capital that afternoon. It was ten kilometres to the bus stop. Ilya took us in his Zhiguli. Since morning we had been drinking beer and wine, alternating, but that was no problem for Ilya. Chişinău was no problem either, he said, if the bus didn't come. He was short, sinewy, and feared nothing, having seen both Dresden and Moscow. But the bus came, and we hugged each other tight on the dusty road to Congaz. We vowed that we would meet again. These were wonderful people. They said, "This is how we live," and showed us their life as naturally as others would give a tour of their house. Elena's sister had got up at four in the morning to kill a rabbit and a chicken for our breakfast. The mother of the two sisters, paralysed, sat on a chair in the shade of a grapevine and watched, grinning, as we drank wine. The father shared with us his slivovitz coloured with raspberry juice. Plates of melon and watermelon slices. Now we embraced Ilya on the dusty road to Congaz and vowed that we would meet again, though none of us believed it.

Chişinău, ah Chişinău! White apartment blocks on green hills. You saw them from the north, south, east, and west. Massed like high cliffs gleaming in the sun. A paean to geometry in the rolling, irregular landscape. There is nothing larger or taller in all Moldova. Giant tombstones stuck in the fertile, plump earth. Stone tablets of egalitarianism. Termite towers of universal progress. A New Jerusalem dying a technological death.

At the exits from the city stood trucks loaded with plastic kegs, jugs of wine, Weck jars, a thousand containers into which Moldova had stored its wealth to make it through the winter. Marinating, pickling, fermenting, pasteurizing, salting, canning the produce of its gardens and plots. Downtown, on the Boulevard of Stephen the Great and Holy, among stores selling Japanese electronics and Italian boots, people went burdened with jars. They carried ten, twenty cleverly packed, brand-new mason jars at a time. Or shiny galvanized pails. Or sacks bulging with cucumbers and tomatoes. Pickup trucks loaded with melons, cars pulling trailers loaded with melons. Old Chişinău was really more village than town. A little off the main walkway, you found one- and two-storey homes wrapped in green, separated by wood fences, cats strolling, people sitting on front steps. That was downtown: twenty criss-crossing streets, and the last wafts of sleepy imperial province. If you took away the cars, everything would be as it was a hundred years ago.

So that was Chişinău. I spent many hours under an umbrella in Green Hills Nistru on the Boulevard of Stephen the Great and Holy, at the corner of Eminescu. In the pub sat a more international gathering, speaking in English and German. Probably office workers who had chosen to throw away their European and American money in this particular spot. Besides them was the growing Moldovan middle class, the men wearing gold, sporting sunglasses, in the common style that combines hood, pimp, and gigolo, the women like the women you see on television, practically all with cell phones on silver chains round their necks. I recalled something like that in Romania. I ordered my beer, coffee, and so on in Romanian, but the waiters pretended not to understand entirely; they answered in

Russian. Of course they understood, but Russian was for them the mark of refinement, urbanity. It's possible they took me for a Bessarabian hick — or a spy who had been incompletely briefed.

A strange city. Frightened eighteen-year-old cops patrolling in threes; men in Land Cruisers who think they own the streets; shady types by the post office selling additional minutes for phone cards; people hauling utensils; bald juveniles in oversize trousers, their meek eyes fixed on the ground, making a humble, Franciscan-monk kind of gang member; and young women with exposed bellies and unsteady on their stiletto heels as they strut the main street as if it were a beauty pageant runway, a Romanian-Slavic mix of loveliness and risqué make-up: peasant modesty in dance-hall gear. The general impression that everyone is playing at being something other, each according to a private notion of a world not here. For that reason we finally left Chişinău.

Kola said that for thirty euros we could ride all day. He had an old Renault van with a plastic outer-space ornament. In the Soviet time he taught the samba. A heavy, moustached, good-natured fellow. To Old Orhei, Orheiul Vechi? Sure. He'd never been, but no problem. We headed due north. At an exit, perhaps Ciorescu, not far from the road, in the shade of a tree, stood an old desk. An overweight cop sat and watched the younger cops in big round hats stop victim after victim and without a word take twenty lei. But we were going to Old Orhei. Someone told us we had to, and he was right. The Răut River had dug its way deep into the earth, as if to reach the other side. A thin spit of land risen several dozen metres. The Golden Horde built a city here once. They had good taste. The landscape was from before Creation. In the beginning, a sketch only, a rough idea of how the planet should look, an abstraction really, the most basic shapes: vertical cliff, valley flat as a table, and a slow river in search of its tectonic shift. No change in 100,000 years, except the water had sunk deeper into the earth and had a mud-grey colour.

A whim of the river formed a steep, long peninsula. The monastery was carved into a wall of rock. A few tiny windows looked out on the primeval scene, on beauty still not sure what shape to take. You reached the cells only from the cliff, by a chain ladder. When the friars pulled the chain up, there was nothing but solitude and empty space. As in the Egyptian Sketis, where the Desert Fathers challenged demons to battle. I saw other monasteries later, but they seemed imported. They actually were imported, because the Russians built them, in the grand imperial style. Orhei, however, was nothing but holes bored into rock, an attempt to escape the curse of time and live in eternity. In the cells — so low you could only lie down or kneel — were seashell outlines, round crustacean ornaments, traces of the first days, when the deep was separated from the dry land, the darkness from the light. I tried to picture monks crawling in the dimness, like animals in caves, on all fours, how in a way unimaginable to us they left behind their corporeal forms, their humanity. Abandoned their stinking, lice-infested bodies, because the visible and the palpable exist only to keep us from the truth.

But that was long ago. Now the few brethren lived in a village at the base of the cliff. We found one monk in a small chapel dug out of the earth. He was gaunt, bearded, voluble, and evidently conversant with the world, because he took us for Slovaks. He gave us a summary of the history of the monastery, showed us the clean-swept cells without windows in which you had to bend, then turned to three officers from the Russian, Moldovan, and Ukrainian armies, respectively. They looked out of place in their uniforms, holding cameras instead of rifles. The Russian, in an aviator hat, was the oldest and seemed to have the highest rank. The Ukrainian, the youngest, handsome, and wearing mirror sunglasses, looked like a Hollywood actor playing a soldier. They were quite odd in this timeless landscape, with this monk in the role of guide. Later we saw them having their picture taken with the cliff and the twisting Răut behind them. They handed the camera around and stood taut, as if facing not a barren waste but a battalion at least. These were peacekeepers patrolling the border of a non-existent country, patrolling Transnistria, Trans-Dniester. They were probably on leave here.

Transnistria is not recognized by any government. It has a length of about two hundred kilometres but is narrow, a kind of European Chile. Thirty kilometres, maybe, at its widest point. We were a little nervous about going there. They told us that if anything happened, it wouldn't be clear who to talk to. In a phantom state, the etiquette is phantom too. We went anyway. Valerij drove us in a ten-year-old Vectra. Valerij feared nothing: yesterday Kiev, tomorrow Moscow, Vienna the day after that, and Transnistria — sure, why not? The Communist time, when he worked as an agrotech engineer, was better, but you could manage now too, you just had to make the effort. Valerij was all right and took everything in stride. We wanted to see the non-existent country at its most out-of-the-way, going through Răscăieţi, because the Dniester divided there, its branches meandering, weaving, a blue ribbon thrown at random across the map. First, a long, empty bridge and not a single vehicle, only two kids on bicycles from the Transnistrian side. In their baskets they carried tied bundles of twigs. Then cornfields began, and in the midst of them stood a sentry box with a solitary Moldovan customs officer in a black uniform. Moldova obviously does not accept the secession of this would-be state, according it only the status of an autonomous region. Since the border also is unrecognized, we didn't need to show passports. But Moldova keeps its customs officers on duty just in case. After all, it's in Transnistria, at Cobasna, that you have one of the largest ammunition depots in Europe. From there, from Tiraspol, the Soviets planned to launch their liberation of the Balkans, Greece, and so on.

The customs officer didn't want anything from us. He didn't even put on his cap as he consulted the road map with us — all the river's bends and turns, marshes and lakes, the stream occasionally looping back — spread out on the hood of the car. He tapped a finger and said that this place was the best, but our Vectra probably couldn't make it there. Not a blink from him at our camera or camcorder; the man was in his early twenties, and the spy obsession had not yet poisoned his mind. He waved as we left. When we came to another Transnistrian sentry box, the situation changed: the same kind of makeshift hut but containing four guards. These men were dishevelled, in uniform but as if just pulled out of bed and half asleep. Their shoelaces (the shoes entirely civilian) dragging in the dust, their post-Soviet shirts and trousers crumpled, their solemnity quickly assumed. The moment they took our passports, we felt that we were enemies. They wouldn't look us in the eye, looked up instead, at the sky, to the limitless horizon of an all-union republic gone forever. Could this really be the first time they set eyes on a foreigner? In the next dozen minutes, a wagon with hay went by, a woman with a hoe. The wagon and woman passed without questions asked and were gone among the rows of corn. At last the guards told us to go back, to the town of Bender, where the headquarters were, and people who would know what to do with us.

On the thoroughfare in Bender, a shambles: barracks, plywood, corrugated metal, crumbling concrete, makeshift structures, barriers. Dissolution and melancholy with an undercurrent of menace. First thing, they saw the camcorder, which roused in them the primal fear of those who have something to hide. They said we were filming the border crossing. Of course we were, but we insisted we weren't. They took our passports, and three or four went with them into the plywood hut. We were left out in the burning sun. A. was covered with sweat. He sat on the edge of an open car boot and slowly, inconspicuously removed the cassette from the camcorder and put a new one in. No one noticed. Occasionally a guard emerged from the hut, glared at us, and retreated with a few stiff steps. No question but that we were the enemy, lurking to take their possessions. They kept our passports, which they couldn't even stamp, assuming they had a stamp, because no nation would recognize it.

Valerij finally went to the guards. After a while he came back and said that they knew we were filming, which was a serious matter and forbidden, but for a hundred lei we could move on. We gave them the money. They didn't want the cassette. We were the enemy, but we had paid. We received a scrap of paper, a kind of receipt. On the back was written, in pen: one car, four persons, and a camcorder. That was our Transnistrian visa.

Transnistria broke away from Moldova in 1992. It was a regular war; several thousand people died. Historically Transnistria had never really belonged to Moldova. When after World War II the Soviets took from Romania the lands between the Prut and the Dniester and turned them into yet another SSR, Stalin attached to the Moldovan SSR this narrow strip on the left bank of the Dniester. There was industrialization there, a power plant, an arms factory — and obviously the Russians, who kept their paws on it all. Across the river were farms, cornfields, vineyards, a village, cattle, and Moldovans speaking Romanian. It's not impossible that the Georgian ruler foresaw all this and planned accordingly, making sure that the collapse of his aborted empire would cause as much trouble as possible. He simply had no other idea about how to be remembered. And so in Transnistria there were too many weapons and too many Russians for an independent, green, and poor Moldova to do more than dream of acquiring Transnistria.

From the border to Tiraspol it may have been ten kilometres. There are landscapes and towns that are impossible to recall. You seem to see something, but it's all vague, dull, as if you were inside someone else's oppressive dream. There's nothing there. Two lanes, grey square houses, the gaunt red of Soviet slogans along the road, rusty Zhigulis with new licence plates that pretend to be German licence plates: the ground floor of the imagination. That's what the ride to the capital looked like. We stopped at a bazaar. I wanted to see what their money looked like. Right at the gate, the exchange booths. One simply went in and gave Moldovan lei to a person in the dim interior. I saw no face, only a hand with a gold bracelet. For one leu you got two Transnistrian rubles. A five-ruble bill measured five and a half centimetres by thirteen. On the front, naturally, was Suvorov; on the back, a four-storey building in the style of the 1960s, at the bottom of which were the words *Kwint Factory,* the local producer of cognac (which actually wasn't bad). So on the front you had history, conquest, the Slaughter of Praga, the glory of the Russian military—a glory mainly abroad—and on the back you had booze (however you looked at it) as government accomplishment or national pride.

In any case, Valerij took a satchel and went shopping for groceries. Everything was supposed to be cheaper in Tiraspol than in Chişinău. He bought melons, watermelons, peaches. We drove to look for a place to have lunch but found nothing. In general, this was more outlying district than city. As if an attempt had been made to start something, but it petered out. At last we were shown the way to the centre: a wide street lined with old trees. An occasional car came through—an antique Moskvich, humble Zhigulis, and among them, once in a while, a big SUV with tinted windows and usually black. Tiraspol was not a place where you would want to stay. Soldiers everywhere. They probably made up half the population of the city. We came to a huge bookstore that had practically no books. Instead, portraits of Lenin and blank certificates of honour with his picture on them. In one pub, bald men sat in tracksuits drinking beer. From time to time one of them would leave, but he soon came back, because in Tiraspol there was nowhere to go. These people were waiting for something to happen, waiting to be called, to be needed.

But in Tiraspol, it seemed that everyone was expendable, a fifth wheel to affairs that were foreign, major, and murky. These people were auxiliary—auxiliary to the troops, to the arsenal, to the Russian Fourteenth Army stationed here, to the black SUVs, and to the omnipresent firm of Sheriff which belonged to Smirnov, the shadow president of a shadow nation. If there was anything new in Transnistria, anything not wrecked, it bore the name Sheriff. All the petrol stations in Tiraspol were Sheriff, and the supermarket too. The yellow star of the Wild West gleaming with absurd brightness in this post-Soviet diorama. Anything was possible here. An old apparatchik dressed as an American lawman won the hand, raked in the chips, in this land of un-pleasant miracles.

We drove north along the Ukrainian border. Corn grew every-where, and in that corn, across paths in fields, stood red-and-white barriers and sentry boxes. It all looked a bit surreal but on the other hand, it held a sad beauty. The guards were protect-ing space, a vacuum, borders that were merely an idea. On the map it looked completely awkward, angular, drawn with a ruler, soundless, lacking the fluid grace characteristic of territories in which history merges with geography, with human presence, and with ancient clutter. The proportions of this frontier on the map brought to mind African borders drawn across the Sahara. "They mark the borders of the former *sovkhozy* and *kolkhozy*", I was later told by an acquaintance who knew a little about Mol-dova. Now the barriers divided sandy lanes on which cattle went, horses, swine, wagons on rubber tyres, boys to visit girls at night, women to exchange gossip, drunkards to get drunk, thieves to thieve, relatives to see one another, people to meet people. We drove down an empty highway, and the men in uniform in the sea of corn resembled scarecrows. Most likely they were armed and had orders, but in that agrarian expanse, what could they do? They could make the birds overhead veer, search peasants who carried bundles of twigs, turn back carts piled with hay, and return lost animals.

There was no one, nothing on the road. Far off the beaten track, we passed the ruins of petrol stations. In places this country looked like the set of a film. Between Mălăieşti and Butor, for instance, someone had built a wide highway that had not a single car on it, and someone had built petrol stations that were reverting to the earth. Everything seemed cast away, thrown aside, of no use or value. People sat in their homes and were completely isolated. You stepped from your door, opened your gate, and wasteland began, a no-man's-land. Perhaps that was why Valerij took us to his family, to a normal house with a garden in Grigoriopol. He wanted to show us ordinary life.

We passed a high wall and entered the cool shade of grapevines. We were greeted by Misha, enormous, big-bellied, and naked to the waist. He talked continually, or rather orated, delivering florid, ceremonious speeches. He took us into the garden, presented to us the patches and beds, and praised self-sufficiency and the fertility of the Moldovan soil. The garden was in fact as green and lush as the tropics. The vegetation towered, trailed, twined, spilled over, so that you had no place to put your foot and the ground was invisible beneath the profusion. But Misha pranced like a ballerina among the cucumbers, tomatoes, beans, paprikas, melons, moved like a thickset Moldovan Pomona. He explained to us the various uses of cucumbers, and it was a bit like being among the Gagauz: once again we were barbarians who came from a land that had no vegetables.

Then an obligatory visit to the cellar, which was roomy, with a high ceiling, and cold. Everything that grew in the garden lay here in jars, vats, jugs, bottles. Over and over, Misha poured red wine into glasses and talked, talked, talked. Still half naked but completely comfortable. Surrounded by his cellar abundance, he spoke of how in earlier, less happy times, the eighties, he visited Warsaw with a Moldovan-Soviet song-and-dance troupe. Having plenty of rubles, he drank champagne and cognac, took taxis everywhere, and was a king in that haggard city. He was accompanied by a Polish friend, a Party secretary as poor as a church mouse. Refilling our glasses, Misha asked us to find his buddy and convey his hugs and greetings. I drank what he gave me and promised to locate the former secretary in the city of two million.

All this was preliminary to the real hospitality. We went to the house. Misha's father was celebrating his patron saint's day. On the table were wine, cognac, and grape moonshine. We ate and drank continually, not wanting to offend our host. Before long, I was both drunk and stuffed. Our hosts were Russified Ukrainians. On the walls hung their youthful portraits, the celebrant and his wife in Soviet military uniforms. New dishes kept arriving. A Moldovan Eden: a garden, a feast, toasts made among family and friends. Misha recalled the time he served as a prison guard. His mother recalled her days teaching Romanian. Valerij insisted that there was no such thing as a Romanian people. Everyone agreed that life was better before. Even I began to agree, but resisted and hoped Valerij would soon give us a sign that it was time to go.

On the border bridge in Vadul lui Vodă stood armoured transporters. No one stopped us, and in a few minutes we saw the apartment blocks of Chişinău.

We drove to the city of Soroca with W., who had business there. Soroca lies to the north of the Dniester, and beyond it is Ukraine. As you head north, the vineyards are gradually replaced by corn, which becomes omnipresent. We went to Soroca to meet Gypsies, who had a mini country of their own there.

Even from a distance, from the boulevard along the river, you could see it: on the hill above the city and down the steep bank to the Dniester, the Gypsy district. You could see that it was unlike anything else in Moldova. Tin roofs agleam in the sun like fish scales, looking like a Baroque-Byzantine-Tatar-Turkish encampment — good words, these. Roofs piled high, roofs bellied like wind-filled sails, roofs budding one from the other like living tissue. This from afar. Closer, it was a roller-coaster ride through centuries and continents. Victorian mansions, Mauritanian residences, Chinese pagodas, classic Greek facades, the Romanian Renaissance, and a reduced replica of the Bolshoi Theatre in Moscow with three plastic steeds on top. Before a pavilion with twenty front windows, amid a green garden tangle, rose a six-metre fountain of white stone in an austere rococo style. At its base rested a crocodile, life-size and of the same material. Two Moldovans were finishing the monument, smoothing the last sharp edges, as Gypsy women watched, smoking cigarettes with holders of gold. I asked Robert who designed all this. Robert had a black-and-gold business card, owned a bakery, was building a mansion, had a BMW 700 with Slovak tags in his backyard, and was a kind of grey eminence in Soroca. "We did," he answered. "It's all from the imagination."

Robert also owned a pub. That is, it was jointly owned, but he was the main entrepreneur. We took seats on the veranda. In the centre were tables, the bar, and ten computers. Kids sat at the computers — mostly Gypsies, with a couple of Moldovans. The dads could comfortably chat, drink, and keep an eye on their Internet-marauding progeny. We sipped cognac and ate watermelon. Robert said that times had changed and now one had to keep one's children off the street. But things were good otherwise: the borders were open, you could travel, do business, all you needed were a passport, ideas, and connections. You could go to the Chukchi, if you wanted, and sell them Chinese linens. No one would forbid you. It wasn't that bad before, but there were fewer possibilities then. That's what Robert said, over a cognac.

Artur arrived, and Robert invited him to join us. Artur was a king—or baron. His business card read, in English: "Gypsy Baron of Moldova." He had a grey beard down to his belt, plaited grey earlocks, and resembled a holy man of distant India. He was fully aware of that heredity and told us that the Nazis had collected the blood of their Gypsy victims, which held exceptional value for them because it was the purest Aryan blood. He said this without expression, entirely confident of our belief in what he said. He made marks on a card, deriving the Russian alphabet from the Sanskrit, and mentioned in passing that women ethnography students from Poland had visited him that summer. Yes, Artur was an important figure. In the courtyard of his palace he had a collection of Soviet samovars and two dusty limousines on flat tyres. In the windscreen of one limousine was a bullet hole. After he concluded his lecture on the Aryans and Sanskrit, Artur said goodbye, rose, got into a green BMW X5 driven by his son, and took off to attend to his royal duties.

Others slowly gathered, but this was not Moldovan hospitality; it was simple courtesy. They drank two bottles of cognac with us, ate three watermelons, spent three hours of their time, revealed as much of their life as they considered proper, until we went our separate ways, each to his own world.

We returned, according to the itinerary, by minibus. I sat next to the driver. He did some kind of hocus-pocus with the tickets, selling them and collecting them or yelling at passengers to hold them up. I couldn't figure it out. In the middle of an empty field, a woman got on. She cut her leg stepping on a sharp piece of metal and bled. The driver yelled at her for not being careful. He was lean, low-class, neurotic, and drove furiously. After thirty kilometres we were stopped by a patrol. A cop waved a black-and-white-striped stick, and we pulled over. The driver took a twenty-lei bill from a box, got out, walked over to the policeman, and gave him the money. The policeman, wearing a sort of aviator cap, waved us on. It was 150 kilometres to Chişinău, and we were stopped three more times. The same performance each time, this submission to power, acted silently and in full view. The cops' faces stony and dull, the driver's face resigned and resentful. I asked him if it was always this way on this road. "Always," he said. "Ever since the end of the Soviet Union."

The entry point at Leuşeni was as deserted as it had been two weeks before. I was waiting for an acquaintance who was supposed to come from the Romanian side. He was late. No traffic in either direction: no point, apparently, and nowhere to go. There weren't even bicycles loaded with bundles of sticks. Just void, immobility, heat. I stood an hour, an hour and a half, and watched how this small and solitary country ended.

At last Alexandru drove up and stopped on the other side. I waved to him and proceeded to the guard booth. They were pleased to see me, remembered my arrival two weeks before. I imagined that I was the only traveller they had recently let through. I threw my backpack into the boot, got in, and we drove off. Twenty minutes later, we had passed Huşi.

The Ferry to Galaţi

So, SPACE IS just a kind of eternal present. The cold air from Ukraine and Russia descends on Romania. My Bucharest friend says in the receiver, in English, "Very, very cold." I try to imagine a naked Danube Delta, blue ice covering the canals, but it's not easy; first I have to cross, mentally, the space that separates me from Sfântu Gheorghe and Sulina: Šariš, Zemplén, Szabolcs-Szatmár, Maramureş, Transylvania, Baraganul, Dobruja . . . I have to imagine chill entering all those places I knew in spring and summer. I have to shake off their heat as a dog shakes off water, because I can't believe that it's freezing now between Samova and Niculiţel, that the pigs aren't rolling in the dust of the concrete-hard clay yards behind cane fences, and that snow now lies on the thatched roofs of the mud huts along the curved pavement from which you can see Ukraine and the white ships sailing the Chilia arm of the Danube. It is hard to imagine hot dust not rising from the floor of the bus, hard to imagine the poplar grove by the ferry to Galaţi leafless, empty, devoid of characters drinking vodka at 15,000 lei a flask, purchased in a store sided with sheet metal and hot as an oven. It seems impossible that Bratianu now is completely different, that the drunks have most definitely all gone away, and the dogs too, the pack of scruffy mongrels near the ferry that looked like the younger brothers of the drunks, man and dog equally sad and withered by the sun.

I lack the imagination. For that reason I have to pack, stuff into my pockets odds and ends, passport, money, and go to see what it's really like. Whenever the time of year or the weather changes, I have to pack up whatever I can't do without and visit all those places I've been before, to make sure they still exist.

And the ferry to Galaţi, embarking from the low shore, where gaunt horses once grazed on faded fields? On board, among a few newly washed cars, came a faded Dacia pickup carrying a huge sow that stank to high heaven. They must have come a long way, because the animal was covered with shit. I took in the foulness with pleasure as I leaned against the back fender of a black Mercedes in which a clean-shaven guy wearing mirror glasses was sitting with a blonde, gold on her ears, and I looked to the far bank of the Danube, at the big rusty cranes of the port. This was my Romania — this momentary brotherhood of Mercedes, gold, reeking pig, and industrialization whose tragic abandonment was on the same grand scale as its size. In five minutes the sow, the limos, and my group parted company forever.

It gives me no rest, my wish to know the fate of all these scenes that entered my eyes and have remained in my thoughts. What happens to them when I am no longer there? Unless I have taken them with me, immobilized them for all time in my mind, and they will be with me until the end, untouched by the change of seasons and the weather.

What will become of those two characters in dark trousers,

white shirts, ties, and shoes that gleamed as if just polished? They extricated me from the middle of Tecuci, a flat and dusty town, took me out for a few kilometres' spin, and with a fountain pen on a scrap of paper wrote "Bacau" so I could have something to wave in the face of the drivers. In the stifling Moldovan dusk, they looked like angels. I didn't ask them for help; they simply appeared because I was tired and lost. Nor were these Orthodox angels. Later I read what was on the reverse side of the makeshift flier they handed me — this sentence among others: "Creaza o buna imagino publica Bisericii Adventiste." My angels were Seventh-Day Adventists and understood me, because in Tecuci they were just as lost as I was.

Now it all seems so simple. Events intersect free of any logic of sequence; they cover space and time in an even, translucent layer. Memory re-creates them from the back, from the front, or sideways, but to them it makes no difference. This is the only way in which meaning will not trip us up, not knock from our hands the thing we were grasping for. Where did Moldova end and Transylvania begin? No doubt somewhere along Route 120, somewhere near a place called Tasca, the transition began. I was picked up by a hundred-year-old Audi. Inside, everything hung, peeled, fell apart. Loose wires from the dashboard, strips of upholstery from the ceiling, wind and dust from the floor. The man behind the steering wheel sat in shorts and an undershirt. A gold chain round his neck, yellow flip-flops on his feet. He was brown from the sun; only a little white showed from under his broad watch strap. On the rotaries the engine would sputter, so he kept his foot on the petrol and didn't slow down when he should have. We were to cross the deepest ravine in Europe. We tried conversing. He was from Satu Mare and hated Hungarians. To show me how much he hated them, he passed, with his wreck, spotless Passats and Cordobas that had Hungarian licence plates. The road was not the best for passing, full of curves. He passed uphill, his head out of the window to see a metre or two farther. I was afraid but I had a flask of Romanian brandy on me.

By Bicaz-Chei it was almost dark. The walls of the ravine were several hundred metres and we drove as if through a giant cave. I was in awe of this wonder of nature but at the same time wouldn't have missed the moment of our crash for anything. My driver muttered curses and punched the steering wheel when he lacked power and for several dozen metres had to stare at the silver rear of a Seat Ibiza with a Budapest license plate. At the mountain pass were stalls with handmade goods for tourists. Then we descended. After one curve, a herd of horses on the asphalt. Some with bells. We swerved left, directly into the path of an oncoming bus. Both we and the bus managed to stop athwart the road. Apparently this was normal, because my driver made the sign of the cross only three times, and we continued at the previous speed. But now he crossed himself each time he passed. I got out on the main street in Gheorgheni. Two men got into the car, both like the driver, only less brown and with thicker chains. I saw him give them large packs of bills, ten-thousand-lei notes, which throughout our drive had rolled back and forth in the back seat.

And that was all. Part two might have taken place in the evening, in Slovakia somewhere. In a roadside pub, let's say, between Šariš and Zemplén, where two truck drivers ate potato pancakes with braised liver and onions. They drank tea and looked at a dripping tap topped by a gold pheasant. From the small room by the bar, every now and then, a dark-haired young woman came out. She ordered four borovičkas and disappeared with the shot glasses behind a wood partition from which wafted cigarette smoke and male laughter. Each time she appeared for a new round, she whispered with the barmaid at length, as if wanting to put off the moment of her return. Only when voices were raised through the flimsy wall did she break off her nervous, rapid chatter. I couldn't figure out if the drinks on the tray belonged to her, or why she was serving those loud, invisible men. Coaxing them to commit a crime — or perform a good deed? Because she paid for each and every round, pulling from the tight pocket of her jeans rolls of red hundreds. All this happened in a place and season different from those I'm trying to summon now. Most likely it was between Nemecká and Predajná, on the road to Banská, and it was winter.

With events that have passed there is no problem, provided we don't attempt to be wiser than they are, provided we don't use them to further our own ends. If we let them be, they turn into a marvellous solution, a magical acid that dissolves time and space, eats calendars and atlases, and turns the coordinates of action into sweet nothingness. What is the meaning of the riddle? What is the use to anyone of chronology, sister of death?

At midnight in Kisvárda, bass speakers rumbled, and boys revved up and made their tires squeal, to stop ten metres further on. In the sultry night at the border, their shaved skulls glowed like milky lightbulbs. We were seeking a place to sleep, but this town had insomnia. The proximity of the border drove away sleep. In suburbs, the hedges of gaudy villas built in a month or a week. Vampire pistachio, rabid rose, venomous yellow. Downtown was old, hidden among trees full of deep shadows that swallowed up alleyways. But the crowd at Krucsay Marton Street, insect-like in its movements yet also lethargic, brought to mind a party of conquistadors at an aborted conquest. Or a herd of animals that found itself in the city but could derive no benefit from it. The young men shifted here and there, engaged, sniffed each other, parted, and again approached, joined by unseen threads of business, fear, need. They circled in the light like moths. The neurosis of the border: swift victory, swift defeat. Twenty kilometres farther on was Záhony, the only way from Hungary to Ukraine, so everything here budded, swelled, inflated, gathered strength. At the Hotel Bastya, a huge bleach blonde from another time wouldn't take dollars or marks, only forints, which we didn't have.

The hotel outside the city had Paris in its name, or Paradise. It looked like a set for a local remake of *Caligula:* plaster fountains, statues, plush, drapery. In the parking lot, the black gleaming fat asses of BMWs and Mercedes. A guy whose eyes were both empty and sensitive told us there were no rooms. But he took forints from his pocket and sold them to us at a relatively decent rate of exchange. We asked him who was staying here, Hungarians only or Ukrainians too? He regarded us as if we were children. "Ukrainians?" he replied in English. "They aren't European people."

We drove in the direction of Vásárosnamény and suddenly found ourselves in darkness and silence. Passing Ilk and Anarcs, we could hear the sound of sleepers breathing behind wooden shades in the windows of the low houses, and we could smell the nocturnal damp rising from the gardens. In the town we knocked long at a hotel door before a sleepy porter in carpet slippers opened for us. On the lobby walls were trophies: a zebra skin, the stuffed head of an antelope, exotic antlers. In the dimness of a side corridor, a spotted thing that could have been a leopard. Aside from the woman who finally turned on the lights in the kitchen and this porter, there was not a soul in the hotel.

Sometimes I get up before sunrise to watch the way the dark thins out and objects slowly reveal themselves, the trees, the rest of the landscape. You can hear the river below and roosters in the village. The light of dawn, cold and blue, gradually fills the world, and it's the same in every place I've been. The dark pales into the district of Sękowa, in the town of Sulina, on the edge of the Danube Delta — and everywhere time is made of night and day. I drink coffee and picture the light of another place.

Pitching One's Tent in
a New Place

IT'S THE MIDDLE of November, and still no snow. For two months I've been preparing for Hungary but am not yet prepared. I think of the north-east, of driving to Szabolcs-Szatmár, because winter must come eventually. I recall the road in Hidasnémeti and how almost a year ago on the day before New Year's Eve we crossed the border in rain. A wet December covered Zemplén like a curtain. Hungary was naked; the black trees hid nothing. Perhaps that is why we were constantly getting lost — in Gönc, Telkibánya, Bózsva, Pálháza, Hollóháza, Kéked, Füzér. The semi-transparent land a labyrinth. In the summer this seemed a region of endless noon, even at night. Streetlights in the towns and villages burned long tunnels through the dark. Behind the fences, in muggy gardens among the leaves of walnut and apricot trees, flickered the pale fire from television screens. Now an aqueous light filled all the places that in the summer had lain in shadow. Tokaj was as empty and flat as an old stage set. The Bodrog and the Tisa had lost their smell. Calmly and ruthlessly the weather had taken over. Actually, little had changed since the time when there were no houses here, no cities, and no names. The weather, like the oldest religion, then reigned equally over Beskid, Zemplén, the swamp below the Tisa, Erdőhát, Maramureş, the Transylvanian Hills, and all the other locations in which I spent months in the vain hope of seeing them as they really were. Rain in Mátészalka, rain in Nagykálló, rain in Nyír-bátor. Soggy yards with deep hoofprints of hogs; stripped plots; gardens glistening like glass; houses lower and lower, as if pulled into the soft soil. In Cigánd or Dombrád, on both sides of the road, a chain of puddles looked like flat scraps of grey sky. But that could have been in Gönc as well, or anywhere in Poland, Slovakia, Ukraine. And not a soul in sight. As in a dream, long streets with single-storey buildings on either side and no busi-ness, no pedestrians, vehicles, or dogs.

The scraps of sky were probably in Abaújszántó, on the main road, a blue house to the left, a church to the right. A little farther on stood a yellow house with bay windows and a green gate in a low surrounding wall. Several willows there too. But this, I think now, was on the way back, on New Year's Eve. It was in that unpopulated town, at a deserted cross street leading to a windy valley below the massif of Szokolya, that we found a pub, an *italbolt,* because we wanted to get rid of the rest of our forints. Cigarette smoke and talk hung in the air, and some kind of sedentary holiday was being observed, in which you didn't leave your chair, only raised your voice, made slow gestures, had shining eyes. Through the cloud of tobacco, it seemed that absolute silence had to be maintained on the street and that only in this dark room did the rule not apply. All these citizens sitting at tables had left their homes to make some noble, far-reaching plans, as if an enemy had come or an epidemic, and, unable to endure the solitude any longer, they huddled together here like chickens. But then the cigarette haze parted a little, and I saw a few Gypsies in black leather jackets, and two Gypsy women who had dyed their hair blond.

Except that this was the day after, when we were on our way back. Now we were looking for lodging in a maze of roads and refused to slow down, so the light-blue signs with names of localities had to be read quickly and with that pleasant sense of amazement we always got from Hungarian, which freed our trip from geography, letting it follow instead the path of fairy tale, legend, towards a childhood in which the sound and music of words mattered more than their meaning.

We stopped, I believe, in Hollóháza. Around a gravel lot, long, one-level houses with arcades. We were given rooms and asked no questions. Everyone was occupied with tomorrow: smells from the kitchen, the clatter of pots and pans, garlands, streamers, and balloons in the hall where the guests of this roadside inn or camp building were served food. We left our things and drove on. Spruce trees in the village squares; cardboard angels and stars on them, wet and losing their shape. This was a year ago, and now I cannot distinguish Tokaj from Hidasnémeti, Sárospatak from Pálháza. I remember the brown roofs of Mád on the right side of the road. They were like clay deposits on a hillside. Bright, soaked, bare because there were no trees, only dead grapevines with rows of wooden crosses that followed the rise and fall of the land and went on forever. But Mád was the day after, and we were probably on our way then to Mikóháza, to find that solitary pub outside the village, the pub like a campsite. Embers glowed in the mist at dusk, and you could smell smoke. Men fanning big grills in the open air, under the eaves; women putting things on tables. Everyone as if they had just come down from the mountains or up from the swamp: covered with mud, in the paramilitary dress of hunters. All that was missing was horses, the quiet neighing in the dark, the clink of bridles, the stamp of hooves. People drank palinka. Its smell mixed with the smell of burning logs and roasting meat. Behind the pub was a scummy pond and the mess of a village yard: chicken coops, hay, a green wallow, a wire fence. Beyond that, the dying day, and from deep in the landscape I could smell the wet presence of mountains. We entered the wooden hut to eat goulash and drink red wine. At the tables sat people in thick sweaters and heavy boots. No one paid attention to us. It's not impossible that in this rain-sodden end of the world, in the dead of winter, foreigners were a daily occurrence.

Now, a year later, I consult the Slovak map of Zemplén and see that I was right about the swamp and mountains. Just beyond the pub, beyond the duck pond, flows the Bózsva, and after that is marsh, and then, in complete darkness, the Ritkahegy range. This information is of no use to me, really, but I collect it, as if to fill in a space, to keep returning to the beginning, keep renewing, to write an endless prologue to what was, because this is the only way that the past and dead can be brought back, even if only for a moment, in the absurd hope that memory will somehow work its way into an invisible crack and pry open the lid of oblivion. So I repeat my hopeless mantra of names and landscapes, because space dies more slowly than I do and assumes an aspect of immortality. I mutter my geographic prayer, my topographic Hail Marys, chant my litany of the map, to make this carnival of wonders, this Ferris wheel, this kaleidoscope, freeze, stop for a second, with me at the centre.

Then came Sátoraljaújhely and a night as glossy as a silk lining. On Kossuth Street, moving curtains of rain. We looked for an ATM or anything open, but in the windows we saw only cashiers in stores going through receipts, people sweeping, mopping floors, guys making small talk in doorways as they let out the last customers.

The first time I was here, four years ago, it was July. I hardly noticed the Hapsburg ochre-and-gall yellow of the facades. We sped down the tunnel of shade that was the main street, and the town vanished as quickly as it had appeared. To the right, grapevines going up; to the left, an occasional gleam from the Bodrog. Route 27 cut the scenery in half. The east was the dark-green marsh of Bodrogköz, the west a mountain chain where dry heat reigned in the heights and from the volcanic soil jutted, here and there, limestone that looked like fragments of a primordial spine. Here was where the Great Hungarian Plain began, reaching as far as Belgrade. Its northern limit practically touched the Carpathians, and the western edge gently brushed the Northern Medium Mountains, Zemplén, then Bükk, Mátra. In the flat wetland forked by the Tisa and Bodrog stood groves of poplar, and only remnants of the true *puszta* west of Debrecen could surpass the melancholy of this region. You smelled water everywhere, and the spongy earth sank beneath the weight of the sky. The villages were islands of yellow brick. The world clung to the horizon, and from a distance everything assumed the form of a horizontal line. From the road through Tisacsermely and Nagyhomok you saw the mountains behind Sárospatak. They climbed suddenly, without warning or introduction, like pyramids in the desert, and their shape was just as geometric. But Sárospatak was some other time. Now we were watching the rain and an increasingly deserted, shuttered Sátoraljaújhely. *Sátoraljaújhely* means "a tent pitched in a new place".

Delta

I'VE BEEN DREAMING of water since I got here. I dream of many places in the world, but all are water. They have substantial names—London, Bulgaria, the GDR—but invariably they swim in the whirling deep. I accept this, because the voyage from which I returned was itself a dream. Transylvania, Wallachia, Dobruja, the Danube Delta, and Moldova were filled with heat, and I doubt now that my memory can re-create the things that continue existing back there without my participation. I search my pockets and my pack for evidence, but the objects I find look like props: thousand-lei banknotes with Mihai Eminescu on them, who died as Nietzsche did, from syphilis and dementia. You can buy nothing with them; only Gypsy children are happy to take them. The kids gather images of the national bard and go to a shop to exchange him for sweets and chewing gum. So it was in Richiş, Iacobeni, Roandola. On the five-thousand note is Lucian Blaga, who wrote, "The cock of the Apocalypse crows, crows in every village of Romania." The ten-thousand note goes to Nicolae Iorga, who was murdered by the Iron Guard, although, as Eliade states, "he was a true poet of Romanianness". I saw them all tied with string into thick packets. In Cluj, at eight in the morning on Gheorghe Doja Avenue, a van stopped and out stepped a fellow in a suit covered with such packets, like Santa Claus bearing gifts. At a bank in Sighişoara, piles of low-denomination bills, tied with twine, lay on a counter, but no one showed the least interest. The guard explained to me that foreigners were not allowed to sell Western currency. He shrugged apologetically and in a whisper advised, in English, "Black market . . . black market . . ."

Now I take from a pocket these venerable faces, smooth them out, and am amazed that they haven't disappeared, that they didn't melt into thin air when on the return trip at four in the morning I crossed the border at Curtici. Above the station was a deep-blue sky. As I was getting off, the border guards and customs officials combed the Budapest train for currency smugglers. I saw them gut the luggage of the English travellers who boarded at Sighişoara. My conscience clean, I calmly drank a Bihor palinka. The uniformed officials stepped off, and the train was about to move when a girl jumped down with a backpack, her eyes wild, her hair loose. It could have been fear, it could have been fury — I'll never know. In any case she belonged to a group of foreigners. She ran across the platform and disappeared into the station building. No one chased her. The train left. Mine would come soon, with the silver light of dawn rising over the Bihor Mountains.

The compartment and the corridor were empty. I could easily see on either side. Along the depot, in intervals of several dozen steps, stood soldiers. They had boyish faces and uniforms that didn't fit: the trousers were too short, and the jackets didn't quite match in colour. The nearest soldier wore civilian black boots with big buckles. These men looked as if they had just been pulled out of bed and taken prisoner. Without weapons, without belts, shivering in the morning cold. Staring into space, as if to avoid seeing the train, as if to avoid making eye contact.

I take the bills from my pocket and see not Eminescu, Iorga, and Blaga but the faces of those kids.

But I have other evidence to prove that I didn't dream it all. This ticket for a hydrofoil ride for 120,000 lei. "Rapid, Commodious, Efficient," I bought it in Tulcea, to go to Sulina. To see the continent sink into the sea, the land slip beneath the surface, leaving behind people, animals, and plants, escaping its business, shaking off all the noise of histories, nations, tongues, the ancient mess of events and destinies. I wanted to see it find repose in the eternal twilight of the deep, in the indifferent and monotonous company of fish and seaweed. And so I got up early to catch the train, at the Gara de Nord in Bucharest, to Constanța.

Branești, Dragoș Vodă, Ștefan cel Mare — on the steppe-like plain the houses all burrowed into the earth in search of coolness. They were low, scorched by the sun, and brittle. They resembled stones, crusts. On occasion I saw distant horses and people, their silhouettes as black as their shadows. The sky in these parts, I thought, if you rapped on it, there would be a metallic clang. After Fetești the train went up an embankment over marsh, and in the Cernavodă district it clattered across a bridge that spanned the Danube. A nuclear power plant rose like a phantom, then disappeared. Grey cliffs filled with bird nests. I thought I could smell the sea, but at the station in Constanța the smell dissolved.

At the bus station on the other side of town, it was like being in a village. Kerchiefed women sat with their hands folded over their bellies; the children flitted about them like sparrows. I bought cheese and bread and went to a nearby pub to have a beer. A teenage girl crawled in. She had a pretty face. She moved along the floor using her arms. The men laughed and threw cigarettes. She gathered them, laughing too. It was a game they were playing, one they knew well. Later I saw her in the station. She gave the cigarettes to an old woman who sat motionless among children.

The first minaret I ever saw was in Babadag. I was on the way to Tulcea, to take the Sulina boat. The microbus was operated by two men. One drove and sold tickets; the other, younger, jumped out at every stop to open and close the door. In Mihai Viteazu someone tried to ride without paying. The second man pushed him from the door so hard, the guy went rolling.

The yellow, bare hills of Dobruja resembled dead anthills. The heat penetrated the earth and tore it apart from inside. To the right somewhere was Histria. Greek ruins, marble columns from the seventh century BC — but I was unimpressed: the farther back the past, the more wretched it is. Human thought wears at it, the way a telephone book gets worn by human hands. The minaret in Babadag was simple and severe, a pencil pointed at the sky. We had a five-minute stop, but no one went to take a leak. Everyone drank water, which immediately appeared on the skin. A dark stain spread between the driver's shoulders. The tape kept playing: folk melodies in that strange, moaning key that went with the minaret, with the heat and dust. I could feel the continent ending, the sigh of the land casting off its responsibilities. We would remain with our property, with our curses and our nerves, as we watched the naked back of the land slide under the smooth surface of the water.

I saw Tulcea from a distance and from a height. We descended by gentle zigzags through the hills. A blue-grey mist hung over the city and the river. The Danube divided into three branches here, into dozens of canals, lakes, backwaters. The river's arm became a wide, splayed hand, whose fingernails were sandy beaches, whose bracelet was ponds and pools, all covered with the green skin of marsh and with endless reeds. Tulcea was the wrist.

Horses grazed at the port, cropping wisps of something on the barren square among cranes, train tracks, mounds of scrap metal. Their roan backs were lost in the rust red of the ships behind them, of the belt conveyors of ore. No one was about, only a couple of boys jumping back and forth between the shore and the wreck of a tugboat. I sniffed the air for the sea but smelled only river: a warm fish-and-slime odour mixed with motor oil.

A hundred and twenty thousand lei. "Rapid, Commodious, Efficient." A crowd had gathered early at the ramp. The hydrofoil was of Soviet vintage. Those who had tickets boarded first — God knows where they purchased them. The rest had to wait and see if there were seats left. Two young Frenchmen slowly, sleepily counted out banknotes. They passed them to each other, as in a game. The banknotes fluttered in the breeze. The two seemed stoned. There were peasants with bundles, boxes, bags, and a few fishermen carried loaves of bread in backpacks. And men in uniform, of course. I saw four kinds of military or paramilitary uniform. Each soldier was wearing a holstered pistol. I couldn't tell which were protecting us and which were simply taking the boat somewhere. All had the same face: grave, drawn.

I don't really remember anything of that trip. Seventy kilometres with three stops, and the seating as on a bus. Once in a while, when we crossed someone's wake, the belly of the hydrofoil slapped the water in a soft, fishy way. Around Crişan we passed a Turkish freighter as large and black as an old factory.

It was carrying sheep. In dozens of stacked cages, several hundred white-grey animals standing up, lying down. Pieces of straw jutting. I went out on the upper deck. The Frenchmen were on their backs at the stern, their eyes shut. Two Turkish sailors, smoking cigarettes, leaned against the railing of the freighter and contemplated the endless green of the Delta. For a moment I thought that their boat was named "Bethlehem", but that was just my imagination struggling with the extraordinary.

In Sulina we arrived at the main street. A crowd at the shore was waiting for family and friends. Along Deltei Street, trees and shade. At the nearest pub, I got a coffee and sat under an umbrella. Waiting for it to sink in, awareness of the end. The river had emptied into the sea, and the land, with all its events, had come to a halt. There was no returning by the same route. I could feel how time, until now given human aspects, was dissolving to its original form. Here, in Sulina, it was as palpable as the humidity in the air. It ate at the houses and ships, etched faces and landscapes, the glasses in the bars, the merchandise in the stores. It consumed like a fire the delicate envelope of minutes, hours, and days and took possession of all that was seen and unseen, including thought.

The way to the sea led through desolate, treeless pasture. Hulls of ships, tugs, motorboats rusting in sand. The stink of manure hung over this region. Salty gusts from the sea disappeared in its hot fog without a trace. In the marsh, shoals of litter gleamed white among stunted, thorn-bearing shrubbery. A plastic bottle, blue-grey, shone like the belly of a dead fish. Concrete bunkers were stuck in dirty yellow land; angular military ruins stood along the shore in this baked, windswept place; in their shadow, an occasional horse, untethered, tried to rest. From across the bleached, shaggy dunes, the sound of waves crashing, as old as the world and as monotonous. The sound overflowed the levee and made for the town. Quiet loss filled every corner, every low house and garden, the tenements along the promenade. Grass grew on the driveway to the Hotel Sulina. The Hotel Europolis was shut and still. The Association of Victims of Communism had its quarters in a building not much bigger than a dollhouse.

About five in the afternoon, wagons, handcarts, and bicycles began to gather at the harbour. People came. From the west, from Tulcea, the ferry *Moldova* brought news, goods, passengers. It docked majestically and dropped anchor. Those who carried little disembarked first, then the cargo was unloaded, everything that Sulina lacked: cases of bottled water and beer, cartons of bread, jars of fruit, foam mattresses, sausages in foil that sweated from the heat, coffee, white wine in plastic jugs, rubber boots, glass and porcelain, a market of miracles, rolls of tarpaper from my hometown, reins, T-shirts, Balkan cheddar and Romanian Hochland, contraband, soap, jam, beads, notebooks, Nescafé, chairs, a cuckoo clock, and a bunch of beach umbrellas. The wagons, carts, and a white Dacia pickup truck transporting it to a couple of shops on Deltei Street could barely hold all this stuff.

I walked towards the sea between the dead hulls and bunkers. I climbed up onto a giant concrete platform ramp, from which someone, someday, might want to launch land-sea missiles. From there I could see the sun dropping to the Danube. The river glowed phosphorescent green, like a taut lizard skin. A ship approaching from the open sea was several storeys high and black as pitch in the dying light of day. It slipped through the narrow estuary and crossed the red sun. I did not see any movement on deck — no one stood at the edge, no one smoked, spat, or watched the port. When it got dark, I followed its path. The ship anchored at the end of the shore, not far from the Hotel

Sulina. Ship and hotel were equally dark and silent. The ship sailed under the Lebanese flag. Stopping for the night, to continue upriver at dawn.

In the room where I slept, the tapestry over my bed depicted Mecca.

To Sfântu Gheorghe, directly north, it takes less than three hours. My boat was sky-blue, sleek, and had a Honda motor. First it went a little above the main current, then took a network of canals. The craft couldn't have been wider than 1.2 metres, but it was long. A fifty-year-old man sat at the bow and signalled to the man at the helm. The canals were narrow and full of tricky spots. Sometimes we had to turn off the motor and lift it to get across a sandbank or keep the propeller free of seaweed. At the narrowest places, we passed through a tunnel of green reeds. "Vietnam," remarked the captain, lighting up a Snagov cigarette. Now and then the reeds thinned and you could see plots of corn and cabbage. Plots not much larger than a gravesite mound or flowerbed went right to the water's edge. Some were guarded by dogs on short chains. We returned to the main channel and looked for the next canal. A patrol boat blocked our path, and a cop, standing a metre above us, asked the captain our origin, destination, type of motor. Finally he waved, and we headed due north.

We passed old-fashioned boats with diesel engines and structures like sentry boxes. White pelicans glided over Roşu Lake. We passed a fishing village. Only men on the shore, puttering among their boats and nets. The canal was straight as an arrow and smooth as glass. Geometry kept a tight rein on the reeds, with nowhere for the eye to rest, nothing that stood out, that was irregular, in the monotony of green lines and rectangles under an endless, clear sky. The Delta here was infinity done in simple parallels and perpendiculars. Every now and then, on the border of vegetation, fishermen stood in high rubber boots, motionless, aloof, grey, like large herons.

At the landing in Sfântu Gheorghe lay a pile of rotting hay. I walked towards a two-storey concrete building. The ground floor was unoccupied, full of crap. People lived above — you could see curtains in the windows. Heat hung in the dusty, empty square. The sky was the colour of sand. I looked for a little shade. A few high trees grew before an outdoor pub. In a shed they had seven kinds of beer and twelve wines, and men sat at plank tables. It was now two in the afternoon. I got a Ciuc beer and sat too, because I had finally reached a place from which one could only return.

The ferries to Istanbul left from Constanţa. Trains to the outside world left from Tulcea, possibly also from Galaţi. I sat on an island separated by mud, swamp, and time, a time decomposing over the Delta like organic matter, mouldering, giving off the smell of a beginning that preceded the cycle of life and death. The continent here burned slowly, like the edge of a fabric. Sand, dust, dogs, and siesta without end. Men got up from the tables, disappeared, reappeared. Women sat on benches a bit to the side and listened to the conversation, their bodies calm, languorous, heavy. A cart went by, harnessed to an unbelievably thin horse. The boy driver wielding a broken stick. Carrying mineral water and yellow cases of Bergenbier. They turned a corner in ridiculous, neurotic haste.

A man approached me and asked if I needed a room, a place to sleep, because if I did, he knew a "babushka" here who would be glad to take me in, but I had to decide now, because he was leaving. He spoke in Russian, like many in Sfântu Gheorghe. I really didn't know what I would be doing next, I said, I had to give it thought. I didn't care to rush my beer, to leave the shade. The guy left but remained in sight. He hurried across the pub, said words here and there, but went on, not waiting for an answer. Quick, busy, as if serving as an emissary in a paralysed village. He wore a grey shirt, old trousers from a suit, and, on his bare feet, flip-flops. He wasn't interested in taking care of any business for me. One of the times he passed, he said that the girl working at the bar spoke Russian and could help me find a room. Before I could open my mouth, he was gone.

After an hour or two I went to the babushka after all. She lived not far from the pub, in a small white house. Green posts held up the porch. A burst of flowers in front. At the back, the thick shade of nut trees, pear trees, apple trees. The old woman was as small as her house and full of chatter. She would ask a question but continue talking, or nod: from Poland, yes, staying for a few days, of course, arrived by boat, what I did, where I lived, in the country, in town — a mix of gentle prying, indifference, and goodwill.

She opened the room. Tiny, it smelled like the room of my grandmother. The still air was of old wood, sheets, and damp. No one, at least no stranger, had used it for a long time. A table, a chair, and the bed took up the space exactly. Everything in its place since time immemorial. When I moved the chair out to hold my backpack, I felt like a criminal, as if I were destroying this piece of dark-brown furniture by exposing it to the present moment, that it would die as a sea creature dies when wrenched from the depths to the surface.

"And God you have?" she asked, pointing to the icon hanging

in a corner right below the ceiling. "I have," I answered in Russian. She nodded, gave me the key, and left. At the same height as the icon and right next to it was a cupboard filled with boxes for Western perfume, deodorant, and coffee. No doubt from the son in Bucharest or the daughter in Constanța, because the old woman, in the course of fifteen minutes, had managed to tell me about her children too. The icon and that Western trash bin were the only ornaments in this spare interior. I didn't care to consider the symbolism or the semantics of their juxtaposition. I felt old, no longer having the strength for the obvious. I left my luggage and went to look at the sea.

From the bank along this arm of the Danube, you had a view in both directions. On the right, the river's water flowed slime green. The dark boats anchored in the shallows, their bows and sterns turned slightly upwards, were sleek and quaint. In the ever-changing waterscape, among the glinting mirrors of the current, among the tide pools roughened by the breeze, their shapes seemed unreal. Particularly at dusk, when you couldn't tell boat from shadow. They hung in the lucent space like cardboard cutouts, carvings from coal. Bringing to mind remnants of the most ancient night, when they were used to ferry souls. In the Delta I saw nothing more beautiful or more simple.

To the left stretched a village of reeds. Fences, roofs, walls, sheds for cattle and for fowl — all made of dry, hollow stalks. Cut reeds lay loose in piles, were tied into sheaves, stood waiting in ricks. A flat human habitation, since nothing high could be built from such material. Bits of clay had fallen from earth-plastered walls, exposing the construction of poles woven with reeds. The village was like a vast campground. All that these people possessed seemed in constant peril. Barely raised above the ground, barely attached and joined and marked off by fence and stake and a few twigs, Sfântu Gheorghe had a heroic resignation about it: exposed to the elements, filled with uncertainty, doomed to oblivion, it held on to the land as a sparrow's nest holds on to a branch.

Then, just as in Sulina, a bare stretch began and continued to the beach. At its edge, just past the village, stood radar towers. I saw a few camouflage trucks behind an enclosure. I was not drawn to it at all. The military in my part of the world, in times of peace, is always the same: sad and giving off a faint stink. I preferred to keep my distance. The black latticework of the antennas loomed above the huts of reeds and mud. I tried to imagine the tedium of a post like that, the tedium of empty sky and green computer monitors. Card games, booze smuggled in, talk about women, radio stations on which you might catch Western rock and roll or a folk number. Sleepiness, coffee, and no barbarians on the horizon.

But it's quite possible the place was simply a point from which to observe the rest of the world, that monster with no shape or boundary that always lays siege to a people preoccupied with its own existence. I considered the cowpats drying in the sun and tried not to think about history. I couldn't help it, of course. Once again geography had made me prey to all the unclear events, murky pseudo-facts, muttered truths, and unimpeachable falsehoods cobbled together into meaning. Danger indeed lurks beyond the horizon and always has. As we wait in time for what we desire, space brings us unsolicited things: armies or ideas, and there's no escaping them. The age of portable, movable nations, nations whose history depends on an unending present, is long gone. Today there is nowhere we can go to start over, and that's why we live mired in a past that permeates our territories, just as an animal's den is filled with its smell.

The radar was aimed, I am willing to bet, at Turkey.

People lay on the beach. Several sun umbrellas were stuck in the sand, not much larger than rain umbrellas. Otherwise, as far as the eye could see, no shade. The thornbushes on the dunes were shoulder high in places. I walked south along the shore and soon reached the spot where the river current joined the salt water. The Danube, darker, fed into the transparent silver of the waves, like a cloud passing across a mirror. A gleaming black snake swam up on the beach and slithered over the sand towards vegetation, its small and supple presence an apparition on this great bare stage, so I followed. Sensing my shadow, it stopped and coiled. I left it in peace. It waited a moment, then proceeded landwards.

Sfântu Gheorghe came alive in the evening, as if everybody had been waiting for the lights to go on. It was no cooler, only darker. People came from the houses, the beach, the boats, from their fishing. The pub under the trees, unable to accommodate them all, resembled a bivouac: dozens, hundreds of people in constant motion, in patches of flickering light, their gestures beginning in light and cut off by a dark that magnified everything. Echoes came from deep in the night, as if the village were next to another village and that next to yet another, as if Sfântu Gheorghe had siblings in this void or were a dull, small planet attempting, without much success, to reflect the sounds and brilliance of planets many times larger than it. The sky now and then flashed mercury. *Eto mayak*, someone told me in Russian: a lighthouse. The beam, majestic in its repetition, made everything taking place on earth seem random, coincidental. The people expended their energy in quick, nervous bursts, like lizards. I got a Ciuc at the pub and stepped aside to watch the fiesta from a distance, a party whirling about inside a cave. The night pressed in on all sides, so one had to keep moving, talking, shouting over the canned music, clinking glasses, gesticulating, so that the hot dark wouldn't congeal and close up like a scab over a wound. This was a carnival, a European tropics, the fear of the harsh light of day, the bliss of oblivion, everything pierced by the quivering, plangent sound of a clarinet in that scale one encounters south of the Carpathians.

To cool off, I walked to the water, to the dock where the ferry was moored. You could see nothing here. I heard the slap of waves, of fish, smelled the warm, muddy breath of the river, felt its enormous pulse and indifferent presence. I imagined green blood flowing out of the body of the continent, which went on living anyway, as it has done for thousands of years.

I understood the pub frenzy. It was simply a sign of existence. People met in this poor light, drawn like moths, to see if they lived. They had to examine one another and raise a racket. Between the infinite sky and the dwindling land, there was no room for them. At this edge, this swampy island edge, they had to find their image in the eyes of others, for there is nothing worse than nothingness that takes the shape of geography.

Bedbugs bit me through the night, and at dawn I got up and left the old woman's house. The air was blue-grey and a little cooler now, though heat still filled the sandy streets. The flame had been turned off for a moment, but there was no ventilation. Heat oozed from the walls of houses, from the ground, from gardens and fences, it oozed like thick juice from fruit, like the current from a sticky battery. I passed the wreck of a delivery van on four flat tyres, the only vehicle in Sfântu Gheorghe. I walked to the end of the village. After the last houses, trash: non-recyclable plastic, cans, glass, rags, tinfoil, cardboard, old pots, a bucket without a bottom, containers collecting humidity and decay, Tetra Pak and crushed PET bottles as far as the eye could see. The spit of the dump extended into a canal and at the water's surface lost some of its massiveness, spilled in an avalanche of jutting bottle necks, inflated bags, an even mix of wet corrugated board and aluminium wrap, the metal and broken glass resting somewhere lower.

That's when I noticed the cross. It stood in the middle of the dump. It wasn't big, a metre, a metre and a half, fashioned with two rough planks and painted brown. The ends of the horizontal piece had been carefully rounded, to give the raw wood form. No inscription, no base. The thing was simply stuck in the ground. Its neighbours: a pail with holes, a broom, a paint can, a boot coming apart, and a box for Lux soap showing the face of a brunette. Had the cross been here before the dumping began, or had someone planted it in this cemetery of objects? But surely no one in Sfântu Gheorghe hoped for the salvation of things, dared think of their resurrection, their immortality. Probably few believed in their own resurrection — hence the symbiosis of the cross and this inorganic mortuary.

I went back. It had to be after six, but not yet seven. A group of men sat at the pub, a bucket, a trowel, and a level at their feet. They looked like proletarian freemasons. Drinking vodka straight, with beer as a chaser. No trace remained of the evening carnival; the ashtrays on the table were clean. The men hardly conversed. Heat came from the east, and the shadows of people diminished like wet blotches drying. The masons drank up and left. The babushka promoter appeared, brush in hand, a rag wrapped round it, and wiped everything along his way:

the kerb by the pub, the concrete divider, the pavement. He did this quickly and efficiently. The rag, dry, left no mark. He disappeared round a corner, appeared again at the far end of the sandy square before a store, and did his hurried cleaning there too. For almost an hour I saw him come and go, in a constant rush, trousers bagging as he did battle with dirt and dust, a Buster Keaton of the Delta trying to stem the chaos of volatile substances and defend Sfântu Gheorghe against the rain of particles from outer space.

The masons returned, but now without their tools. Once again, glasses of vodka with beer chasers. Evidently they had started a job and so now with a clear conscience could, without haste, take the measure of the new day. More people gathered at the tables. It was after seven; the sky took on a dull milky hue and began to swell. I drank Ciuc and Ursus, alternating, wanting to be less conspicuous in this morning company, to participate in the fatigue that came from their faces and bodies. Sleep in this place, apparently, took as much effort as getting through the day. I would have loved to sit at the wooden table until my soul sank out of notice, until my limbs became immersed in this strange soup of dawn and dusk. It is possible that my perverse love for the periphery, for the provincial, for everything that passes, fades, and falls apart had found peace at last in Sfântu Gheorghe. I could sit here for years and grow comfortable with death. I could go out to the ferry dock every day and watch death come in. The worn, threadbare measurements of time would hasten its arrival, or delay it, and eventually I might acquire a kind of immortality. Because if life was extinguished here so easily, death would have to take on some thinned-out, spectral aspect. In my daily walk between the shadows of the pub's lindens and the harbour, I would keep just enough of my energy so my mind wouldn't shut down, so I could continue imagining the world, make sure I had lost nothing. At noon, when boredom struck, I would walk to that flat sandy stretch along the shore. From inland would come mirages of distant cities. Between the mirror of the water and the clouds, Bucharest might appear, Berlin might float, Prague, London, Istanbul, and, with the right combination of light and convection currents, a fusion of New York and Montevideo, Tokyo and Montreal. Atmospheric-optical flux might also let me view my past life, my gestures and actions preserved among the layers of air, frozen in stratosphere lockers but now reanimated for my amusement or moral instruction. In Sfântu Gheorghe anything could happen—I was convinced of this around seven thirty, when the first guests sat down at the tables. There are places where only potentials exist. And in this place the only way out might indeed be a miracle, a sign, a sudden revelation. Void, paralysis, the horror of decline, the sorrow of elements forced to assume geometrical shape, earth and sky pulling at weary, sleepy humanity in either direction—all this in itself was miracle and sign, stopping the imagination in mid-stride, replacing it with implacable reality.

I finished my Ciuc or Ursus and got up. The schemes I had dreamed of were so alluring that I needed to take some action. At the dock, a couple of boats were anchored. On a board hammered to a mast, someone had chalked "crap 35000, som 38000". The prices for carp and catfish. Two men sat by a wooden shed. I went up to them and asked how people got out of here. Was there a boat to Sulina? They mulled awhile. Finally one said no, there was no such boat, not in the whole village, no one was going out, and there was no ferry until tomorrow. I heard the same thing from men who were tarring a dinghy that had been hauled from the water. Anyone I asked, it was the same: No one is going out. I didn't really want to leave, I just wanted to know. Everyone spoke of the ferry and sometimes of a tractor that at five in the morning set out through the marsh towards Sulina. The thought of tomorrow's ferry depressed me; I intended to take it but not that soon.

At a shop I bought bread, caşcaval cheese, mineral water, and white wine in a plastic flask. I made for the beach. At eight, it was as hot as it is at noon at home. The ground smelled of cow dung and dust. I found an isolated spot. When I waded into the sea, the water was as warm as the air. The bottom barely dropped. I went out so far, the land became a thin line, but even so the water hardly reached my chest. Now and then I felt a cooler current, but it was gone in a moment, and once again it turned as warm as if I were sinking in enormous, churning innards.

It's possible that everything I've written so far began
with this photograph. The year is 1921, in a small Hungarian
town, Abony, seven kilometres west of Szolnok. A blind violinist
crosses the street, playing. He is led by a barefoot boy wearing a
visored cap, a boy in his early teens. The shoes on the musician's
feet are worn, broken. His right foot at the moment rests on a
narrow track made by a cart's iron wheel. The street is unpaved.
The ground must be dry: the boy's feet are not muddy, and the
tracks are not deep. The tracks arc gracefully to the right and
disappear into the blurry depths of the photograph. Along the
street, a wooden fence, and part of a house is visible — a reflection of sky in its window. Farther on stands a white chapel. Trees
grow behind the fence. The musician's eyes are shut. He walks
and plays, for himself and for the unseen space around him.
Besides these two pedestrians on the street is a child of a few
years. He is turned towards them but looks beyond, as if there is
something of greater interest following them outside the frame.
It's a cloudy day, because neither people nor things cast a sharp

shadow. On the violinist's right arm (so he's left-handed) hangs a cane, and on the guide's arm what appears to be a small blanket. Only a few steps separate the two from the edge of the photograph. They'll be gone in a moment, and the music with them. Leaving only the toddler, the road, and the wheel tracks.

For four years I have been haunted by this picture. Wherever I go, I seek its three-dimensional, colour equivalent, and often seem to find it. That's how it was in Podoliniec; in the side streets of Lewoczy; in white-hot Gönc, where I was looking for a train station, which turned out to be an empty, ruined building, and no train departed until the evening. That's how it was in Vilmány, on an empty platform amid vast fields melting in the heat; how it was at the marketplace in Delatyn, where old women sold tobacco; how it was in Kwasy, when the train had already left and there was not a soul in sight, though the houses stood close together. And in Solotvino, among the dead mine shafts covered with salt dust, and in Dukla, when a heavy, tedious wind blew from the mountain pass. In all these spots, in 1921, André Kertész put his stamp on the transparent screen of space, as if time had halted then and the present was revealed to be a misunderstanding, joke, or betrayal, as if my appearance in these various locations was an embarrassing anachronism, because I came from the future, but was no wiser for that, only more afraid. The space of this photograph hypnotizes me, and all my travelling has had only one purpose: to find, at long last, the secret passage into its interior.

On the Road to Babadag

I HAVE COUNTED THE stamp marks in my passport. In seven years, 167, but there ought to be more, because some of the officials were too lazy to lift a finger. They waved me past in Oradea, for example. A couple of days later, I returned through Satu Mare; no one else at the crossing, noon, but they said, "Pull over, leave your car." Nodding for me to follow into a glass hangar, a hothouse, fifty degrees Celsius, Amazonia. A door, another, then finally the control centre, ten dead computers, a guy with his feet on the desk and a pile of sunflower seeds. He gnawed the entire time. He did take his feet off the desk. We were alone; the others had left, no doubt to the sentry box, lest someone dangerous sneak through. I understood a little — *Cinde? unde? intrare, ştampila* — but played dumb. He inspected my passport from every angle, from the back, from the front, upside down, my driver's licence too, my registration, my *carte verde,* and finally told me to go out in the corridor. I watched him through the glass door. Again the feet up on the desk, and more sunflower seeds. He was waiting for me to soften in this oven, to confess to spying, smuggling, having plastic surgery done, and to be willing to wipe away these crimes with the help of a few dollars. I leaned against the wall, shut my eyes, and pretended to sleep on my feet. After half an hour he called me back and again said something, but I answered in Polish that it wasn't my fucking fault if his colleagues in Oradea had failed to do their job. In this vein we conversed. At last he threw me a look of reproach, handed me my documents, and waved me away.

So they don't always stamp, but neither do they always give you a hard time if you didn't get stamped. There's no rule. The Hungarians sometimes won't stamp but then won't fuss, they just make this slow, heavy gesture, my favourite, which means, Screw the lot of you. Generally I like Hungarian border guards. Particularly at Sátoraljaújhely in the summer. They're lazy, a bit unbuttoned-unbuckled, holsters hanging carelessly, but they move with dignity, as if to say, Once this was all ours, but you wanted Trianon, so now you have to stand in this stupid line. I say "jo napot" to them, and they let me by. This *jo napot* I owe to a border guard on a train at a crossing at Lőkösháza. I was returning then from Sibiu, and it was something like five in the morning. The man appeared at the end of a corridor, and my heart sank. He was two and a half metres high, had a head shaved bald, wore a field jacket much too small for him, and carried an enormous gun at his side. A dog of war, a mutant mercenary. I sat in my compartment, put my hands on my knees, and held my breath. Then the door opened, I saw a big smile, and heard, in Polish, "Hello, your humble servant — is that how you say it? Any drugs, weapons, pornography, Semtex? No? Thank you. Toodle-oo — is that how you say it?" And he was gone.

But the Romanians are no worse. Or the Ukrainians, or the Slovaks. Even Austrians can be cool. Occasionally someone slips a cog—like the Slovenian at the border in Hodoš who insisted on knowing how many dinars we were bringing in, because he had forgotten that for the past ten years his country was part of Yugoslavia. Occasionally someone draws a blank—like the Greek at Corfu who couldn't believe that we had spent two weeks in Albania for pleasure and who looked at our dirty underwear under a strong light to find the answer to the mystery.

Yes, 167 stamps, and if you include the stamps not made, a good 200. Red, violet, green, black; smeared, with a word or initial added in ballpoint pen, with pictures of antique locomotives, automobiles, with childlike outlines of planes and ships, because it is all childishness, a game of tag, blindman's buff, hide-and-seek, a pointless amusement that, once set into motion, cannot stop. Some stamps are indistinct, as if a carved potato were used, an amateur printing kit, or even as if I had made the mark myself with chalk or a fountain pen, as a joke.

I wonder what the stamp of Moldavia is like. That is to say, the Republic of Moldova, east of the Prut, its capital Chişinău. I must find out. I hope it's green. That's how I picture the country: green hills, with a forest now and then. Gardens and plots in the sun. Watermelon, paprikas, and grapevines growing. In the side streets of old Chişinău, the shade of chestnut trees. The cuisine, I understand, is rich, hard to digest, but delicious. The only problem: no vodka on the menu; instead, a sweetish, heavy brandy. According to one German newspaper, the most important thing in the Moldovan economy is the trade in human organs. Generally they sell their own, but sometimes those of foreigners. I'll go in the summer. I love travelling to little-known countries. Then I return, consult books, ask people, and gather a mountain of facts to determine where I actually was. It's hopeless, because in time everything becomes stranger, resembling a dream within a dream. I have to look at my passport to verify that those countries even exist. Because what sort of countries are they anyway? Memories of a dead past, projects for a dim future, vague potentials, promises, and "We'll show you yet". I ought to cross a true border, to a place where women walk in snakeskin boots and nothing reminds you of anything, where life is suddenly interrupted and carnival begins — or some kind of trauma, or transgression. My 167 stamps aren't worth a rat's ass; I always return as clueless as when I left. Everywhere guys stand at street corners and wait for something to happen, everywhere seats on trains have holes from cigarette burns, and people putter and watch calmly while history presses the accelerator to the floor. I'm wasting my time and my money. I might as well not leave my house; I have everything here.

Wherever I go, I see Gypsies. In Prekmurje, I used a tank of petrol in search of them, because I was fed up with that buttoned-down country and with the Slovenians, traitors all to the Slavic pigsty, but I found not one Gypsy, though I had read they were definitely there. Hiding, most likely, having smelled me from a hundred kilometres away, me with my love of disintegration, my sentimental fondness for whatever doesn't look the way it should. They smelled me even as I left my house, and back in Slovakia, when I passed their slums outside Zborov, a place by the road, on a hill, an ad hoc, slapped-together thumbing of the nose at the charms of order and plenty. It never fails to thrill my soul that one can say fuck you to the world and practise the ancient art of rag picking in the midst of the postmodern and post-industrial. The women carry tied bundles of twigs, the men drag carts heaped with scrap metal, the kids pull bottles from garbage. In front of plywood huts stand cars without wheels, carpets are drying, and plastic bags flutter everywhere.

Basically these people are doing what we all do: trying to get by. Yet they don't pride themselves, don't write down their history, preferring their legends, folktales, fables passed from generation to generation, their "once upon a time" instead of, say, "on the thirteenth of December of the aforesaid year in Copenhagen". And so wherever I go, I look for them, for that living image of Mediterranean-Christian civilization, that nation without land, those people who, the moment something is built, must discard it, burn it for fun or in despair, and move their portable kingdom to a place where the white European horde heaves a little less with hatred of them. I look for the Gypsies — as in Slovenian Prekmurje — and am disappointed when I don't see them, feel that I've strayed too far and it's time to go back. I am related to them, in an illegitimate way: I learned how to put words together, and my words survive somewhere, and yet I cannot create a credible account. My nouns, verbs, and other parts of speech all detach from the world, fall off like old plaster, and I return to legend, fable, ballad, to things that truly happened yet are lies, rubbish, metaphoric claptrap. The existence of what I wrote was simply too brief to take on meaning. Or it lived on only in my brain.

Once, in Okęcie, an official at a control booth inspected my passport from every side, flipped through it, gave me a look, again glanced at the worn pages, until I thought, not a chance, I wasn't going anywhere, but finally he slid a glass panel open and asked, "Sir, what's the point of all this?" Fifty times I had travelled from here, going south, my heart in my mouth, feeling the delicious fear of what awaited, and he was oblivious, though his counterparts at my destinations sat and stamped with the same spring-loaded, hand-held devices. There, everything begins for me: happy young men on the Slovak side selling five-litre bottles of juice — red, yellow, orange, green — the sun shining through and making them gleam like Ali Baba's treasure; selling vodka, beer by the case, the hardiest buying red Modranské wine, horribly dry but only five złoty a bottle; the women selling sacks of sugar, flour, rice; and three duty-free shops in an open field, by a forest, rocking like boats, like ships filled with emigrants crossing the ocean a hundred years ago, carrying the same mob, the same faces — even the cloaks and caps haven't changed that much. An abundance of cheap crap swaying among the gentle green of the Beskids, and a chance of getting something knocked down to half price animates my village, Konieczna, like the prospect of the Promised Land. I stand in line under the pretext of buying dark Thirsty Monk beer or bitter Demänovka herb liqueur, but in fact I am imagining that in "Na Colnicy", in this shop begins the south that leads to the Ionian Sea and the shore of the Peloponnesian peninsula, and along that shore, like birds on a wire, sit folks no different from those here. Their bags full of stuff, their heads full of schemes for getting by, with their own shabby, red-haired, bespectacled customs officials, and always with too little cash, so they must keep moving, dodging, to trick reality and come out on top by the close of day. Košice, Tokaj, Arad, Timişoara, and Skopje are the bright beads on this southern thread. From the shop called U Pufiho is a great view of the Kamenec valley. Peasants drink beer and look south. The light in that direction is better, more distinct, so there's more to see. Košice, Tokaj, Arad, Timişoara, Skopje . . . Yes, you could transport Poles from Małastów, Zdynia, Gorlice, and place them in front of a shop in Hidasnémeti, where the last forints are available at the border, or at the marketplace in Suceava, or in Sfântu Gheorghe, where the Danube in swampy mist feeds into the Black Sea, or even in Tirana, when a fume-heavy dusk hangs over Skanderbeg Square and the harmony of the world is undisturbed. No one would know that they are foreigners. At least, not until they opened their mouths.

Not long ago I was wandering at night in Grójec, looking for the road to Końskie, and I had much the same feeling as I did once in the town of Abrud in Transylvania. The same darkness and doubtful light, the same uncertainty of human presence. Space not altogether wiped clean, still carrying the primordial gloom from which it was scraped. It's that way with these guys: begun but not completed. As if they had stopped to wait for the next step in evolution or creation, for events to unfold; as if they dwelled in an endless present endlessly turning into the past. The future is a fiction. It will come, of course, we hear about it all the time, but the old wisdom knows that only what is, and what was, exists. The rest does not, because no one ever saw it or touched it. And so at U Pufiho I too gaze south and plan trips into a present mixed half-and-half with the past. I cannot think ahead without looking back. Sometimes it seems to me that things hold together only thanks to the borders, that the true identity of these lands and peoples is the shape of their territories in an atlas. It's a stupid thought, but I can't shake it.

"To sum up, Romanian folk culture is one of the richest and most complex in Europe." Once, in Milan, I asked Francesco, "What are the Romanians — Romance brothers to the average Italian?" He answered, "To the average Italian, all Romanians are Gypsies." In Sibiu, I was looking for music in a record shop near Nicolae Bălcescu Avenue. The saleswoman asked where I was from. When I said Poland, she began to recite, *U lukomorya dub zyelony* ("By the bay, a green oak stands"). "You have it all wrong, ma'am," I said with a sigh. In a Kraków pub, Jabłoński, trying to impress two Slovak women, spoke to them in Czech for three hours, and they looked at him with diminishing interest. At last Kamil, who knew the women, entered and told Jabłoński, "They're Slovenian and have no idea what you're saying." The English are familiar with the name Czesław Miłosz but think he's the guy who did *Hair*. And so it goes, in a circle, and I'm fine with that. It's good to live in a non-obvious land, one whose borders contain more locations than any geography indicates: the vastness of the unknown, the expanse of guesswork, the retreating horizon of puzzlement, the sweet mirage of prejudices that no reality will correct.

One summer, for a week, I wended my way through eastern Hungary along the Romanian border and pictured what lay on the other side. I went through Szabolcs-Szatmár, sandy villages, the sticks, air stifling with pig shit, somewhere between Mátészalka, Nyírbátor, and Nagykálló, and imagined a Romania I knew not a blessed thing about, yet my imagination soared, I walked in a waking dream, dreamt without agenda, without form, touched by the unreal that everyone knows is more real than what is real. Then, at Záhony, I crossed over to Ukraine and, along the Tisa, took a slow train east, again with Romania on my right, at arm's length, and it was only when I got to Sighetu Marmației that I turned north and could free myself of this illness. A year later I went to Romania in earnest, but that "in earnest" was a repetition of the old dream, of my hallucination on the border, and it lasts to this day, despite the successive stamps in my passport, because you cannot stamp hallucinations that are larger and more permanent than any border or boundary in the world.

I know something about stamps. A hundred and sixty-plus over seven years, and the greater part of them in "the belt of mixed population", in a region where B follows A without logic or any consideration for the bigger picture, where vampires and werewolves still mate and the mind finds no peace, because only it can do battle with the chaos of what, though invisible and impalpable, is confirmed by misfortune. South, south-east . . . Everything here reminds you of freedom and childhood. As if you are travelling back in time and have an unlimited number of paths to choose from. In Konieczna, oblivion hangs in the air, and in the Zborov district a man begins to lose his identity. It dwindles with each kilometre, just as, proceeding back to infancy, you finally part with yourself as something different from the rest of the world.

On the way to Hungary, as you pass through Slovenské Nové Mesto, at the intersection of the road with Route 55, begins a ten-kilometre stretch on which you can see what your car can do. If it's spring, the Zemplén Hills are yellow with blooming rapeseed. The place is so empty, you're not sure whether you're looking at a landscape or a diorama. The road climbs hill after hill, descends, and runs straight, as if someone had tossed a ball of grey ribbon. For those ten kilometres, I felt that I had found at last the seam of existence; it was like beholding the world from the other side: everything the same as before yet different. At Čerhov I slowed down for a railroad crossing, and things gradually returned to their places, probably to allow me to feel that I had survived, to allow me to weave these tales that provide a break from a reality I don't understand and don't particularly care to. I know that at the Slovnaft petrol station I should go straight — not right, as I usually do — to see the village Borša, the birthplace of Francis II Rákóczi, hero of an episode from the French series entitled *Great Escapes* and leader of the Hungarian popular uprising against the Hapsburgs in 1703. I know I should take the straight path, to face reality at least once in my life, but instead, like Dyzio the

Dreamer, I flee into sweet fantasy, and if it isn't a railroad crossing that distracts me, in another ten minutes I'll be driving into the shade of old trees growing on the main street of Sátoraljaújhely. This shade, it gives me no peace. Its contrast with the green semi-desert of the final Slovak kilometres: the perfect scenery versus the perfect town, where venerable trees block the facades with such cunning that you can't distinguish the moving patches of sunlight from the lichen on the stucco. It's the same in Satu Mare in the main square, the trees obscuring the light-blue signs, so you drive in circles looking for the road to Cluj or Sighetu or Oradea or Baia Mare, until finally you park — anywhere — and sit on a bench in the green shade, cursing Romanian vegetation and waiting for autumn, when the leaves will fall and reveal the world's directions.

And it's the same in Chernivtsi: the ancient light and shade trying to break down the walls, the stucco, to smooth away the complicated surfaces, get rid of all the cornices, pilasters, balconies, oriels. But my memory of Chernivtsi is hazy, because Sashko, in his indescribable hospitality, set such a pace that the next day was like being in a furnace, albeit an inviting furnace. At the bus station, heavyset cab drivers said that nothing today was going to Suceava. They swung their key rings: car keys, house keys, keys to basements, gates, safes, mailboxes, God knows what else. They rattled this metal and were put out that no one believed them, that no one was willing to go with them to Siret for a lousy fifty, and they stood — or rather, fidgeted and paced — and peered above the crowd, because cab drivers in that part of the world, even when they are runts, see farther than anyone. It's rough for a guy with wheels who can't give anyone a ride. Ditto in Gorlice, Kolomyia, Delatyn, and Gjirokastër in Albania: they charge as much to take you one kilometre as in

Berlin, in these places where the gross national product is $1,500 per capita. They sit in their twenty-year-old Mercedes wrecks, in a line, and no, sorry, German prices only. Zero negotiation.

Heat beat from the sky, no shade, horses digging with their hoofs through overturned garbage cans, men picking their noses, balling the snot, and flicking it into the dust of the street, exactly as our Polish cab drivers do at their eternal stands. But I had to go to Erind, where the road ended and the Lunxherise massif loomed, unpopulated, a long piece of moon embedded in the wild and lovely body of Albania. They must have seen the need in my eyes, must have sensed it with their seventh cab driver sense. I got into a green 200, its rear practically touching the ground, and off we went. I had to make it to Erind, so I could understand. We crept uphill — in second gear, second, sometimes in third — the tailpipe clanging on the stones. "There was no shade along the road. Travellers slogged through the dust as if it were mud and gazed at the withered yellow slopes on either side, slopes from which flooding, strong winds and the sun had taken everything that a hungry wretch might grasp at." A fair description. Then the rubble that was Erind. Houses like caves, heat-resistant greenery, and a few kids among white walls, the rest of the people no doubt gone to plantations in Greece. No dogs, not even a chicken, only a monument at the very end, in a small burning square, to fallen partisans, with tombstone photographs in porcelain frames. One of the fallen was Misto Mame, another Mihal Duri — twenty-one and twenty-four, respectively. The cab driver stood there and waited for me to take it in. He thought I had come for this, because what else was here? To hell with the German prices, I thought to myself as I saluted. The guy had shown me what they valued most in this place. He might not get a passenger here for another two years, so the money divided over that time amounted to nothing.

Sometimes I think that this is how it should be: the entire world's treasury, all the dough of the Frankfurt banks, the vaults of the Bank of England, the virtual funds of corporations circulating in electronic space, the contents of the multilevel underground coffers on Bahnstrasse in Zurich, all the paper, all the ore, the rows of digits coursing through the icy bloodstream of fibre-optic cables, should be thrown out, should lose its value, should be exchanged for zeroes in such loci as Erind, Vicşani, Sfântu Gheorghe, Rozput, Tiszaszalka, Palota, Bajram Curri, Podoliniec, the square in front of the church in Jabłonna Lacka, the train station in Vilmány, the train station in Delatyn at dawn, the grocery store in Livezile, the grocery store in Spišská Belá, the pub in Biertan, the rain in Mediaş, and a thousand others, because the map I look at is a fishnet, a star-studded night sky, an old T-shirt or torn bedsheet, and through all those spots that I visited shines a light stronger than the failing light of simple geography, stronger than the ominous glow of political geography and the moribund glow of economic geography. And nothing will sew up those holes. The future will pass through them like food through a duck, will sift through them like sand through fingers. No big ideas or big fortunes or degenerate time will disturb these places, these rips in the gist and foundation, these traces of my presence. Yes, I know, my attitude is benighted, backward. It's January 11, a quarter past two in the morning, and I'm aware that I'm dreaming of building a reservation of sorts here and that the citizens of the above-mentioned towns and villages, if they got wind of it, would boot me in the ass. But it's unlikely, especially in Erind, that anyone will ever read this.

Indeed, a reservation, an open-air museum bathed in everlasting light, that's how I imagine it, desire it, because my heart sinks whenever something disappears from view, with a bend in the road or in growing darkness, and I cannot free myself of the thought that it has disappeared forever and I am the only one who witnessed it and now must tell, tell — assuming that anyone will want to listen. Moreover, all these places are falling apart, totally wrecked, hardly one stone upon another, the remnants of former glory, so this fear of mine is no figment: if I return to where I once was, I may find nothing. It's a characteristic of my part of the world, this continual disappearance mixed half-and-half with progress, this crafty undevelopment that makes people wait for everything, this unwillingness to be the subject of an experiment, this perpetual half-heartedness that lets you hop out of the flow of time and substitute contemplation for action. Whatever is new here is bogus; only when it ages and becomes a ruin does it take on meaning. Boys from Kisvárda, Gorlice, Preszów, and Oradea with their baseball caps on backwards imitate black brothers in slums across the ocean, because there's nothing to imitate here. Everything new is a movie that has no connection with the past. And so I prefer the old and choose decay, whose continuity cannot be undermined. In Elbasan on the main street I saw great piles of rags. Commerce, apparently, but it looked like a dump. Women poked through the garbage, which went on for many metres, and spread it out on the pavement, as if seeking the bodies of relatives after a catastrophe. They put rags on, took them off, dug for something better. Two truckloads, and God knows where it came from. Greece, Italy, in any case from a place where it was no longer needed. Ideas and concepts arrive here in the same second-hand condition, particularly those made ad hoc for a distant situation. This is a realm of recycling, and the realm itself will be, in the end, recycled.

Such thoughts afflict me in the evening. The wind blows from the north-west, and the white semicircular edges of snowdrifts lie across the road leading to Konieczna. I should invent a graceful story that begins and ends there, provide a first-aid kit that cleverly soothes the mind, alleviates anxiety, and stills hunger. In the darknesses of life I should come up with one piece of evidence that miraculously points the way to what can be followed, what consoles. But no, not a prayer: the world is here and now and doesn't give a flying fuck about stories. When I attempt to recall one thing, others surface. Romania crawls out from under my childhood, Albania from under my visits to grandparents, and now that I am, as it were, an adult, I end up in a region filled with the earliest scenes of my life. I am over forty, yet it's the same randomness, the same hen houses, coal bins, bins for everything — as if someone were showing slides from the time we played cops and robbers, cowboys and Indians. Snow falls on Konieczna, Zdynia, the whole parish of Uście Gorlickie, once called Uście Ruskie. In the monochromatic landscape are shovels of many colours: red, green, blue, yellow. People trying to get to their bins, storage shacks, buildings, outbuildings, where animals and old cars are waiting. Drifts grow at the pass, and no one heads out for the Slovak side. Here too, now, is one of those booths, the size of a kiosk selling magazines: a store, a bar, a currency exchange rolled into one — so says the sign in the window. But there is no one here today, other than the lieutenant in the balaclava, who tells me with a smile that the Slovaks have it better, their snowploughs make the rounds every two hours. He is disappointed, I think, when I say that I don't drive, that I came only to watch the snow attempt to eradicate the border, bury the map, and level the Carpathian water gap. A man appears from nowhere with a blue shovel on his shoulder and says, sighing, "Looks like I'll need a tractor." I return to the snow-filled parking lot and think that in a year all this may be gone: the red-and-white crossing gate, the flashing lights, the rubber stamps, the suspense, and the questions: "Anything to declare?" "Destination?" And the dog sniffing for amphetamines and Semtex. And the small talk, the flicker of risk, the usual "Here's how you get to Konieczna . . ." I will take no delight in their passing

I collect, putting aside black-and-gold hundred-crown notes with the Madonna of Master Paul on the front and, on the back, Levoča; green twenties with Pribin on the front and, on the back, Nitra; and violet thousands with Andrej Hlinka on the front and, on the back, the Mother of God. I also collect Czech fifties, hundreds, and two hundreds, with Saint Agnes, Karol IV, and Jan Amos Komenský (Comenius), all in pastels and faded, like the wrapping for old-fashioned sweets. The Hungarian forints, however, have a fierceness about them. Especially the light-blue thousand note showing King Hunyadi Mátyás (Matthias Corvinus), who was a Renaissance connoisseur of art and science but on this money looks like a man who could live on raw meat if he had to. More than twenty years younger, Francis II Rákóczi gazes from the five-hundred note more mildly, yet a sneer plays on his lips: a magnificent barbarian's contempt for the entire civilized West, for the Hapsburgs in particular. True, he introduced the fashion for the Transylvanian minuet at Versailles, yet his five-hundred-forint visage resembles less a Louis Bourbon than Bohdan Khmelnytsky on the twenty-hryvnia note or our Jan Sobieski. Yes, I love the Hungarian banknotes, because they don't mince words: they say, "Shove Trianon", and they pine for the day when the horses of the Huns swam the Adriatic. But my favourite banknote of all is the Slovenian fifty tolars. On the front is Jurij Vega (1754–1802), who unfortunately is passed over silently in the Polish *PWN Encyclopedia*. The design of the note suggests that Vega was an astronomer. His features: a young Beethoven, a Germanized General Kościuszko. But the reverse side is even better: three-quarters of the note is an intense blue, like the sky over Piran in January. A blue that, like a kindergarten drawing, makes no compromises. Only the Romanian two thousand lei, all in plastic and the national colours and with a transparent window, can compete with it. This last was released on the occasion of a full eclipse of the sun in 1999: "Doua mii lei, eclipsa totala de soare." It will all be gone someday, so I am collecting, for a private museum, to have a few memories in my old age.

On a shelf I keep a black canister for a litre flask of Absolut, and in it there are at least ten kilograms of loose change. When I am low, I dump it out on a table, to revisit all the pubs, shops, bus and train stations, petrol stations, and cabs in which I obtained them. The coins remind me of things and places: the street stalls in Saranda, the lane stanchions on the Slovenian highway A1, the ferries on the Tisa, the parking meters on the Szentháromság tér, Holy Trinity Square, in Baja, the enormous yellow barrels of beer on the streets of Stanislavov, cigarettes, shot glasses, goblets, music boxes, the talking machine for tourists at Saint Jacob's Church in Levoča . . . Whenever I come home, my pockets are full of change, and I can never discard these coins, believing as I do in the lovable bumpkin magic that will lead me back to those places so that I can finally spend them. But what can you buy with a hundred lei that bears the head of Michael the Brave? Not a thing. You could drill a hole in this substantial disc and hang it round your neck like a medal for valour in battle. Even worthless, this treasure lifts my spirits on bad days. I can picture all the hands it passed through, imagine the routes it took from town to town, from village to village. I see the men drinking in taverns, the women shopping in marketplaces, the children buying sweets at kiosks. Who knows how many times my hundred lei with the hole in it went through Transylvania, Moldova and Wallachia, Mutenia, Oltenia, Dobruja and the Delta before it lost all its value? Into this heavy disc, as into a computer hard drive, has been inscribed the history of wealth, poverty, desires, profit, loss, market ups and down and arounds, but I cannot read it, I can only save it. I let the coins dribble from my fist and feel how time and space go by, society, economy, human lives, how the Carpathians, the Czech-Moravian Heights, the Great Hungarian Plain, the Romanian Lowlands, Transylvania, and a part of the Balkans all convert into a soft clink.

Once, on Route 19, a few kilometres beyond Satu Mare, we saw a Gypsy camp in the red light of a setting sun. Three, four carts standing on the side of the road, dirt poverty, gaunt horses, and torn plastic spread over movable goods. Inside were sheets, blankets, mattresses, women, kids, pots, human existence as shit hole, but in the sun it blazed, as if it might be gone any moment, ascending to heaven like a multiplied Prophet Elijah, and the men, adjusting things in a hopeless tangle of harnesses, were darker than their own long shadows. "I must get that," Piotrek said and stopped the car right there. He grabbed his camera, ran out, began negotiating, but the miracle of the light would be over in a matter of minutes, so he waved for me to come and handle the financial end. I dug out of my pocket kronas, forints, lei — according to the route we had taken — and explained in pantomime that we were willing to pay but it had to be within reason. The thin, veiny leader, in a white undershirt, looked at the change, of which the forints amounted to two dollars at least (we were not far from the Hungarian border), finally grimaced and waved with contempt and said, "Nu, țigari." I gave him all the cigarettes I had: a pack of Snags, the few Marlboros left, the few Carpati. He accepted them, went to his people, and distributed. Then the sun went down, and they set off for Satu Mare. The three, four tattered carts became darkness, nothingness, not having belonged to this world in the first place. They did not belong seven hundred years before, when on the Peloponnesian peninsula European memory first made note of their presence, nor on May 4, 2000, when a man resembling his own shadow said to me, "Nu, țigari," because money seemed to him more trouble than it was worth.

A year later I was at a traffic light somewhere past Sibiu — or it might have been Cristian, or Miercurea Sibiului. Roadwork was being done, and our side and the opposite side got the green light in turns. Two children took advantage of this forced wait. They ran up to the cars and put on a little show that combined comedy and begging. I gave one a bill, but the other grabbed it from his hand, and the first kid started bawling. I consoled the bawler with a second bill. Then I saw them both in the rear-view mirror, how in perfect harmony they were enjoying, together, the spoils of their performance.

I dribble the change from my fist, I leaf through my banknotes, and it's like touching photography in Braille, because my fingers can feel the things that happened and my nose can smell the places. The small but heavy hundred-forint coin will forever be for me the emblem of the green hills of Zemplén. It was the price, that year, for a glass of palinka in the village taverns. In Gönc, Telkibánya, Vilmány. The worn thousand-lei note with Eminescu on it will always evoke Transylvania and the tiny dark shops in Biertan, Roandola, Copşa Mare, Floreşti, which were cool caves dug into the Transylvanian heat, and when I bought bottle after bottle of wine, the change I got was wads and stacks of these rags heavy with sweat and dirt. What is memory, anyway, if not the endless exchange of currency, a continual allotting and distributing, a counting in the hope that the total will be right, that what once was will return with no shortage, whole, untouched, and perhaps even with interest, through love and longing? What is travel, anyway, if not spending, then reckoning what's left and turning your pockets inside out? The Gypsies, the money, the passport stamps, the tickets, the stone from the bank of the Mát, the cow's horn smoothed by the Danube current in the Delta, *blok na pokutu*, the fine in Slovakia, *račun parkiranja*, the parking ticket in Piran, *nota de plata,* the bill at the pub in Sulina: two fried catfish, two salads, a carafe of wine, one Silva beer, in all 85,700 . . .

This was off Deltea Avenue. You entered from the street, into a room with four small tables. Upstairs was a small hotel. Behind the counter stood a willowy young woman with short hair, her face delicate and sad. She did the cooking herself, wiped the glasses, served the food, a moving shadow. Men came in stinking of fish and diesel fuel. The chairs creaked beneath them as they drank their beer, smoked, muttered, and returned to the shore, to the rusting barges and tugboats, iron in scummy water, to a river that in despair had opened its arteries. The young woman cleaned the ashtrays and bottles and went back to the counter to insert a tape cassette, a medley of stuff in English: Elton John, Gilbert and Sullivan, the Carpenters, the seventies, the eighties. A bony black horse outside the window was hitched to a cart on rubber tyres behind a blackened wood house. A beanpole cop for the seventh or twelfth time that day paced the length of the sandy walkway. A little farther on, at a wire fence, a man in striped pyjamas stared into space. The building seemed abandoned, but the sign said it was a hospital. On the driveway to the Hotel Sulina, uncut grass. The continent ended here, and events too had run their course, but the grass quietly waited for something that would happen nevertheless. With a barely noticeable smile, she brought us the bill, then returned to her world.

And this *parkovaci preukaz*, parking permit, at the small hotel in Ružomberok . . . We ended up there late one evening after an entire day on the road. The town stank from a cellulose factory. The black silhouette of mountains darkened against the sky. In the centre of town, everything was cheap and throwaway. Things normally made from solid material here were all plastic. Walls, doors, and furniture pretending to be bona fide. In the pub, the owner and his family were being entertained. Two musicians in shirts and cherry waistcoats on the bandstand adjusted the Yamahas and microphone. The singer held a notebook stuffed with songs. One of the musicians improvised. Seven, eight people danced. Two little girls watched the stars: they were the boss's granddaughters. A fifty-year-old character — wooden face, gold watch, gold chain — tried to preserve his dignity on the dance floor. Everyone moved frugally and stiffly, as if afraid of bumping into something, though there was plenty of room. An imposed task for them, this, or a game they were still learning, or a rehearsal for completely new roles. The lightbulbs, dim and melancholy, were as tentative as the guests. The women had high hairdos and trouble with their high heels. The boss took off his jacket, wore a grey waistcoat and white shirt. Moved his massive body as if hearing music for the first time in his life. Three or four more people entered, led by an enormous guy in a black suit, shaved bald, with dark glasses. Making exactly the impression he wanted to make. Someone behind him held a bouquet. They stood there waiting to be greeted, but there was no greeting, so they slowly made their way into the lifeless party, and only the enormous one, his neck thicker than his bare skull, remained at the entrance and surveyed the room as if it belonged to him. These folks must have watched all three parts of *The Godfather*, especially the party scenes, and now they were trying to re-enact it among plastic chandeliers, artificial flowers, and beet-red leatherette upholstery, to the rhythm of the indomitable hit "Comme Ci, Comme Ça."

I keep all these events in a shoebox. Sometimes I take out one or another, like a parrot plucking a slip in a lottery drawing. Valabil-2 Calatoria, a thin strip in green, red, and orange, and a tram ticket, punched twice, from Sibiu to Rășinari. The tram shuttles between the city and the village. Even my most detailed maps don't show its route, yet I took it at least twice and drove along its tracks four times. From this scrap of paper you could segue to a few good stories: about Emil Cioran's insomnia in Sibiu; about the Păltiniș madness of Constantin Noica, who wanted to breed Romanian geniuses; or Lucian Blaga, who in the summer months in Gura Râului attempted to establish a Mioritic ontology . . . All three men had to take this tram that harks back to the Austro-Hungarian time. The shoebox works exactly that way, my brain like the parrot plucking slips in a lottery. The metal canister for Absolut vodka works that way, too, a magic lantern of coincidence, accident, and adventure making a story that goes in all directions and cannot go otherwise, because it involves memory and space, both of which can commence at any point, both of which never end. You can see this just by driving to Konieczna. By driving there and returning after a week or two, to find that time is dead, or was waiting for us to come back, not accompanying us at all, and everything that happened on our trip happened simultaneously, without sequence or consequence, and we did not age one minute. It's a kind of illusion of immortality when the red-and-white crossing gate is raised, a cunning version of tai chi, meditation in motion, and ultimately — let's be honest — a most ordinary escape.

But it's great, in the middle of winter, to say, "Fuck this, I'm going to Abony, that hole in the centre of the Hungarian Lowlands near Szolnok, I'm going from one nowhere to another." And only because six years ago, I saw a picture that André Kertész took on June 19, 1921, and that I can't get out of my head: a blind fiddler crossing a sandy village road as he plays, led by a teenage kid. It hasn't rained for a while, because the road is dry — the kid's feet are not muddy, and the thin tracks made by the metal wheels of a cart are not deep. They curve to the left and leave the frame, blurring first. In the washy background sit two figures by the kerb. The two white daubs near them are probably geese. There is also a toddler standing midway between the focus and the rim of the photograph. He looks to the side, as if not hearing the music, or perhaps the appearance of these two pedestrians is an everyday thing. Because of this, I went to Abony in the dead of winter. And found nothing there. I filled my tank on leaving Budapest but in four minutes had driven through the town. A woman hanging up laundry, then there were no more houses. I was not really looking for anything, because, after all, nothing could have lasted; it all remained in the photograph. I turned towards the Tisza. A reddening dusk over the Puszta. A few scattered houses, groves of poplar, two children walking to the horizon over naked earth, black and empty stork nests, all this beneath a limitless, blazing sky. Darkness fell somewhere after Tisaalpár.

The next day, in the photography museum in Kecskemét, I bought an album of Kertész, to discover that the blind fiddler is not left-handed: the picture I had at home was flipped. I needed to drive to Abony in January, pass through it without stopping, to discover, a few dozen kilometres farther, that the boy leading the musician was his son. This information is of no use to me. I cannot know, can only imagine, their life, unfold that day beyond the frame of the picture, fill that ancient space with their fragile presence. The father's shoes are worn, falling apart. He wears a dark jacket, but over his right shoulder he has thrown another covering, which resembles a torn blanket. The son also carries something like a blanket or towel. They are prepared for bad weather and the cold. The boy holds in his hand a small bundle. Under the brim of the fiddler's hat is a crushed white cigarette. At least I think so. I must gather what facts I can, to flesh out that day. On June 19, the sun rose at 3:14, and an hour or two later the heat of the Puszta set in. There is no shade here. It's far from one town to another. The roads to isolated homes beyond the horizon are straight and scarlike. It's fourteen kilometres to Újszász, fourteen to Újszilvás, ten to Törtel and Kőröstetétlen, seventeen to Tószeg. The air is still and smells of manure. When the breeze comes from the east, it brings the swamp reek of the Tisza. You can hear the birds over the bogs. A trained ear distinguishes even the dry whistling beat of their wings. Sometimes a heavy team of grey, big-horned oxen passes, or a clattering carriage. Then you get a whiff of tobacco, untanned leather, and horse sweat. These conveyances, passing, grow silent, are gone, leaving only dust.

This is my Hungary; I cannot help it. I realize that it all

belongs to the past and may not actually have ever taken place. I realize that eighty-five kilometres farther and eighty-two years later is Budapest, then Esztergom, et cetera, and the glory and the power and everything that gets collected over the centuries in minds that want to live beyond their allotted time. But my Hungary is in Abony, where I didn't even stop. No doubt because the blind musician could show up in any of those places that no one knows and where no one ever goes, places never mentioned but that make the world what it is. Only a miracle saved him and his son from oblivion. "I took the picture on a Sunday. The music woke me. That blind musician played so wonderfully, I hear him to this day" (André Kertész).

I can take my Hungary with me wherever I go, and it will lose none of its vividness. It's a negative, or a slide through which I shine the light of memory. In Tornyosnémeti, two men emerged from the dark and began to play. One had a harmonica, the other a guitar with a dull sound. It was freezing cold and foggy. The waiting tour buses formed a black wall. The guitarist's fingers must have hurt. The music, numb, could barely leave the instruments. I didn't make out the melody, only a hurried, nervous beat. A string broke, but they played on, with sad eyes and the stubbornness typical of hopeless enterprises. Then we tried conversing, in a borderland mix of Hungarian and Slovak. It wasn't money they wanted but to change it. They had a handful of Polish coins, tens, twenties, fifties, collected no doubt from our truckers. They sold them to me for forints. We said goodbye, and they were gone. They might have been from Gönc. The younger man, the harmonica player, could have been one of the two kids whom three years ago the bartender refused to serve at the pub next to the Hussite House. I'd ask, if I could, how that skinny one is doing, the one with the homespun coat over his bare back, the one I arm-wrestled that summer and drank with to the health of Franz Josef. If the musicians were from Gönc, they would know him. And know the man who was brown as chocolate, round as a ball, and naked to the waist, who every day went down the main street in a small horse-drawn two-wheel cart. I can still hear the muffled clop of horseshoes on asphalt softened by the heat.

It's winter now, and I need such sounds. From my window I see a two-horse team and, on the cart, four men bundled up. The horses, though shod, step uncertainly on the ice. They all appear out of the mist and in a moment are gone again. If only it were summer — then, instead of returning to their Pętna or Małastów they could head for Konieczna and there by some miracle get around the guards and rules and make it to the Slovak side. And, in Zborov, say, they could blend in with the locals, being exactly like them in style, dress, expression, general appearance. May would be a good time; there's grass for the horses and only occasionally a touch of frost in the morning. I'd go with them, to look at the passing world and at their faces, so different and so familiar. I'd sit to the side like a ghost and listen to their words. Probably they would talk about how things change as they travel, but not so that a person feels at any point the bump of a border. Slovak names would imperceptibly become Hungarian, then Romanian, Serbian, Macedonian, finally Albanian — assuming that we keep more or less to country lanes that go along the twenty-first line of longitude. I'd sit to the side and drink with them all the varieties of alcohol that change with the changing land: borowiczka, körte palinka, cujka, rakija, and eventually, around Lake Ohrid, Albanian raki. No one would stop us, and no one would stare as we rested at a place off the thoroughfare. That region is full of forgotten roads. Turn down one, and time slackens, as if it has evaded someone's supervising eye. Time wears away gradually, like the clothes of the men travelling by cart. What seems ready for discarding persists as it degrades and fades, until the silent end, the moment when existence shifts invisibly to non-existence. My mind in this way wandered after they vanished into the mist. I see them cross the Hungarian Lowlands, Transylvania, the Banat, as if they were born there and returning home from the marketplace, from a visit, from work in the field or in the woods. Time parts before them like the air and closes again as they pass.

Whenever I come home from Romania in the summer, the undercarriage of the car is crusted with cow shit. One evening, as I was descending the switchbacks from Păltiniş and found myself among the first buildings of Răşinari, I heard under my wheels a series of sharp, loud splashes. The entire road was covered with green diarrhoea. Moments before, a herd had come down from its pasture. I could see the last of the cattle finding their paddocks. They stood under the gates with lifted tails and shat. Had I braked, I would have slid as on ice in winter. Cows and steers turned this crossing into a skating rink. Completely filled with crap, a route that Sibiu society would usually take to their vacation dachas in the mountains. Crap from one shoulder to the other. Crap drying in the last rays of the setting sun. People on motorcycles had the worst of it. The animal world had invaded the heart of the human world, which was fitting. Now whenever I drive at dusk through villages in Transylvania, the Puszta, or my own Pogórze, I think of that splashing, think that we have not been altogether abandoned.

Another time, before Oradea, I turned off Highway 76 and got lost in a tangle of village roads. It might have been Tăşad, or

Drăgeşti, I don't remember. In any case, in the distant east you could see the gentle cones of the mountains the Hungarians call Királyerdö, the Romanians Pădurea Craiului, and we Poles the Royal Forest. It was late afternoon, and the slanting light threw gold on everything and lengthened shadows. In an hour I was to leave Transylvania and enter the Great Hungarian Plain, so I wanted to have a last look. And ended up in this village. The houses, side by side, were arranged in a wide ring. In the centre was a commons overgrown with young birches. A village, but it was like driving through a grove. The slender trees shone like honey. Here and there the gleam of a white wall, but no person in sight, only heavy pink pigs trotting through the scenery. Maybe ten of them. They sniffed, their snouts to the ground, looking for prey, as if they reigned here and were tracking down a foe. In the golden light, their hundred-kilogram hulks were an exquisite blasphemy. Clean, as if they didn't live in a sty. Under the dull and bristled skin, flesh swollen with pulsing blood. I will go back someday, to learn the name of that village. Without a name, it is too much like a vision, and I need real things to have faith in.

Last summer I took a bus to Saranda. The bus, an old crate of a Mercedes, barely made it up the Muzinës pass. Below, at the bottom of the cliff, rusted chassis of vans and sedans that would lie there until Judgment Day. On the other side of the Gjëre Mountains, near Delvine, we drove into a cloudburst and entered Saranda in pouring rain. Two men — they looked like father and son — unloaded from the bus bundles, bags, sacks, packs, parcels tied, parcels taped; it could have been a lifetime's accumulation of possessions. A sad, sodden move someone was making. Finally they pulled from the bus's cavernous luggage bay a scruffy mutt. The little animal was added to the baggage, as if that was now its home. Then the bus took off, and the curtain of rain closed on them.

I recall all the animals and see them as clearly as I see the people. The horses grazing untethered in Chornohora, the big-horned cattle of the Puszta, the cows belly-deep in the muddy current of the Delta, the Bucharest dogs, loose, moving freely, seeking food in a world that draws no borders between man and beast. In Sfântu Gheorghe, at dawn, I went to an outhouse in the backyard. The shed was so low, you dropped your trousers before you entered, because inside you had to bend in half. And you stepped out to pull your trousers up. Precisely then I was attacked by a red rooster, its beak aimed at the very thing I wished to conceal. The hens stopped scrabbling for a moment to look at him with admiration while I ran across plots to the protection of the house door. The rooster was no longer in pursuit, yet I still felt fear, because of this momentary crack in the world. In Përmet, or maybe it was in Kosinë, a woman rode a donkey on a side path. She was so ancient, so burned by the sun, and so wrinkled and shrivelled, that if it hadn't been for her clothes, you could have mistaken her for part of the animal. In the dust and heat, the two had passed this way hundreds of times. Their shadows on the white stone of the path fused into a single shadow, just as their fates were fused into one.

My four men on the cart, I see them always at the same hour, trying to get home before nightfall, exhausted after a day in the woods, in melting snow and mud, and the horses too are exhausted, heads lowered, hoofs sloshing, the same heaviness in their movement as in the men sitting slumped, heads nodding. Enfolded in the mist, the human and the animal cannot be separated. I watch them pass, I smell them in the chill air: horse sweat, damp clothes, shirts that stick to backs, the worked leather of the harnesses. The odour of monotonous labour chained for centuries to matter. That's how the two shepherds smelled in the German pub in Spring, how the plots smelled in Nagykálló, how the train smelled, the Red Ruta leaving Delatyn at dawn for Kwasy, how the old houses smelled in Sulina. I stayed in one of them, south of the river. In the middle of the day I entered and saw a dark interior. People lay on a large mattress, three, four, more. In the mingling of half-naked bodies I could make out the narrow shoulders of a child, and feet sticking out from under a cover. Possibly an entire family, men and women, deep in sleep. They had taken shelter from the merciless white sky, but the heat had pursued them, or the heat came from them. Their skin was almost black against the sheets. I had entered someone's home and saw strange people in the moment of their greatest vulnerability. They made no attempt to conceal themselves, as pets sleep openly before us. I went to my room and never saw them again. I remember only dark bodies saturated with materiality and so heavy, it seemed they would never get up again.

Clearly I am drawn to decline, decay, to everything that is not as it could or should be. Whatever stops in half stride because it lacks the strength or will or imagination to continue. Whatever gives in, gives up, does not last, and leaves no trace. Whatever in its passing stirs no regret or reminiscence. The present imperfect. Histories that live no longer than the relating of them, objects that *are* only when someone regards them. This is what haunts me — this extra being that everyone can do without, this superfluity that is not wealth, this hiddenness that no one explores, secrets that, ignored, are lost forever, memory that consumes itself. March draws to a close, and I hear the snow slipping off the mountains in the dark. The world like a snake sloughing another skin. The same feeling each year, and it deepens with each year: the true face of my region, of my corner of the continent—precisely this changing that changes nothing, this movement that expends itself. Some spring, not only will the snow melt, everything else will melt, too. The brown-grey water will wash away towns and villages, it will wash away animals, people, everything, down to the naked skeleton of the earth. Meteorology and geology will join forces, ruling in a dubious coalition with history and geography. The permanent will seize the transitory by the throat. The elements will resume their places on Mendeleev's eternal table, and no more tales, no more narratives will be needed to interpret existence.

On the shore of Lalëzit Bay, around Jubë, I saw a military encampment. Tents and occasional barbed wire. Faded canvas torn and sagging. The jutting bare feet of soldiers asleep on cots. It was Sunday. A little farther on were people from Tirana sunbathing. The barbed-wire fence served no dividing purpose: neither side had anything. Each side could gather all it possessed and leave. If you folded up the tents and beach umbrellas, the shore would look as it had looked before. Only the bunkers of a previous era would remain, of no use to anyone, and they were now slowly becoming part of the natural landscape.

People soak up time like sponges. They steep themselves in it, amass it like those who stockpile a thing they fear will run out. Sometimes I get into a car and drive a few hours, thirty, forty kilometres from home. I enter a maze of highways, lanes, short cuts across meadows or through groves, because I saw on the map a hamlet called Lower Gaul or Bethlehem, or three huts given the name Ukraine or Siberia. I'm not making this up. Check *The Lower Beskids and Foothills,* the Eugeniusz Romer State Agency of Cartographic Publishers, Warsaw-Wrocław, fifth edition, it's all in the upper left corner. But along the way I forget my destination. All I need do is turn off the main road, and space thickens, resists, deigning to grace these homes and farms, the miserable little patches behind fences, the vegetation that has barely emerged from the ground, barely raised itself above the surface, and is now attempting to survive. This surviving is done day by day, without hope; fatalism alone holds things together. Concrete, bricks, steel, and wood combine in random proportions, as if waxing and waning can reach no final agreement. The old looks bedraggled, cast off, impotent; the new struts and challenges, wanting to overcome both the shame of the past and the fear of the future. Everything is temporary, ad hoc, a verb whose action is never completed. This could all disappear in a second, and space would accept the gap, fill it in, and smooth it over as if not a thing had happened. An introduction to what never begins; a periphery that has no centre; a suburb that stretches to the horizon without ever reaching the city. The landscape devours, and space patches up the holes, because these backwaters that I drive through and love with my despairing love are emptied in the very act of their becoming, their sense drained in their very struggle to be. They are so like nature that on a misty day in early spring they can scarcely be distinguished from their surroundings. In a moment the low sky closes like a door, and everything is gone. That's why I rush to make these trips, why I'm so avid for details that will soon vanish and need to be re-created out of words. I don't know why all this is, and I lost the hope, long ago, that I would find an answer. Therefore, to be safe, I write down everything as it happens, substituting consistency for justice and meaning.

A few days ago I drove through Duląbka. The shadow of Cieklin Mountain filled the valley. Up the clay slope climbed a horse harnessed to a plough held by a bent man. Behind them, a woman, doubled over as she tossed ploughed-up stones to the side. A scene of biblical poignancy. The wind blew, and through the clouds on occasion came the slanting rays of early evening. The three silhouettes on the hill stood out so sharply, they seemed not of this world. Duląbka a few days ago, Turza a few days before that, and in a week from now some other nowhere town in Moldova or Macedonia. But if you wrote, "I was driving through Golden Prague" or "Once in Budapest" or "In Kraków one day" or "In Sosnowiec", that wouldn't work either, there's nothing there, no key or legend to use, no metaphor, no language that will travel beyond the gates of the city. "One day in Warsaw" makes no sense. Cities in this neck of the continent arise on the spur of the moment, by coincidence. No good reason for them to be there. Try navigating Budapest during rush hour. There's no way to get around it: it sits like a spider in the middle of its web of streets. Or try making it through Warsaw, through Bucharest. A city on a trip is a disaster. Especially in countries that are like large villages. Villagers don't know how to build a city. They end up with totems to foreign gods. The downtown area takes a stab at copying something, while the suburbs invariably resemble an aborted farm. The hypertrophy of storefronts with the melancholy of lost illusions. Whenever I am driving along and suddenly an edifice looms in the centre of a small town, I am stunned, because nothing prepares for or explains it. At every opportunity I skirt such centres, taking bypasses, trying roads barely visible on the map, going way out of my way to miss the long shadows of downtown towers and highrises. Any place with a population over 100,000, I cross it off my list: Go ahead, build in the hope that someday it will completely block the view of where you come from.

Thus goes my litany in the swirl of ring roads, overpasses, throughways, as I squint at road signs and route numbers, my map spread across the steering wheel, with honking behind me as I glance in the rear-view mirror, as I sit in the stinking shadows of trucks, at dawn in Duląbka, in the evening in Bratislava, and on to the knot of Viennese arteries, breaking through to the other side of the enormous imperial capital, then south to reach a sleepy village in the middle of the night, by the Zala River, then to Bajánsenye by the Slovenian border, where the fifty-year-old Mr Geza runs a pension in an old watermill, and at two in the morning, over red wine and bacon and eggs, he repeats, "Budapest is different now. People don't talk to each other any more." If January has no snow, the willows and reeds in the early sun are the colour of faded wrapping paper. The soil is always wet. Or else the sky is low, unusually low even for Hungary, and its weight squeezes the moisture from the earth.

Twenty-two kilometres from Mr Geza is where Danilo Kiš lived during World War II. His father made mad travels through this region and drank "handcrafted Tokay from Lendava" in its taverns. Lendava is now a border town on the Slovenian side. And Uncle Otton rode here on a bicycle. The uncle's left leg, frozen, hung while the right foot, tied to the pedal with a belt, pedalled. He took the dusty clay roads to Zalaegerszeg, to oversee his complicated business affairs. If Kiš's father was a character out of Bruno Schulz, his uncle was straight out of Beckett — that's how I see them when I read Kiš's *Garden, Ashes* in a black-green cover that by some strange twist of fate or accident has the photograph of a dark-brown clay bird on it. Two years before, in the winter, in that region, in Magyarszombatfa, I bought two clay angels of exactly that colour. It's a place of potters, but the publisher, Marabut, was probably unaware of it. So this is a sign for me to go there once more, to find the Count's Forest and all the other topographic features scattered throughout the text, because a story should defy time and logic, just as our imagination separates itself from events. There should be a to-be-continued, which may have nothing to do with the beginning, so long as the story is nourished by the same substance, so long as it breathes the same (albeit somewhat stale) air. I tell myself it doesn't matter if I find nothing.

On the map I see the blue vein of a river. It's called the Kerka. In the underbrush along the bank, an eight- or nine-year-old boy, living in the memory or imagination of the grown Danilo Kiš, crawls on all fours, chews the leaves of wild sorrel, and suddenly sees, in the sky, God's image. "He stood on the edge of a cloud, dangerously leaning over, maintaining an inhuman, superhuman balance, with a burned wreath around his head. He appeared unexpectedly, and just as quickly and unexpectedly disappeared, like a falling star." Even if nothing remains of those days, the river is still there, and the underbrush, and the clouds in the sky. Theophany needs nothing more, just like eternity, which never comes to our cities, because such a visit would put them on an equal footing with the earth . . .

So Kiš finally arrived. "To travel means to live," he wrote in 1958, quoting Hans Christian Andersen but giving the words an altogether new meaning. *A Schedule for Buses, Ships, Trains, and Planes*, his father's project, in its full and perfected version would describe — more, would duplicate — the whole world in units of time and space. Empty places between hours of departure and between distances would be filled with accumulated knowledge of continents, bodies of water, culture and civilization, history and geography — information taken from every field, from alchemy to zoology. If such a book were published, all travel would become pointless, would be replaced by reading. I wouldn't need to make the trek from Dulągbka to Bajánsenye, then go another twenty kilometres down to the Kerka. I could sit at home, knowing that whatever I saw as a traveller would be no more than a copy, a pale reflection of such and such a chapter and paragraph in the Universal Schedule. I wouldn't bother to pick up a pen, because the road from Dulągbka and all other roads would exist in a pristine and ideal state untouched by human foot or vehicle wheel. The bus to Jasło would stay forever in its shed, the bus to Kraków also, and the 22:10 international to Budapest, and so on, to every corner of the planet, and no matter where people went, they would find evidence of the presence of the mad genius of the Schedule. Unfortunately this magnum opus was never completed, and the initial sketches, notes, and diagrams, on typescript covered with scrawled corrections, were lost in the 1940s somewhere by the Zala River.

It is for this reason, among other reasons, that my passport looks the way it does. Without a schedule, a guide, a plan, and abandoned to chance, I try to find out things on my own, and always have to start from square one. I go to Baia Mare, let's say, as if no one had ever been there before. Or, at noon in the middle of the summer, to Dukla, where your shadow contracts to a small patch at your feet and the solitude at Market Square thickens as if Judgment Day might come at any moment. Or I cross Pusztaradvány and climb the high barrens towards Slovakia in January, to see how dead the borderland there is and how the rows of hills appear untouched by human eyes, and how at Buzica the red-and-white crossing gate and the guard suggest a vigil for the repentant souls of smugglers. I went there one day in order to bypass Budapest, drove up the northern slopes of the Bukovec Mountains and Mátra in the hope that in a few hours I would reach, by some miracle, the Danube's bend, at Esztergom, where one August on a side street near the intersection of Pázmány and Batthyany I discovered a pub that inside was like a village cabin done up for a wedding reception: a few simple tables covered with chequered cloth, a few chairs, and that was it. A fat man in braces appeared and brought a menu on which the dishes, only a few, were written in longhand. The writing quaint, calligraphic. The room was cold, quiet, empty. I felt like a party guest who had come too early. I ordered *gombaleves,* mushroom soup. Braces brought it and placed it before me as one puts food before a person who just got off work. I could eat with my elbows on the table, even slurp, no one would care, though not far from here, more than a thousand years ago, Saint Stephen was baptized, making all Hungary Christian in one fell swoop.

It was August, and Basilica Hill shimmered like a mirage in the heat. I no longer recall where I had arrived from, but right after the green bridge over the Danube, Slovakia began, sleepy Slovakia, with its tranquil peasant waiting for what should come but might not. Cement-grey plaster and villages that ended abruptly; pot-bellied men in white undershirts drinking beer and sitting on plastic chairs in front of a *hostinec,* in shoes without socks, as if they hadn't left their yard, as if their home encompassed the entire village, the entire region, the rest of the world as far even as two, three bus stops away. Sometimes women would be standing beside them in dressing gowns and slippers — not sitting down, just there to exchange a few words.

Sleepy Slovakia, a deepening afternoon, with only the Gypsies astir and getting into things, turning in the swelter like scattered black rosary beads. It's five, six, and the Košice and Prešov beltways are as empty as dawn on a Sunday. In Medzilaborce, too, not a soul, but in a dark-grey pub at the exit to Zborov, where the only ATM in town stands, someone's hand holds a shot glass. Except that was another time. I was driving to Ubl'a, due east, above the Ukrainian border, because someone called Potok had had adventures there, a couple of times barely escaping with his life, and for weeks at a dusty border marketplace he drank the cheapest and vilest booze in that part of Europe, losing over and over again the pistol that he had stolen and that held only one bullet, kept for the darkest hour. I went to check all this out, in particular to find that fucked-up international bazaar at which the Moldovans spread out on the ground all the treasures of Transnistria in the hope of exchanging them for the riches of Transcarpathia, the jewels of Szabolcs-Szatmár, the inexhaustible goods of Maramureş. I wanted to take it all in, hear the Babylonian cacophony of tongues, Slavic, Finno-Ugric, Romance, see the eastern hotchpotch of tents, pubs of canvas and plywood, old buses turned into brothels on wheels. I wanted to smell Gypsy camps stocked with marvels that no woman or man could resist, because they came from a realm no one yet had reached or—more to the point—no one had returned from. Thus I set out for Ubl'a, east of the volcanic mountains of Vihorlat, mountains no one in his right mind would venture into, as they are haunted by the ghosts of field officers and front-line soldiers of the Warsaw Pact, and by pallid ghouls, deserters, who sell arms and uniforms as souvenirs. I drove through the town of Snina, where among weeping willows stood two-storey garrison buildings with red roofs, all looking as if they had been thrown together that same day and had aged and fallen apart just as quickly. On benches in doorways sat women with children. Soldiers' wives, widows of the officer ghosts? Snina was a dream dreamt at the edge of a country that had lost all its enemies.

I drove to Ubl'a, through Stakčín, Kolonica, Ladomirov, in

the shadow of the Bukovec divide, through Transcarpathian Rus, because a few years before, Potok gave voice, supposedly, to the spirit of these lands and times, because the genius loci of this corner of the continent spoke in tongues, as if in a kind of early capitalist Pentecost. Somewhere around there, perhaps a little to the south, was the square, the commons, the market to which the cursed of the earth were drawn as soon as the crossing gates lifted. The miracle of liberty, of the free exchange of commodities in dust, dirt, an open field, a city rising from nothing and unlike anything the world had seen. Because it had to be as it was once: caravans, troops on the march, migration. The super-natural reality of different prices, different currency drawing entire families from their homes, entire tribes, and making them walk an uncertain path, as once it drew people to the farthest seas, to the ever-retreating horizon of adventurers and discoverers. So I went to Ubľa, beyond which lay Vyšne Nemecké and Čierna nad Tisou, not unlike travelling between the Tigris and the Euphrates to a new Nineveh. Not two rivers met here but three borders, like three currents carrying the fertile sediment of smuggled riches, cunning, greed, fake vodka, pipes for which no excise tax was paid, Siberian skins, exotic parrots and turtles, bullets for Makarov pistols, and Hungarian pornography. Three borders like three rivers, each gathering the best from the depths of each land. I imagined that somewhere between Čierna, Chop, and Záhony a city would grow from the naked soil like a hallucination of the damned, with twenty-four-hour commerce, unlimited supply and demand, and that consumption and capital expenditure would be joined forever in mystical marriage. Such thoughts accompanied me.

But there was nothing in Ubľa. Only two rows of tidy houses, one on either side of the road. A Slovak cop stopping an old

Ukrainian Mercedes driven by some bald bozo. Nothing happening aside from that. You drive and drive, and suddenly the
country ends, for no reason, it seems, almost as if it simply got
bored and quit. The uniform waved; the Ukrainian slowly continued on his way. Two girls emerged from between houses and
were gone in a moment, swallowed by the international wasteland. In this wasteland, odd thoughts occur. We think that on
the other side of the border we will be someone else. Meanwhile
it is May 26 today, tonight, and to the south, above the Republic of Slovakia, the sky brightens now and then from soundless
lightning. I returned from Ubl'a, and nothing had changed.
Back to square one. Which is where everything should begin.
That's what it depends on, on the imagination, which draws no
conclusions. Memory, meteorology, visions.

Should it rain tomorrow, I'll reconstruct that day when in a
small town we boarded a ferry to take us across a lake. Sheets
of grey rain passed over the water. No one was at the pier. Dun
reeds, a solitary purveyor of souvenirs in a shop, and faded signs
for ice cream from a season long gone. Hard to believe it ever
got hot here. The greasy overalls of the crew were soaked. For
the thousandth time they released the anchor, raised the plank,
started up the rumbling diesel, but there was no escape: these
inlets could accommodate at most a child's boat of cork, a raft
of twigs. To ease the dreariness of inland sailing, I pretended
we were at the end of a long transatlantic voyage and heading
for the coast of a country mentioned only in mist-shrouded
legend. The border of the real world lay nearby. Up ahead,
everything seemed familiar and authentic, yet only the natives
could believe that their land existed, that it wasn't a reflection,
shadow, mirage, or parody of an actual land. Raindrops fell on

the deck. On the faces of the crew, boredom competed with indifference. Meanwhile I imagined we were now entering a strait in which space loses its thread, matter its concentration. I leaned against the railing, lit a cigarette, and played the stranger who has ventured into questionable territory without a guide, preconceived notions, or proud knowledge. It was the end of April, and the air, landscape, and whole day were filled with spring. Humidity wafted like grey smoke. We passed boarded-up houses. On the other shore now, the dingy mirror of water still in view, we drove through lethargically expectant country. The entire region idle. It would all change in a month, maybe even in a week, when the sun rose on a Saturday or Sunday, because this was an area of health resorts, a vacation spot, which right now was waiting, dozing, conserving its breath and energy, only half alive. It would endure strangers with their brief excitement, immoderate activity, carnival prodigality, then stillness would settle once again and life return to the old and tested ways, leading to a relatively painless end.

Later, we left the lake and found another, much smaller one, known for not freezing even in the bitterest winter, and smelling as if it were fed by an underground stream from Hades. The rain continued. Wooden pavilions and footbridges stood in murky water and were rotting from both the water and the heat. The white bodies of old men floated on childish inner tubes. Walkways on slippery boards. The men were mostly German or Austrian retirees, but also some spoke Slovak, and some Hungarian. Steam descended from structures on stilts, the structures thick with blindingly white bodies. When naked and crammed together, people seem dead, even when they move. An ominous scene: the stink of swamp decay and sulphur mixed with the smell of steaming flesh. I went inside one structure for a moment, then left. I recall it now as a persistent vision, or as something one only reads about. Nothing remains; Ubľa, Heviz, Lendava, Babadag, Leskovik, et cetera, leave no evidence that quantity eventually becomes quality, that one meshes with the other and like the gears of a marvellous machine begins to produce sense.

Two days before, I was back in Gönc. A sweet shop the colour of lilac appeared to be closed. A padlock hung at the door, and through the dusty windows I could see black, empty oven pans. Each time I come here, there is less of Gönc. One day I will come and find no Gönc at all. The town will have disappeared from the map, and only I will know what it looked like, only I will remember the man with the chequered hat and fishing rod waiting for the yellow bus that went to the other side of the green Zemplén Hills. But all places are wearing out, wearing away. Almost as if they were already in my head only, as outlines, fading colours, shapes blurring at the edges. I drank coffee, looked at the street, and felt oblivion encroach on every side, from the air, the walls, the pavement, from the vastnesses of the past and future. A man in a green shirt passed my little table. I saw his back: old, worn cloth that someone had carefully repaired, preserved, with white thread.

It was Sunday, and I met no other car all the way to Tornyos-németi. Nothing afterwards either: thirty kilometres in total solitude. It was only on the approach to Košice that an occasional car moved on this absurdly many-laned blank. I took Road 547 and at the edge of Rudohorie, the Ore Mountains, turned north-west. As usual, I saw Gypsies, their desperate liveliness in the slumbering monotony of Slovak towns and villages. As if everyone, exhausted by the everyday, was taking a nap, hidden behind curtains, behind rambling roses in gardens, behind the windows of furtive cars, in the stuffy interiors of grey homes, and only these dark-skinned and cursed people were surrendering themselves to life, making use of the world and their few minutes in it like a winning ticket. So I always keep an eye out for red, rusting roofs and blue wisps of pine smoke. And for patches of bare clayey soil on which not a thing can grow, because the Gypsies are constantly on the move, stepping, visiting, going to endless parties under the open sky, passing stories from mouth to mouth, and peering into every corner, for the earth belongs to no one, and no one has the right to claim it for himself.

In Krompachy, their settlement rose. To the left of the road, on an almost vertical incline, house grew atop house, and the highest jutted into the boundless blue. Structures resting insanely on empty space. Jagged, exposed to wind and rain, hanging in defiance of gravity, they brought to mind bird nests perched on rock. Protruding, sagging, as if at any moment something would fall into the road — poles, pieces of sheet metal, sticks, parts of old houses hauled from who knows where, houses no one wanted to live in any more, with mud and moss in the chinks between boards, scraps of tarpaper pressed with stones. Everything had been found and made use of with paranoid cunning. From discarded matter, the magic of a domicile. It seemed that it all fluttered in the wind, that in a moment it would take to the air, fly away, and no sign of this aerial town would remain. I imagined the Gypsies sailing skywards like a tattered cloud, a great patchwork raft carrying a mountain of possessions, the whole dump and scrapheap of things nobody needed and only the Gypsies could put to use. I saw them fly over Rudohorie, over Šariš and Spiš, over the entire world, in the nebular wealth of their poverty, the shreds and shards from which they had cobbled — pointedly without dignity — an ordinary life.

Then a small town and the usual industrial shit in a valley of the Hornád, to the right. Rust, the wretchedness of inert metal, the despair of outdated technology. Tanks, stacks, conduits, conveyor belts, sidings, hangars with broken windows, and pustules of installation among the greenery. Granted, it was a Sunday, but nothing suggested that by some miracle this equipment would return to life on Monday. Or ascend to heaven. It would have to sit here for all eternity, unless the Gypsies took pity and disassembled it and sold the parts for cigarettes, alcohol, ornaments for their women and sweets for their children, or built out of the parts vehicles not of this world, in which to travel through Europe, exciting among the local population — as they have done before — superstitious dread mixed with envy and admiration. Once people asked an old Gypsy why Gypsies didn't have their own country. "If a country was a good thing, the Gypsies too would have one, for sure," was his answer. So a united Europe is for them an improvement, making it easier for a person to move and live than any single nation can.

I close my eyes and see the Gypsies from Gjirokastër leaving their draughty huts assembled on the rooftops of concrete communal buildings, in which they couldn't endure the poor air and the heat. Those from Krujë leave their lime ovens; those from Iacobeni leave their scattered Saxon houses; those from Porumbacu and Sâmbăta de Sus leave their clay hovels; those from Vlachy leave their log cabins; those from Podgrodzie leave their single-storey houses in a former Jewish district; those from Miskolc leave their slums, which barely rise above the ground along the road to Encs; those from Zborov leave their white barracks cut out of the mountainside; and the Gypsies leave all the thousand other places, the list and description of which I promise myself I will put together someday. A Europe without borders is a Gypsy dream, there is no denying it. White folk, lazy, rooted, fearful, stay in their homes, as one does on a Slovak Sunday. You see only the Gypsies, walking in their solitude, in twos and threes, on the roadsides from village to village, and the green countryside closes after them like water. It's as if they could not live without space. Freed from the workings of time, they are indifferent to the nothingness that will claim Gönc and all the other places we have given names to, because only by naming can we grasp the world, even as we condemn it to destruction.

By an empty field before Brezovička, a swarthy ten-year-old boy was doing push-ups in the middle of the road. He was naked. At the sight of my car, he stood, covered his genitals, and dived into nearby bushes, where three of his buddies, dressed, were laughing their heads off.

Old women carrying brushwood on their backs, men gathered around the open hoods of old cars, a boy in Podgrodzie cradling a puppy in his arms. A cart in Transylvania hitched to two horses, and in the cart a frightened foal, a couple of weeks old, its legs splayed, a child embracing its neck affectionately, face in the brown fur, as if the child had found a creature smaller than itself and more defenceless. Red Kalderash petticoats on the road to Mount Moldoveanu, bare feet covered with yellow dust. A smouldering dump in Erdőhát; small, slender figures plucking metal, plastic, and glass from the smoking rubbish. A dump in Tiszacsécse, by the road that winds above the river, where an old man with a pipe in his mouth pulls long pieces of wood out of the hills of junk; he ties them in bundles and sets them beside a relic bicycle . . . I should create a catalogue, an encyclopedia of these scenes and places, write a history in which time plays no part, a history of Gypsy eternity, because it is more enduring, and wiser, than our governments and cities, than our entire world, which trembles at the imminence of its demise.

Yes, Gypsies are my obsession, also the border wasteland, and the river ferries in eastern Hungary. The ferries in particular. The ferry on the Tisa ten kilometres beyond Sárospatak was a veritable Noah's ark. Hay wagons, tractors, cattle and sheep tethered, men in rubber boots and baseball caps; rakes, pitchforks, bottles of beer; as if these people were leaving their land, because it bored them or had gone barren, and were seeking a new one. Houses were the only thing missing on the wooden deck eaten away by the water and the sun and covered with cow shit. Mr Ferenc Lenart of Gávavencsellő was the owner of the boat — this fact was recorded on the blue ticket costing 290 forints. Living by the Tisa is like living on an island. You're constantly crossing. The river winds, turns back, can't make up its mind, oozes to the sides, pulls swampily away from the land, and Szabolcs-Szatmár and Erdőhát float uncertainly, unmoored from the earth by a semi-aqueous layer: bogs, quicksand, reeds, the sweet stink of rot and standing water cooked in the sun, houses on stilts and levees erected a kilometre from the main current so the spring waters from the Gorgany, Chornohora, and Maramureş have somewhere to go. Two hundred and ninety forints is nothing for a drowsy excursion across the flowing green on the back of this beautiful and strange device that like a weaver's shuttle joins the torn fabric of roads. Its wake immediately seals up, and everything is as it was before. In Szamossályi the price is even less, only twenty a head, or thirty and change.

Where the high bank descends was an enclosure filled with goats and sheep; on the other side were a small house and a board with laughably low prices for crossing. Black roof, yellow walls. The ferry trying to leave the opposite bank. It was the motorless variety, moved only by the river. Connected to two pulleys, long lines stretched across the current, it had to wait for the water to take it. Drawing in a cable with two winches, now this one, now that, it went back and forth like the simplest, earliest machine, barely conscious of the law of gravitation. The sole passenger a woman with a bicycle. The engineer cranked, shoved off from the bank with a pole, all without effort, without haste, submitting to the will of the river. Sometimes he left the wheel and oars to chat with the woman, who was sitting hunched on a bench. I saw it all from above: two small figures on a rectangular deck of thick planks the colour of the sandy shore, waiting for this strip of land to detach itself from the Great Hungarian Plain and, like a much-burdened flying carpet, bear them to the other side of the Szamos. It was maybe fifteen kilometres to the Romanian border, and again I felt time subsiding, growing still, yielding the field to pure space — it was that way in Ubl'a; that way in Hidas-németi, where immobile trains baked beneath the high heaven like grass snakes; that way also in stricken Buzica and in my own Konieczna. But eventually the ferry moved, drifted, arrived, and now I could drive down to the platform. I looked upstream and tried to remember when and where I saw this river last.

Most likely a year ago, in Satu Mare, when I was on my way to Păltiniş, but only for a moment. The bridge was in the centre of town, and as usual I was seeking a detour, reading the rusted sky-blue road signs, so this didn't count. Two years earlier, I spent a whole day wandering along the river. I had come from Carei and wasn't sure whether I wanted to continue on to Cluj or to Oradea, whether to go south-east or west — or anywhere. On the 1F to Bobota was truck hell: tank trucks, dump trucks full of gravel and earth, honking. Transylvania was a possibility, but I wasn't quite up to the Balkan method of driving after a long Hungarian night of pear brandy and Kadarka wine from

Szekszárd. I checked out Crişeni on the map and headed there, north, and in Jibou entered a valley of the Szamos. Except I remember nothing of that drive, other than the coffee in some godforsaken place and a hailstorm among green hills. It is only Baia Mare that I remember clearly, hallucination that it was. Conveyor belts like black viaducts, mining cars for gold hanging lifeless above the earth, and the hopelessness of a suburb where people milled before worker compounds that looked like gutted ruins. The town had chewed its way into the mountains in search of ore, but the rust of poverty in turn eroded El Dorado. Baia Sprie perished in the same way, a victim of its own greed.

To the gap at Gutîi it was ten kilometres. There, at 987 metres, the world fell in two. Nearly a kilometre above sea level, continuity ended, chaos celebrated. The mocking memento of Baia lay at our back, and on the other side, along the northern peaks, lay, amazingly, the past. Deseşti, Hărniceşti, Giuleşti were dreams carved out of wood. In the sculpting of the homes, gates, and fences was an unending abundance of time: the eternity required to chisel and cut and shape and free all this from the elements. The miracle of patience had to have been performed in some other age, because ours could not accommodate each and every separate motion-gesture needed to fashion this Arcadia of wood. No minute or hour of ours could have contained the birth of this calm insanity of forms. Almost as if it simply grew, the next stage in the slow development of tree rings and branches, nature abandoning its previous designs to try something in the vein of human habitation. Insanity indeed, this Maramureş thousand and one nights, this Sagrada Familia of xylem, all the way to Sighetu, where the Pietri peak cut the sunset off from the rest of the world.

In the morning, I walked along the Tisa. On the Ukrainian side lay Solotvino, where two years before, I got off a train to take a chance at Stanislavov.

And again Babadag, exactly as two years ago: the bus sits for ten minutes, the driver's gone, kids beg without conviction in the southern swelter — nothing has changed. The thousand-lei notes with Eminescu have disappeared, replaced by aluminium discs featuring Constantin Brancoveanu. It's easier to identify them in your pocket, take them out, and press them into an outstretched hand. Thirty-seven of these aluminium coins equal one euro. As I ride to the city, I see three women in dresses that trail on the ground — Dobrujan Turks, no doubt. They look pretty but strange among the crumbling walls, the houses falling apart before they have aged. Babadag is weariness and isolation. People get off the bus and stand, with small shadows at their feet. A white minaret like a finger points at the empty blue. I distribute some of my change. The little beggars take the coins indifferently, without a word, not lifting their eyes. I am travelling from Tulcea to Constanţa, the opposite direction from two years ago. Everything is the same, except that the bills are now plastic.

Babadag: twice in my life, twice for ten minutes. The world is made from such fragments, pieces of burning dream, mirage, bus fever. The tickets remain. From Tulcea to Constanţa it's 120,000 lei. *Păstraţi biletul pentru control.* Gara de Sud, the South Station area in Constanţa, is the shame of the Balkans, a black web of cables over streets, crap, horns, dogs, flies, food stands all jumbled. Tinfoil, lighters, cellophane, trash, a vortex of throwaway stuff, the reek of fried fat, smoke, men in uniform, fast operators without work but in constant motion, gold chains, flip-flops, a holstered pistol — civilian — barely covered by a shirt, watermelon rinds, a kaleidoscope of colour, high heels, mascara, an anthill greenmarket camp. You can only list; description is impossible, since there is nothing here that lasts but weariness, weakness, decomposition, and frenetic toil under a sky bleached by the heat.

From Constanța you pass through Valu lui Traian, Trajan's Bank, a village of dirt-floor huts, thin donkeys, old women in black gazing with wise eyes at the dust and emptiness. If you got out here, you wouldn't have the strength to leave. The present reigns in this place, as it always has. Hence all the names of heroes, rebels, leaders, governors, politicians: Nicolae Bălcescu, Mihail Kogălniceanu, Cuza Vodă, Vlad Țepeș, Mircea Vodă, Ștefan cel Mare, Dragoș Vodă, Ștefan Vodă, Alexandru Odobescu, and there's Independența and Unirea (Independence and Unity), Valea Dacilor (Valley of the Dacians). Not a thing to be seen, just villages scattered in the steppe along Road 3A or a little to the side. In this flat land they are hardly visible over the horizon. Goats, corn, horse harnesses, people stooped in fields, the same movements made a hundred, two hundred years ago, a thousand, forever, movements as unchanging as those of animals. The names are meant to give inert time a sense and direction.

A couple of days later I was driving north-east. I crossed the Seretu valley and in Tecuci recognized the crossroads and the fence where two years earlier I had spent an hour or two taking in the sight of the other end of the Carpathians. This time I kept the mountains on my left, and the landscape flattened. Delivery vans carrying melons. Fruit piled along the road. In the fields, cornstalk sheds. No trees, so the men were waiting out the afternoon heat in these rustling lean-tos. After Crasna, the hills began again — long, sleepy ridges of the Moldovan Highland. An old and crumbling plateau excavated by the river and enervated by the sun. Grassy slopes, white scree, sickly crests of groves presented a kind of geologic metaphor for the acceptance of one's fate, of erosion and decline. The earth showed its bones here.

Then Huşi, where in 1899 Corneliu Zelea Codreanu was born. I should have stopped there but didn't. The town appeared for a moment, then was gone, like a hundred other Romanian towns I had driven through. It was in no way different: low to the ground and pitiful. Gardens hid the decay. I should have stopped. Codreanu was half Polish, half German, but considered himself more Romanian than the Romanians. He thought of himself as a Romanian messiah. God the Father, Christ, and the archangel Michael were constantly included in his plans. In some photographs he appears in folk dress: a white linen shirt to the knees and white breeches. Under short trouser legs are stylish city shoes. He greets the crowds with a gesture like Hitler's heil, but it denotes a purely Roman legacy, unsullied by any connection with the barbaric Germans. On a white horse, he visits Moldovan and Bessarabian villages. The peasants listen and nod, because he tells them that all the evil comes from outside.

I drove through Huşi in minutes. It was twenty kilometres to the Prut and the border. Sheep grazed on the hills. At dusk they returned to their enclosure in the waste, a few fences with few crossbars. Nearby were the huts of the shepherds, with bulrush roofs. One could erect them practically without tools. They were part of the landscape in every respect. If all this vanished, it would be without a trace: no ruins, no lingering memories. Inside the huts there must have been objects — a bucket, a knife, an axe — but on the outside all was vegetation and ageless. Composed of the most basic elements: wood, grass, reeds. A few animals, sheep dung.

Before Codreanu on his grey mare, an icon of the archangel Michael was carried, they say. It is not hard to imagine the procession precisely here, among these low hills and huts, or a little farther on, in Valea Grecului with its single church, cow field, and a green speckled with white geese. That's where I felt sure that I was beholding the immutable "it was always thus" or, in any case, a past that could never become the future, because from the very beginning its purpose was to endure.

Codreanu in his knee-length shirt and with his procession through miserable towns and villages brought the good news that nothing would change, that what had been would continue, having achieved perfect form long ago. It merely needed cleansing of the scum borne by the wave of modernity, cleansing of the slime of democracy, the dirt of liberalism, the contagion of the Jews. Poverty and impotence were ennobled by their heroic heritage. Codreanu's comrades wore amulets containing soil from battlefields in which their forefathers had resisted the Romans, Goths, Huns, Slavs, Tatars, Hungarians, Turks, and Russians. Magic, ancestor worship, and Christianity were treated as a tribal religion, an occult science to save the people. These few lines from Codreanu's text are essentially a howl: "Wars were won by those able to summon invisible forces from the beyond and enlist their help. These mysterious forces were the souls of the dead, the souls of our forefathers, who were tied to this land, to our fields and forests, having fallen in its defence. Today they are summoned by us, their grandchildren and great-grandchildren, because we remember them. And above the souls of the dead stands Christ."

Anyone who was born in Huşi and spent his youth there is entitled not to believe in the future. I assume Codreanu visited Valea Grecului too; he was a young man on the move. He hated the Communists, who believed in the future, as much as the Jews. His dull, provincial mind probably had trouble telling them apart. Basically, he never stopped being a prophet from the sticks. The world was divided into Romania and the rest, and the rest had no value because it wasn't Romania, let alone Huşi.

During his studies in Berlin, he wears Romanian folk dress. At the same time, poverty forces him into trade. He buys salt pork and butter in the villages, sells them at a profit in the city. His Berlin life becomes a parody of the life of a Moldovan peasant. He is now no different from his conception of a Jew. In Grenoble, to survive, he and his wife sew Romanian folk costumes and sell them. Little enters his head other than Romania and folk merchandise. In a courtroom (he also tried his hand at lawyering), he pulls out a pistol and shoots the chief of police. His comrades murder "traitors" and despicable politicians, then surrender to the cops, as an act of Christian martyrdom. "Love is the key to the peace that our Saviour offered to the peoples of the world . . . But love does not release us from the duty of discipline, the duty of carrying out our orders," he ranted in 1936.

Parody and delirium. One must be born in Huşi to smell the poison of melancholy that eats into mind and soul. One must be born in Huşi, where even the crows turn back, to grasp this dream of glory of the native land, to understand this nightmare. Madness is left, because only in madness can one overturn, if for a moment, the order of a world that gives not a damn for Huşi, for Valea Dacilor, or even for the village of Decebal, cursed with its Gypsy multitude on every corner. Huşi dismissed, Huşi scorned, Huşi half asleep and dragging its feet, Huşi scratched by chickens and stuck like a broken cane in a crevice of time forever and ever amen. The train terminates there. To come into the world in Huşi is to live in eternity made flesh.

So thought Corneliu Codreanu. Because the past was sacred, it had to last forever, had to be resurrected constantly, driving off the spectre of the future. The future always came from outside, was foreign, like an invader. The future was a violation of the perfection of enduring, which constituted the sense, the essence, the deepest mystery of Huşi and its environs.

I really should have stopped in Huşi. Now I must imagine myself going back. Autumn would be the best time, when the leaves are falling, for me to find confirmation of my ideas, to probe the cracking, the rotting, the mould that quietly, imperceptibly enters stone and wood and Sunday outfits kept on shelves. Microorganisms, gravity, humidity — these are the fundamental components of my part of the continent. They should be listed on the ingredients label, should appear on the coat of arms. Whoever thinks otherwise is in for a rude awakening. Codreanu's paroxysm resulted from his complete misunderstanding of the genius loci, which he wanted so much to change. Possessed by the need for his people to be great, he fell into the absurdity of imitating a foreign destiny. All that he bequeathed, then, was counterfeit.

I can't help it, I love this Balkan shambles. It begins right after Satu Mare. Everything half-assed and fucked up, and God only knows where the edge of the highway is, where the shoulder, plus the horse-drawn carts, and suddenly there is more dust in the air than there ever was in post-Hapsburg Hungary, and at every step you have to swerve because of something on the road, as if these Dacias and Aros were not properly tightened and lost parts or maybe had too many parts to begin with. Stocky Gypsies stand by Mercedes with open hoods, as if the radiator burst or a belt slipped, and desperately they wave at you to stop, then thrust gold or precious stones in your face at half price. The kids dart back and forth across the road, no doubt trained from the cradle in the famous Romanian indifference to death, in

Geto-Dacian fatalism. No one uses directional signals, because times are tough and a person must conserve his strength. Horns, on the other hand, are heard constantly, because they don't wear out. It was that way in May 2000; it will be that way forever. I dwell on the memory as one dwells on one's childhood. It turns out that a man seeks only what he has seen before. It turns out that the Szatmár chaos, the empty lanes of Sulina and Giurgiu by the Danube recall my Sokołów Podlaski and Kałuszyn. The same material, the same improvisation desperately trying to be permanent. In the buses, the same smell of soap and milk when the villagers set out; on the rotting benches in the shady lanes, the same contemplation. The same carelessness with time, a watch no more than an ornament, like jewellery. Time, really, is just a piece of eternity you cut out for your own consumption.

Between Bozieni and Valea Parjei I saw two men by the road in the middle of a green field. For ten kilometres in one direction and fifteen in the other, there was nothing, no one. They sat in the shade of an Italian pine and played cards. They didn't even look up when the bus passed. A few days later I returned the same way and saw them again. They had moved maybe a kilometre, but the landscape was unchanged: a row of stone pines along the road, corn, and the men still immersed in their somnolent, monotonous game, as if their deck held a million cards. It's possible that night overtook them as they played and that they slept in the open field, to resume at dawn. Someone may have brought them here to do work, but when the hirer disappeared over a hill, they immediately began their game. They had not a thing with them, no tool, unless it was in a pocket. They sat as if they were at a table at home. Grey and crumpled, like most of the men in this region, yet unfazed by the overwhelming space and endless stretch of hours. The fragile abstraction of the game was their shield. At dusk, who knows, they might have lit a candle, or else the cards were marked and even in the dark their fingers could tell hearts from spades from clubs.

I love this Balkan shambles, Hungarian, Slovak, Polish, the amazing weight of things, the lovely slumber, the facts that make no difference, the calm and methodical drunkenness in the middle of the day, and those misty eyes that with no effort pierce reality and with no fear open to the void. I can't help it. The heart of my Europe beats in Sokołów Podlaski and in Huşi. It does not beat in Vienna. Or in Budapest. And most definitely not in Kraków. Those places are all aborted transplants. A mock-up, a mirror of what is elsewhere. Sokołów and Huşi imitate nothing; they follow their own destinies. My heart is in Sokołów, though I was there for ten hours altogether, at most. Usually during transfers from one Pekaes truck to another in the early 1970s, when I went to visit my uncle and his wife on vacations. But my memory is good. Single-storey wooden houses in the centre of town, lilac bushes, shutters, dogs asleep on the asphalt, leaning posts of bus stops with round yellow signs, frames and planks painted brown and green, sand in the pavement joints, an ice-cream store that inside smells like a village cottage, sugar peas in glass tubes, everything only just sprouting from the ground, only just begun, and of course the rotting, the scraping, the dozing, life without pretension, trying to make things last, the squeaking floorboards, the silly heroism of a quotidian that snaps in two as easily as an ice-cream wafer. I remember it all and could go on and on. It's in my blood. So though I drove through Huşi in five minutes, there being no reason to stop, my heart is in Huşi.

Which indicates that I need my own country. Where I can travel in a circle. A country without clear borders, a country unaware that it exists and doesn't care that someone invented it and entered it. A sleepy country with murky politics and a history like shifting sand. Its present breaking ice, its culture the Gypsy palaces of Soroca. Nothing would last here without running the risk of being ridiculous. But why a country, why not an empire with an unspecified number of provinces, an empire in motion, in progress, driven by the idea of expansion, but also sclerotic, unable to remember its lands, its peoples, its capitals, so every morning it would need to start over? That would suit me, since I have the same problem: I remember things and events but do not know what separates or connects them other than my accidental presence.

Three days ago I was in Bardejov. An afternoon mass had begun at Saint Egidius. Those of the faithful who were late squeezed in through the half-open door. The interior must have been full, because you could hear an echoing rumble of voices, yet new people kept arriving. In a long stream across the square, the faithful wore their best and were flushed in their haste, slowing only in the shadow of the sanctuary to give their movement a little decorum. A scene that has been repeated for five hundred years. The Bardejov square crossing, I thought, must be worn from the touch of feet. A space unable after so many years to keep healing. I walked uphill, in the opposite direction, away from the crowd. Louis the Great gave this city the right to hold eight fairs a year and to do beheadings, activities that must have required a bit of room, but now, without commerce and the functions of justice, the square seemed abandoned. I turned down Veterná, then down Stöcklova, to the right, to find myself in a narrow path between a barbican wall and the rest of the city. I saw some steps and went up. The wall, at least six hundred years old, was crumbling here and there. It looked its age. From my height now I could see yards, gardens, back doors, hutches, chicken coops, doghouses, all the things a small town hides from sight, confining its rusticity. A graceful, relaxed clutter here, the remnants of projects never completed, storage gradually turning into rubbish. Plastic bags, compost, fallen apples, weeds, beaten paths, an eternal present crouched in the shadow of walnut and cherry trees. The Gothic slowly disintegrated here, and its disintegration led to things that had no history, things that had use and significance for a moment only. The new joined the old in a just order, a *liberté, égalité,* and *fraternité* of matter.

I sense this equality everywhere. There is no need for deception. I am blind and deaf to all else. But as a rule there is no all else. It was that way a month and a half ago in Uzlina. We reached it by motorboat from Murighiol. Around us lay four thousand square kilometres of canals, lakes, dead tributaries, bogs, wetlands, and land as flat as the mirror of still water. You could go for several hours and nothing would change. A hot, undisturbed, motionless sleep. The expanse swallowing up all detail. Our path left no trace. The great river carries silt from the depths of the continent and with it sculpts a new, uncertain land. In a kind of genesis, the landscape gathers its strength to lift itself above the surface of the water. A trance, this trip against the current of time, towards primordial childhood.

But Uzlina came first. A hotel there rose four storeys out of the marshy, the flat, and the ancient. It looked like a thing misplaced during a move. In a radius of a few dozen kilometres, there was nothing higher. At the driveway entrance waited a young woman in a miniskirt and stiletto heels. She held a tray with glasses of slivovitz, cujka, simple peasant brandy. An olive in each glass. In front of the hotel, a swimming pool, umbrellas, deckchairs. Our room in the annexe was as God wanted it. The view from the window: laundry tubs, rubble, vegetable patches (private plots), dogs on chains barking to protect the cabbage. The first night, I was bitten by bedbugs and had no air to breathe. In the main building nearby, the air-conditioning chugged. All evening, the employees of Coty Cosmetics Romania entertained themselves around a bonfire to global hit parade music.

The next day Mitka appeared. He sat down at our table in a bar under umbrellas. He wore trousers from a hundred-year-old suit and rubber flip-flops. He was maybe sixty. He seemed to come straight from the swamp and reeds. He drank beer after beer, complaining that he could no longer have vodka, not after the doctors cut something out of him. He spoke to us in Russian but called the waitresses in Romanian. He drank at the hotel every evening and didn't pay, though sometimes he contributed a ram or piglet to the hotel kitchen. The owner tolerated this, wanting to buy land from Mitka, who was a neighbour, to expand his business. Mitka's cows and swine wandered through and around, dozens of them foraging untethered through the mud and sand along the Saint Egidius tributary.

At dusk we went to see his farm, which was large and flat. A labyrinth of pens, sties, plots, half-open barns, and huts with bulrush roofs. No light on anywhere. Above, the bright, phosphorescent sky; below, the thickened dark, redolent of animals and excrement. The pigs ran up to Mitka like dogs. In a corner something snorted, grunted, chewed, belched, huffed, followed by a pulse of body heat, as if in the cavern of this farm a great antediluvian beast were settling down for the night.

In Mitka's cabin, a weak bulb burned under a low ceiling. His long and narrow room contained nothing more than a bed, a cupboard with utensils, and a table. Mitka ducked into a small doorway and emerged with a double-barrelled shotgun. An old gun, metal shining through the oxidized finish. He said we could shoot, if I paid for the ammunition. Night had fallen, and I thought shooting didn't make sense. Another time, I said. Disappointed, he laid the gun on the bed. On the wall hung a framed black-and-white photograph, grainy. The man in it reminded me of someone, but I wasn't certain. I asked Mitka. "Yes, it's Ceaușescu," he said with a smile, pleased that I had recognized the leader. Then, since the subject was photographs, he produced from a drawer a picture of his dead wife.

That was Mitka. He worshipped his dictator, remembered his wife, liked shooting into the dark. He lay down to sleep beside his shotgun. There was nothing near his farm, no houses or people. I'm not even sure all his animals returned at night. He may not have known how many he had, may not ever have counted them. Half a kilometre away, at the Coty party, were women in bikinis around the pool and men resembling gigolos in their white trousers. The old man, small and veiny, slept like a child. I imagined him dreaming of cows, pigs, chickens, and dogs, that they surrounded him in a close circle to protect him from the traps and treacheries of the world. The noisy hotel, beside this dark and foul-smelling farm, seemed a thing made of paper, which could ignite in a moment from a careless match.

It's the second half of October. The weather is changing; the first frosts have come, the first powdering of snow. Winter begins in two or three weeks. Yet again I'll have to imagine all those places I visited in the spring and summer. This imagining makes the world bigger. The continent increases. Rozpucie, Baurci, Ubľa, Máriapócs, Erind, Huși, Sokołów Podlaski, Hodoš, Zborov, Caraorman, Delatyn, Duląbka—they all want to be great. To see Lvov in the spring and then imagine it in the winter is like doubling Lvov, making it twice as lovely, but that's as it should be. The poor road leading through the heart of the

Čergov massif begins there. It is closed to traffic, and a man drives it at his peril, because the Slovak soldiers have no sense of humour. In any case, a beautiful stretch through complete wilderness all the way to Majdan. But I digress . . .

I was speaking of greatness and in praise of memory that, like a lit match, burns a hole in the map, sending places and things into an eternity that can be ended only by cosmic dementia (which eventually will happen) and thus expanding the continent to infinite size, bringing oblivion out into the light. Whoever was in Rozpucie, Baurci, or Caraorman knows what I'm saying. The dark soul of a peninsula smoulders there, and matter slumbers, like bone marrow producing the dense black blood of unrealized desires. To be in Rozpucie, Baurci, or Caraorman is to see a past that has not yet harboured doubts about the future, because it is a past that has not yet got under way. And it may never get under way and share the fate of the rest of the world, whose destiny is to weep over its own demise. Neither Rozpucie nor Caraorman will be depleted unto death. They are old but will die young, are weary but will die in the fullness of their strength, in midstride, on a road whose purpose and destination are beyond their ken. It's October, a cold night rain falls, and the wet and dark engulf the villages and towns. Lying at the bottom of the waters, they have lost their names: great sleeping fish with houses, people, and roads in their bellies. People whisper in the dark, huddled, intent, waiting out the flood and guessing the future. Time hasn't yet started; there is no light, and you must squint for the dawn to come. No news, only promises and myths. The world is so distant that by the time an account of it reaches you, it may no longer be.

On such nights I reach for the plastic box with the photographs. There are about a thousand of them. Like an organ grinder's monkey, I pull out the first that comes to hand.

Usually I have no idea when this or that one was taken, but I always know the place. There's nothing of consequence in the snapshots: horses grazing in a dump, a vegetable garden with a scraped wall, green hills, a village hut, a piece of mountain scenery, a black cat and a manhole, a tree in mist and tyre tracks in snow, the facade of a house on an empty street, and so on, with no pattern or sequence or reason, a purely random collection of insignificant objects and meaningless moments, a child's game-experiment to see if the camera click really does freeze reality. But I remember everything and without the box can identify the geographic names, the countries, regions, and villages. The cat was in Lviv, the horses on the outskirts of Gjirokastër, the triangular corner facade in Chernivtsi, the garden in Tokaj, the mountains at Kočevski Rog. I'm not sure about the tyre tracks in the snow. Definitely somewhere near Kecskemét, west of the city, where I got lost and was frantically looking for an exit, because by every indication the road was taking me to the Budapest highway, which I hated like poison. Finally I found an exit, saw above me the dark arch of a viaduct and the long bodies of trucks creeping north. I became entangled in a web of yellow roads. Mist clung to the ground. Through vertical breaks in it I saw the remains of what were probably Hungarian state farms — rusting tractors, collectivization breathing its last, huge barns and stables — then fog covered the scene, the whole world, and you could imagine whatever you liked, the Great Lowland, Alföld, flat and sodden earth joined with the sky by the thick and heavy air, endless marsh with no horizon, a kind of semimaterialization of nothingness. The tyre tracks in snow were there, and yellow grass, somewhere outside Kecskemét, at Kiskun.

I hold on to this rubbish collection of snapshots to imagine what lies outside them, all that is hidden from the eye and memory. A deck of a thousand worn and worthless cards, the faience shine of Fuji and Kodak, the dull light of the literal — these are the photographs I take. Hardly any people in them. As if a neutron bomb had wiped away everything that moved, aside from the cat in Lviv and the Albanian horses. Maybe it's the Bushman fear that the camera will steal a person's soul. Or maybe it simply shows how unpopulated the land is, how solitary my life. It's good to arrive in a country in which you find no one. You can start from scratch. History becomes legend, then, and reality a personal vision. You cannot grasp, say, Voskopojë; at best, you can imagine it. In the pictures from Voskopojë there is not a soul, only two donkeys nibbling among thistles and stones. I know that their driver, Jani, ought to be with them, drinking brandy and beer in turn, and Greczynka, the owner of the pub, and her silent husband, and Jani's friend, as broad as a barn and with a Slavic face, and the retarded kid we picked up on the road, but then the account would bog down and I would never extricate myself from the confusion of their lives. And so: only two donkeys, stones, and a slate-blue sky over the ruin of a monastery. Ah, but of course I should drive after that to Boboshticë, thirty-some kilometres to the south-east, because the village was founded, supposedly, by Polish knights on some crusade. The inhabitants still know a few Polish words, though they have no idea what they mean. I should go there instead of watching the donkeys, stones, and thistles, but frankly, as interesting as Boboshticë is, it's of no interest to me. I returned to Korçë and for hours looked out of my hotel window at the square as if I were a camera without an owner. It was the same in Gjirokastër. Netting to keep out bugs blurred the minaret. And in Seregélyes, rain, an empty courtyard, the wet branches of chestnut trees, and the tinny gurgle of water in downspouts.

In Prelasko, frost on the grass, a parking lot with one car, and a house collapsing on the other side of the street.

It's the same everywhere. You sharpen the focus to pierce the envelope of air, to cut through the skin of space. A window in a new place does the job. In Cahul, it was the market closed for the night and the shadows of dogs many times larger than the dogs. In Chişinău it rained too, and Vasile Alecsandri Avenue became a grey river. In the tropical downpour I had to close the window. Every morning at nine, a man opened an office on the ground floor across the way. I remember the finial on the gate, a shape like a snail, a wave of the sea, the horns of a ram. I remember little else. I watched the finial for hours and imagined the rest. I am doing the same now. I take my pictures out of the plastic box, my change out of the metal canister for Absolut vodka, my parking tickets and hotel bills out of the cardboard box, my banknotes out of the drawer — nothing more, ever, only this thousandfold multiplication of the everyday.

In Máriapócs in September, on the large, flat, windswept field outside town, merchandise lay on plastic bags on the ground. No treasures here: Chinese schlock, jeans, Adidas and Nike knock-offs. All displayed in neat rows and spanking new. The vendors stood motionless over their wares and waited. Each selling the same stuff, essentially. The grass dry and trampled. No one buying anything, no one even looking. An itinerant tribe from an old tale, which spreads out its wares at the city gates, and the next morning it is gone without a trace. A bit farther on, merry-go-rounds and shooting galleries, then more stalls with sweets and wine, church booths with wonders, and gingerbread hearts, handicrafts, panpipes, weathervanes, and stands with religious literature. Among the trees, people had set up camp, put out food: hard-boiled eggs, bottles of beer, canapés. Some had removed their shoes and were dozing. There were several cars from Romania with *SM* on their licence plates, which meant Satu Mare, and a few from Slovakia. Music issued from one of the speakers, but under the vast sky of the Hungarian Lowlands it sounded quiet and insignificant. Budapest television had set up its cameras before a Baroque basilica. The crowd was lost in this great, flat, sandy area, absorbed like water.

I had hoped to meet some famous Gypsies from Moldova, Baron Artur Cerari or Robert — it was a Gypsy holiday, after all — but I saw no BMW 700 or X5. On the lot were only pathetic Dacias, tired Ladas, stalwart Trabants, and reeking diesels from the Reich. The one ATM had no forints. So yes, Máriapócs seemed the last town at the edge of the inhabited earth. It was not hard to imagine a sudden gust of wind spraying everything with sand. In the churchyard, the Uniate liturgy was in progress. The Maramureş Gypsies were dressed with elegance and dignity: black hats, belts studded with silver, gold chains, cowboy boots. A few had beautiful faces. An ancient, unsettling beauty not encountered today. The women's heels sank in the sand. I had driven three hundred kilometres to see this, and nothing was happening. God knows what I had expected: a city of tents, horses neighing, sword swallowers? I always play the idiot, because reality wins, as usual. In addition I was broke. I could only go back. Máriapócs that afternoon was dust and waiting for the evening mass to begin. To the Romanian border it was thirty kilometres, the town of Nyírbátor and two small villages. People strolled and magnanimously wasted time. Practically no one rode on the merry-go-round. Everyone passed as in a dreamy carnival, and the knock-off running shoes, motionless in the dust, seemed to mock themselves. I could picture cattle coming from the Lowlands, large black swine rooting for genuine food in the schlock, nudging the piles of clothing with their wet snouts, tasting and spitting out the painted plastic, squealing, shitting on the logos of international companies, turning this whole fake market into a sty, and the stink would rise to heaven and drift over Máriapócs and Szabolcs-Szatmár, mingling with the sound of bells, wood smoke, the lowing of cows, and the dry wind, forever and ever amen.

Two days before, it was All Souls' Day. As every year, I bought a few candles and drove to cemeteries. A strong wind blew from the south, so it was hard to light them. But with tin protectors, the candles wouldn't go out. Occasionally someone preceded me and I'd find lamps burning. I always wondered, Who in this godforsaken place is remembering the Bosnian dead? the Croatian dead? the Hungarian? The Königliche Ungarische Landsturm Huzaren Regiment — in Hungarian, Honwedzi. Or the Tyroleans. The Tiroler Kaiser Jäger Regiment. Nothing there. You must make a special trip, and there isn't always a road. In Radocyna, the country simply comes to an end: the way for a horse drawn cart or a four-by-four dissolves into meadow, vanishes in russet grass or scummy ponds two kilometres from Slovakia, and yet soldiers came. Four Austrians from the twenty-seventh regiment, infantry, and seventy-nine Ruthenians, also on foot. There were names: *infanteria,* the child's brigade, brats with bayonets, the slaughter of the innocent. Most didn't know where they were or why. The likeness of one emperor or another had to suffice — and did. There was no way out for them. Four Austrians, which means they could have been Slovenians or Slovaks, or Hungarians, Romanians, Ukrainians, Poles. A cosmopolitan spot. They lie with a view of Wisłoki valley, Dębi Wierch (Oak Peak), and the border gap. So I light a candle for them and set it beside one already burning. The trees are bare, but the sun shines, and it's so still and empty, as if nothing ever happened here. It's all in the earth: metal buttons, buckles, bones.

At Długi, the same thing, except that they lie in a completely open field. No trees or bushes, so the lamp must be shielded by a flap of your jacket until the flame takes. Again, infantry and Feldjägers. Forty-five subjects of the emperor and 207 Russians. But in Czarny they rest more peacefully: trees were planted over the graves, and now there's shade and quiet. Even in summer the light is dim. The crowns of beeches meet, and in the centre is such tranquillity, you could be in a cathedral. That's where they lie. Twenty-seven Austrians and 372 Russians. With the Russians it's the same as with the Austrians: half were Ukrainians, Poles, Kyrgyz, Finns, who knows what else — consult a map. No wind to speak of here, so I have no trouble lighting a candle and setting it on a stone pedestal with an inscription in German. Beneath it, the mortal remains of half of Europe and a piece of Asia. Strange to think of the Adriatic, palm trees, the campanile in Piran, mountaineer huts in Chornohora, the Finnish tundra, the steppes, Zaporoże, Crimean Tatars, the vineyards of Tokaj, Viennese decadence, Asiatic sands, the Prešov secession, Don Cossacks, the Transylvanian Gothic, yurts, camels, and all the rest of it lying here, a metre and a half under, tightly packed, mingled, seeping lower, joining sand, stone, clay, and the roots of the trees that for more than seventy years now have been feeding on the bodies of Estonians and Croats, in a corner of the world no one visits. So I light a candle, stand and watch, and say a prayer for the dead, because the important things take place only in the past. In these regions, the future doesn't exist until it is over.

The cold light of November falls on forest, road, and meadow, making everything too bright and hard, as if it must remain so for ages. They came far from home to die here, five hundred, seven hundred, a thousand kilometres. Manure of Europe. Without names or dates of birth. Complete oblivion, perfect community. I love to come here and walk on them. Beneath my feet I feel it all, the subterranean stream oozing, the rains washing minerals from bones, the water carrying them down into the valleys, to merge with rivulets and tributaries, and farther, finally to where the soldiers came from, because they were innocent at their death and do not need to wander like the damned. They enter their homes, the clocks begin to measure the minutes, and nothing has changed. Time has merely held its breath; it's 1914 again. Because they died once before, there will be no war, no sequence of events; the taut spring of history, rusting through, will snap.

Such was my reverie in November as I walked a metre and a half above their bodies. I picture their places of origin and am certain I visited some. The closed circle that this creates is a ceremony. Some of the fallen, like those in the Beskid Mountains, with a good rain can flow directly down the other side of the Carpathians, then, by the Kamenec, the Topl'a, the Latorica, the Ondava to the Bodrog, the Bodrog to the Tisa, and the Tisa to the Danube. They have a shorter route than those who must go by the Vistula and the sea. The Beskids are the Carpathian divide, and when it pours, the water justly parts in two, flowing north and south, taking the fallen with it. A hundred and sixty-eight Austrians and 135 Russians, all infantry. How much time does it take to flow to, say, Tiszalok, when you are a molecule, a speck of calcium or phosphorus?

Returning from the military cemeteries, I look through old Hungarian photographs to stir a little mourning, to feel a tie with the dead. I don't know why, but Hungarian photographs are the best at capturing the dead. In 1919, Rudolf Balogh took five pictures. A section of a wall, a gallows, five figures. The four men carrying out the sentence wear boots that gleam. The sun on them as on a mirror. The convicted man is calm. No despair or fear on his young face. Sorrow, perhaps, and gravity. The sleeves of his uniform are too long. The mast of the gallows is made of old timber. You can see the carpenter's marks on it. It could be a crossbeam from a ceiling, from a house torn down. The execution must have been painfully drawn out, because in the first photograph, in which the man stands alone by the mast and the three-step wooden footstool, he is accompanied by a shadow from the wall; in the next photograph, as they put the noose on him, he is completely in the sun. Yet no despair or fear. He has taken the three steps up, with still no change in his stance: his hands hang at his sides, his head slightly tilted. He'll be that way to the end. Only when two soldiers jerk the stool out from under his feet does his right arm lift. Then his body resumes its former peaceful position, and you can see that his sleeves are still too long. Whereas the executioners are in motion. As if they are eager to leave this place encircled by a wall, to escape in their polished boots. Their stride is soldierly, moustaches bristling, eyes lowered when it's over. Their shadows on the bare earth around the gallows make a complicated drawing.

The captions indicate no exact date or specific place. Only 1919, and in the narrow space above the wall is a leafy tree branch, so we're somewhere between April and October, it's the Hungarian Soviet Republic, and Béla Kun is writing his "To All!": "The workers no longer want to groan under the yoke of the big capitalists and landowners. Only socialism and communism can save the country from anarchy." In April the Romanians come from the east, the Czechs from the north. The Romanians take

Szolnok and then must take Abony, because there is no other way to Budapest. Kertész's violinist, younger by two years, definitely hears them. In the evenings they rest in villages and burn bonfires under the open sky. They drink and sing, of course, because the amusements of soldiers haven't changed for centuries. They are sad and raucous. Two years earlier, they came this way in Hungarian uniforms, to die in Ożenna; now they wear Romanian uniforms, to conquer Budapest on August 3. The ones from Transylvania, at least. By every indication they are attacking their own country, and so they drink more and sing louder to drown the clamour of their time and of their own hearts, because it must be hard to be a Hungarian Romanian and then suddenly a Romanian Romanian and despise what you died for two years before. In any event, the violinist hears them, and his ear automatically records their melodies, so who knows, Kertész may have heard them that Sunday morning under his window. Heard something from the Carpathians, or a *doina,* the Romanian blues of illiterate shepherds, or a *verbunk* known to every Hungarian recruit and therefore to the hanged man as well.

These are my thoughts, more or less, around All Souls' Day. Still no snow. In the leafless trees you can see abandoned bird nests: irregular black spheres made of twigs. The light knows no pity. The thin shadows resemble skeletons. The day ends at four in the afternoon. The sun sinks behind the mountain. The rest of the road to take is hidden from view. Curious: hidden where usually I picture noon, Konieczna and everything else that lies on the other side of the Carpathians. It's evening here, while there the world is just beginning to burn in golden red. Bardejov charred, Spiš smouldering, Rudohorie and Mátra, and the Great Hungarian Plain, and the little town of Mezőkövesd, which has a museum of agricultural machinery. I stopped there twice in my life, once to find an ATM, once to buy something to eat and drink. Wine and salami, no doubt, and something else, and that evening I slept in Bakoński Woods, and the next day or rather night I ended up in Ankaran, at a campsite by the Adriatic, trying to hammer tent pegs into stony ground after midnight, with no success, so I had to curl up in a limp tent. In the morning I saw that among the tall pines all the vacationers who had gathered here to stay for weeks had built a kind of village. There were large, many-person tents, trailers, umbrellas, canvas shelters, field kitchens, and open dining areas. Some people had marked off their place with twine or strips of plastic bags. Laminates, plywood, sheet metal, and polyester formed ad hoc homesteads, garden plots, the only thing missing was wandering cattle, swine on holiday, cows touring, rams and goats taking a break. The town had come here to play at being in the country, a psychoanalytic return to the past. Spa cachet, gold sandals, baggy trousers with palm trees and parrots, gag glasses, the smell of creams and lotions, suntanned tits and mostly bare asses all created a slightly off-kilter rusticity, complete with folksy looking into pots and gossiping at fences, people in close quarters carefully keeping their property separate. Badminton, football, sunburn, lathering backs, grilling, going for walks, activities to kill time and alleviate boredom and therefore very like activities in the true sticks. Ljubljana and Maribor relaxed, re-creating the life of their ancestors in a Microsoft version.

It's November, and I'm recalling thoughts and places from a year and a half ago. The past, locations — there is nothing else to describe. A perpetual All Souls' Day, with every fact an epitaph. We outlive events. That is all we have. From that campsite I drove to Trieste, but Trieste was not important and now lies elsewhere. So let me head south-east. Across the Balkans, down the shore, then through Cetinje and Podgorica to enter Albania at the border by the village of Hani Hotit and pass Shkodët, stopping only in Milot, since I had spent no more than an hour there once and remember practically nothing of it: low houses, a crowd in the street, horse harnesses, possibly a market day, old women in white harem pants sitting on benches in front of stone cottages — that's really all. Also: the front yard of a one-storey house, a few tables in the shade of trees, beaten earth, a place to drink raki and coffee. A thirty-year-old woman entered, big-breasted and dressed in bright red, a wide black sash round her waist. She was covered with gold jewellery; her sweeping hair was navy blue; she wore high heels and tight trousers and carried a glittering handbag. This was in Milot, among the horse harnesses and women in harem pants, where the Albanian north begins and the old times endure and "You may not enter someone's house without first calling from the fence" or "Bread and salt, a smile, a fire in the hearth, and bedding for guests at any time of day or night". The woman in red spoke to someone in a loud voice, gesticulating. This sleepy spot, grey from the heat and dust, seemed a flame that could ignite everything, and nothing would remain as it was.

Then the village Rreth-Baz, and at the home of Xhemal Cakoni I drank raki with curdled milk for the first time in my life. We sat barefoot at a low table. On the wall was a tapestry with a view of Mecca. We ate grapes. The women brought plates, returned to the kitchen, or stood in the doorway. We made a toast to success, to happiness, to health. Xhemal introduced his son with pride. A small guy, thin and shy. Worked in Germany. Just took off on his own. Xhemal reminisced with Illyet; they remembered the old days, when Illyet was a teacher in this region. He lived in an isolated house by the cemetery and feared vampires. I wondered about the lot of ghosts in the country of Enver Hoxha, who on April 29, 1967, proclaimed Albania to be the first atheist nation in the world. Almost as strange as the sight of Ceaușescu's grave, a year later, at the Ghencea Cemetery in Bucharest. The tombstone was more than a metre high and topped with a white cross. In the place where you would expect the head of Christ in a crown of thorns was a red, five-pointed star. Affected, I had to smoke. Around the grave, an iron fence. The paranoid shoemaker, even in death, was raving mad: the cross and the Commie star would light his way in the afterworld. Fear had eaten at him all his life, so in cowardly fashion he was armed with both, just in case. To weasel out of it somehow. No telling who would be dealing the cards on the other side. Most likely, however, he rotted altogether in his iron cage, rotted body and soul. There were stains of oil lamps there, wax from candles, so someone came to say a pitiful prayer for the dead. Secret emissaries from the English queen? She had, after all, driven him around London in her own carriage, had put him up for the night in Buckingham Palace. Who can fathom the people of the West, who can guess what they feel? In any case, I thought, a fitting punishment, for him to lie in an ordinary cemetery, not covered much, without marble, some two kilometres from the House of the People, that pyramid raised in shoemaker taste, its base measuring 250 by 250. To reach it, even by the most direct path, you'd have to walk a quarter of a kilometre across scorched and treeless pasture. Which I didn't do, observing it instead from a distance. I preferred to see his grave: more interesting.

At the entrance to the cemetery, we were stopped by a guard.

He was large, a swarthy Rambo in military dress, with dozens of pockets and a walkie-talkie. He asked if we had someone here close to us. Roland answered in Romanian: absolutely, family, relatives. So the government was afraid and kept watch, lest he scramble out on a moonlit night, cross the avenue, and dig up Elena. They lay separately, some twenty metres between them. She had it much worse. Only an iron fence and an iron cross covered with black anti-rust paint. In the centre, a patch of dry earth. Someone had planted something there, but it refused to grow. As if both husband and wife exuded a toxin that destroyed roots. All around, bushes, shrubs, ferns, saplings; here, nothing, as if the rhythm of vegetation had been interrupted by a defoliant. Their bodies did this, I thought. Deprived of voice, sight, motion, they sought to communicate through their decomposition, through corpse juices. Then I saw he had another stone, made of brown marble and standing beside the one with the red star. Much higher, topped with a cross, with a faience cemetery photograph that portrayed the shoemaker in a suit, white shirt, and tie. On the plinth was carved, "Olacrima pe mormitul tau din partea poporlui roman," which more or less means "The tear of the Romanian people on your grave". Nothing more, nothing less. Before this inscription, the Romanian people partied till they dropped and roared with laughter. Still another cross, the same kind as his wife's, black and iron. Someone had simply driven it into the ground next to the marble. The three made a dark parody of Golgotha. In a stone pot serving as an urn, a dried stalk. The base of the tombstone was covered with soot, smeared with yellow lamp oil, and there were burned-out lamps scattered on the ground—the melancholy of the makeshift, a cheap copy of eternal rest. Not far off, on a white slab stood a black dog watching, perhaps to make sure that the body would not dig itself out. As we left, the guard approached us and said, "I knew you had come to see him."

Today again the carters rode through. As yesterday and the day before, monotonously, slowly, in mist. Leaving horse shit on the white road. This time, only two of them. Heavy men, over forty. Both horses dun. At two thirty they come up from the valley. At three thirty it gets dark, and they're home. They unhitch the animals, lead them away, give them water and food. You hear straps hit the metal bucket. The horses shift from leg to leg, and the floorboards of the stable drum. It's humid and dark inside; it smells of manure and hay. The harnesses hang on rusty nails.

Several days ago I was in Mezőkövesd. There was rain and a sudden freeze. Ice coated everything. Sunday morning the Hungarians sold their wares in canvas stalls at the square. People skated, holding their bagged purchases. Ice covered the solemn holiday decorations. There was an ATM at King Matthias Street, the same King Matthias on the pale-blue thousand-forint banknote. I pulled out onto the highway. Three cars at the intersection like automotive phantoms in the haze and intensifying drizzle. I drove towards Miskolc. Everything gleamed: bare poplars, yellow grass, blue road signs. Jesus, how empty and plain the landscape. Nothing but a flat surface and once in a rare while a naked tree in the distance, like a comb. The air seemed to ring from this glassy ice. Near Emőd, junctions, roads to Debrecen and Nyífregyháza. Glistening grey Möbius strips got lost in the void of the Great Lowlands, and it was hard to believe that all those cities, towns, and villages were there, with their houses, smoking chimneys, and life. I think it was near Emőd, in the beginning of December, that infinity revealed itself to me for the first time. But only for a moment, as I thought of Esterházy and his *Transporters*. "They are coming! ... The transporters are coming! Their shouts rip the dawn — the distant, grey, threadbare dawn — the silence fragile and empty ... The reins flowed lightly, the tiny pieces of ice clinked under the rims of the wheels." I always wanted to write about *Transporters*. Twenty-five printed pages. The wet air, uncertain, parts, and it seems that they have stepped from a dream, a dream dreamt by one more powerful than we are, to appear on earth as messengers of temptation. Indistinguishable from their big animals, heated and sluggish, made completely of meat. "Their faces, almost all bearded, are broad, but they are not friendly, not at all! In the back of the cart you can hear their short, hoarse laughter. They understand one another, I see. They have powerful thighs; how tight their trousers must be." Indeed, I saw them near Emőd, on a bare plain, on a Sunday morning in December, in weather that evaded time. The world so slippery that even the air could not stick to it. They drove there at the same time of year, when the mud of the road finally hardens and autumn is done. The same trek for centuries. Salt transported from far away, and wine, let's say, from Eger to the south, to the other shore of the Tisa, to Timişoara, all as in a historical novel, action-packed, or a film, when over the flat horizon a horse-drawn cart appears, the music stops, and only the rattle of the axles, the clank of the wrought-iron rims, and the wheeze of the horses are heard. Those who cross the land always disturb its peace and incline it to evil, awakening fear mixed with need. After their passage, nothing is as it was. The horizon, cracked, will never heal.

Luckily the highway ended there, the road became crowded, and there was an end to philosophizing. A Hungarian maniac on the outskirts of Miskolc passed three cars at once with his

Zafir. With the air a little warmer, ice fell from trees. On the other side of the city, by an exit, I saw a herd of cars gathered around a supermarket, their roofs the cold backs of cattle grazing on concrete pasture. After Encs the road emptied again: no one was driving out of the country. I was in a bit of a hurry, but as usual Gönc tempted, and I detoured a few kilometres. In a sweet shop, an elderly man served at the counter. A woman with a small boy ordered a cappuccino to go in a Styrofoam cup. The two crossed Kossuth Street, to a bus stop, where a man waited with a silver tape recorder and two plastic shopping bags stuffed. He was short and smoked a cigarette, protecting it with his hand from large flakes of wet snow. Where were they going with the tape recorder and child, with the worn, much-used bags? They seemed poor, pitiful. A little family on the road two weeks before Christmas. Mother and son drank in silence, taking quick sips, as if they had no time, though the bus wasn't coming. The bus to Telkibánya, Pálháza, Sátoraljaújhely, across the Zemplén Mountains. The snow fell more heavily. Like people out of work, they didn't converse. Being out of work showed in their faces, in their gestures — I knew the signs, from home. Out of the main current of time, cast ashore, aside, left to their fate, a fate that no longer involved others. You wake one morning and the world is different, though nothing has changed. These were my thoughts in Gönc. But maybe they weren't out of work, maybe I invented that as a way not to leave with empty hands. The unemployed, like carters and transporters, are needed: a reason to go home.

This time I returned from Cres Island, sixty-eight kilometres long and with three thousand inhabitants. It takes twenty minutes by ferry from Brestova. Besides us there were only two trucks and an old Mercedes. Before we landed at Porozina, the driver of the Mercedes managed to down two brandies. From the deck, the island looked deserted. The ferry rumbled and stank of diesel. The bartender also appeared to have had one too many. Fifteen crossings a day, after all. The sky was overcast; the landscape took on weight. It all went together: the diesel ferry, the bartender, the inebriated driver, the dark, distinct water of the bay, the empty dock, the low sky, the sleepy movements of the crew, and the December light. A separate life. Cres, inland, was deserted indeed. The road went its length like a spine. White, treeless tract, stunted vegetation, wind. In one spot I saw a flock of sheep. They stood so still, it was hard to tell them from the rocks. They were the same colour as the rocks. No one tended them. On the map, Cres looks like an old bone. The winter strips it of everything, and gusts from the sea fill the tiniest cracks. It was that way in the village of Lubenice at the top of a three-hundred-metre cliff. I never saw a human dwelling more exposed. A few dozen houses of old stone and a few scrawny, unprotected fig trees. The wind had access from every direction: endless air in every direction. In some places you feel you cannot go on, only go back, because reality has said the final word there. These houses were grey, I thought, because of the wind; the wind had wiped the colour from the walls, colour could persist only within. If Cres was an island, Lubenice was twice one, separated from land by water and air both. A gulf yawned behind this bedroom wall. Outside this kitchen window, seabirds rode air currents. Such was life here. At the cemetery, half the dead were named Muskardin. The cemetery lay at the edge of a rocky shelf. Death must have been a curse for the gravediggers. A grave wasn't dug but chiselled out. Everything said purgatory. No one would come here without a compelling reason. People driven by a sentence or by a fear, and once here, they hadn't the strength to leave.

I drove off the asphalt and down a field. A road was marked on the map, but in reality it was more a dry riverbed or broken steps leading to infinity. I covered a few dozen kilometres in first gear. All around, white rubble, rubble stretching to the sky, breaking off, falling off on the other side. Great birds soared above, seeking a living thing. But for us, people, everything was dead, cold, swept clean by the wind. Someone had divided this open area with stone walls. The walls went to the horizon, cutting rectangles out of the emptiness. A paranoid-meticulous marking off of property, I thought, but later people told me that this labyrinth of barriers was designed to prevent erosion of soil from the rain. The way was so narrow sometimes that I had to fold my side mirrors. In the carefully walled-off square patches of space there were only stones, no earth. An occasional twig grew between boulders. I passed a house with a collapsed roof, then another in equal disrepair, then there were no houses. I imagined summer in this place: blazing white, the lizards baking. As far as the eye could see, nothing that might throw a shadow. Then, high among the rocks, Lubenice. I could have reached it by the narrow asphalt ribbon from the other direction, from the sea, from Valun, but that would have been too simple, telling little of the truth about Cres Island, its hollow interior, where birds circled in search of prey.

Sometimes I imagine a map composed only of the places I'd like to see once more. A not so serious map, having nothing important on it: wet snow in Gönc, Zborov and its ruined church, Caraorman with its desert sand and rusted machines that were supposed to uncover gold in the waters of the Danube, the heat in Erind, Spišská Belá and a grocery shop barely visible at dusk, dawn and the smell of cat piss in Piran, Răşinari at evening and the aroma from a gingerbread factory, pigs not far from Oradea, hogs in Mátészalka, Delatyn and its train station on a dreary morning, Duląbka, Rozpucie and Jabłonna Lacka, Huşi and Sokołów, and back again to Lubenice. I close my eyes and draw the roads, rails, distances, and scenes between the wastes, between one insignificance and the next, and I try putting together an atlas that will carry all this on its flat back, to make it a little more permanent, a little more immortal.

A few days ago I travelled to Kraków on the Košice express, taking the 10:11 from Stróże. Snow still lay on the fields. Greys and blacks emerging from beneath. And, God, the pathetic rubbish along the tracks, the wire fences, the strings of forgotten holiday lights burning in the dark blue of January, the naked trees in yards, piles of old lumber, scrap metal, broken bricks, all of it framed by linear geometry, a supernatural precision that suddenly bares the skeleton of the world. Bobowa, Ciężkowice, Tuchów, Pleśna — as if the tongue of frost has licked the human landscape to the bone, leaving only what is most important, what you can't do without, else nothingness takes over. Noon finally, but in some windows of homes near the track I saw the yellow glow of lightbulbs. The yards were obsessively neat. All cleaned and made pretty, like a body at a funeral. It was the snow, its thin layer outlining every object, that gave the form of the ideal to the poverty of the everyday. Noon finally, yet there was no one about. No reason for people to be about. The land was turning towards the abstract, so they preferred to stay indoors. I opened my window to smell the burning coal, thought of pans on hot stoves, skilful pokers stoking, moments when the fire escapes the iron grate, black smoke rises, and a red glow fills the kitchen.

How many such homes on the way? Hundreds, thousands, and the same details in grey, the same sad order set against the chaos of the world.

The train carriage was Slovak. Its seats were upholstered in red fake leather. Before I got on, it had passed Prešov, Sabinov, Lipany. Things were the same there. The houses stood a little closer together and were more alike, but everything else was similar: the crouching provisionality, the uncertain fate, life as improvisation. What had there been in Sabinov two or three years back, in early spring? A hip roof, Gothic dome, church spire, tower clock; beside the church, a yellow building in the Renaissance style, its facade covered with soot, grillwork in the windows, then the remnants of defending walls, puddles reflecting the smoky sky, and a few chickens looking for dry ground to scratch. I'm sure I landed there by accident. I was probably investigating new roads on the Spiš and Šariša border. Possibly I took a short cut off Road 18 with the old idea that someday I'd get to the other side of the landscape and see everything I saw now but greatly magnified, a kind of ultra landscape that in some miraculous way would unite all scraps and fragments, every Lipany and Sabinov, which would all find their places, they and their chickens, mud, coal-fired kitchens, smoke, tidy desperation of yards, expectation, and become twice, no, a thousand times as large and never, ever again fret over their random, stopgap existence.

In Piotrków, equidistant between the junction to Kielce and the junction to Radom, is a narrow-gauge railway. Unused for many years. Two reddish threads here and there covered by the sandy earth, then reappearing on the right side of the pavement. My *People's Atlas of Poland* says that this line was built in 1904 and still operating in 1971. It was Saturday, February, the sun was shining, and I couldn't tear my eyes from what was left of those Lilliputian train tracks. In Uszczyn there was even a little station still standing. The red-brick structure tried to suggest the Gothic but instead looked like a building-block house. Its naive ornamentation had a puppet quality. The whole area seemed childishly miniaturized. The houses on either side of the road were almost all facade. Especially in Uszczyn, Przygłów, and the area around Sulejów. On these facades with neither age nor style would be a cornice sometimes, a circular window, a pilaster, something put there not for function but simply out of the longing to be a little more, a little better than average. Behind these walls was nothing but the wind. The poultry had their coops, the dogs their doghouses, but every effort had gone into the awful facades, this last defence against the form, so like formlessness, of the world. So instead of going to see a twelfth-century Cistercian abbey, I was drawn to Sulejów garden plots full of blue puddles, to atrophied little squares, yards, and balconies where old furniture accumulated, credenzas eaten by the weather, the mortal remains of human employment. On a thin column, like Simon Stylites, sat a local angel. He looked like the homes he protected. Cut from the same cloth, he would stay with them until the end. The Mother of God by the church on the hill had at least a shelter over her, made of L-square rulers and Plexiglas. The angel had nothing, just heaven. A little farther on stood a trash receptacle. Thirty kilometres due south lay the village of Wygwizdów. I was supposed to go and stay there. The sky over the plain that day was cold and bright. On the way I was likely to encounter three or four broken-down cars.

Only one Wygwizdów in the nation, but I had to go on, to reach Solec before nightfall. That was the plan. I had never been in Solec. I had only seen a photograph once; it was of a movie theatre. The entrance overgrown with grass; in the poster marquee, tatters; a cloudy sky. In the background, an old wooden cottage. The theatre was called simply Cinema; that was the word over the entrance. A willow grew nearby. They had shown nothing for years. Inside, in the dark, chairs rotted. I tried to imagine the surroundings. There are photographs and places that give you no peace, though nothing much is there. The movie theatre in the photograph was from a time when direct names sufficed for things. The facade rose in a gentle arc to accommodate the simple letters. Solitude and desertion moved through the frame like a cold wind. That's why I drove there in the middle of February, patches of snow still on the fields. I had the strong feeling that somewhere between Sulejów, Wygwizdów, and Solec time had ground to a halt or simply evaporated or melted like a dream and no longer separated us from our childhood. Perhaps even no longer from the entire past. I left Road 777, turned right, and empty space began. The land lifted, like a plain gradually approaching the sky or like an oppressive dream in which you can neither reach your destination nor escape. I drove to Solec, through country that laughs at you, for one black-and-white photograph.

Solec was like Sokołów Podlaski thirty years ago, like Huşi eight months ago. It was yet another candidate for the capital of my part of the continent. I didn't want to stop, didn't want to get out, afraid that all this would disappear, so impermanent was it, so fragile and fundamentally fake. At the church on the hill everything ended, and I too turned back. Horses wandered free in this parish, their long manes matted by winter. I'll come here before I die, I thought, come here when I no longer want to live. No one here will notice that all my strength has left me. At night I'll sit in the movie theatre and watch the ghosts of films of former years. Death should bear some resemblance to life. It should be like a dream or movie. Reality in this part of the continent has assumed the aspect of the afterlife — no doubt so that people will fear death less and die with less regret.

I stood before the movie theatre. It was like the photograph: existing and not existing, neither dead nor alive. Matter in imitation of the beyond. Possibly the photograph had more life in it than this. Evening gathered, and I felt a chill in the air. In the theatre's dark interior, frost would cut the transparent images on old reels. Yes, there are places in which we are certain that something lies behind, something is concealed, but we are helpless, too stupid or too timid or perhaps not old enough to know how to cross to the other side. I stood like a post, freezing, and imagined the crooked doors opening and me entering, and beheld the narrow passage we all have been seeking, where Solec begins, Wygwizdów, Sulejów, Huşi, Lubenice, and the rails running from Stróże to Tarnov, the red train carriages from Košice, everything that is no more yet endures, indestructible and without end, even that Saturday a few years ago when we drove through Hornád valley, once more at the foot of the airborne Gypsy village, but this time the miracles take place on the ground, on the flat pasture between the ascending road and the river. There was a thaw, and all the kids had come out from the settlement. A great snow fort was falling under the merciless attack of its besiegers. Towers knocked over, walls breached, the defenders with nowhere to hide. But the scene held more than this concluding battle. On a meadow as large as a couple of football fields were enormous spheres of snow. The children rolled each ball till they could roll no longer, then began a new one. Some were a metre in diameter. Several dozen such balls, looking as if they had fallen from heaven. Beautiful and unreal. Among them, colourfully dressed children rolled tirelessly. There was nothing more animated in the neighbourhood, which lay in the shadow of a steel mill. I drove to the mill. Several dozen men were leaving just then. They walked with a heavy, numb step, as grey as smoke, as sad as all Krompachy and the twilight of the proletariat. Meanwhile the Gypsy children converted their energy into spheres of snow that in a day or two the sun would dwindle and turn to water to feed the Hornád River, which flowed in a complex maze of tributaries and catchments to the Black Sea, to which the government of Slovakia had no access.

Later, farther on, somewhere in a village near Sabinov, hogs were being butchered in a stockyard. On a black wire fence hung meat. In that dirty-white landscape of winter thaw, the meat glowed like fire. The house, the road, the sky, the people bustling, the whole village with vigilant mongrels pacing — as far as the eye could see, it lay in mist, was without colour; only from those pieces of meat did the light of cruelty shine. Through the glass of my car window I felt the heat of the red pieces. In the Slovak slumber and stillness and sad tranquillity of my part of the world, a slaughter was taking place. No one hid the shame of death. Dogs and children watched the quick knife move, the innards in bowls and buckets, the blood. All as it had been for a thousand years. Nothing changing. Then dusk.

A red light at the passage to Konieczna. I waited for several minutes. Someone moved in the dimness, walked to the counter where passports are stamped, pressed a button, the green light went on, the crossing gate lifted. Inside sat one of ours; the

Slovaks didn't care who was leaving their country. "Where are you coming from?" "When did you leave the country?" "What's your destination?" I watched as the passport was slipped into the scanner. "I'm going there. I left today," I answered. The customs window opened a little. "Purchases." "All in order." I saw no face, just the gesture to drive on. I had no sense that I was returning from somewhere. Right after the turn, in the village, the mist began.

Notes

OUR LEADER

For the title, the literal translation of *nasz bat'ko* is not "father leader" but "our father", a traditional way — in Ukrainian, in Russian — of identifying the master or leader: the patriarch of the manor, the owner of the serfs, the priest, the ruler of the region or nation. Our leader is our father, demanding obedience, fidelity, and love. This term has been and still is associated with czars and dictators — Stalin, for example, was called "little father" (*batiushka*) — so it points, at least for one in the modern West who knows a little Slavic history, to an old-fashioned, homey kind of fascism.

P.'s joke ". . . Shell, so we might be close" points to the sound similarity of *Shell* and *Szela;* the name in Polish is pronounced *shella.*

Quotations and facts about Jakub Szela are taken from Adam Bogusz, *Wieś Siedliska Bogusz* (Kraków, 1903).

ȚARA SECUILOR, SZÉKELYFÖLD, SZEKLERLAND

The motto in the church in Roşia is from a German hymn based on Revelation 2:10: "Be thou faithful unto death, and I will give thee a crown of life."

Siebenbürgen, "seven fortresses", is the German name for Transylvania.

THE COUNTRY IN WHICH THE WAR BEGAN

The quotation of Emil Cioran is from his *History and Utopia*. The quotation about devils and suicide is from Drago Jančar's *Mocking Desires*. These, and the one from Edvard Kocbek, are translated into English here not from their originals — from Romanian or Slovenian — but from the Polish edition of this book. (The Polish for Cioran was provided by Marek Bieńczyk; for Jančar, by Joanna Pomorska; for Kocbek, by Jerzy Snopek.)

SHQIPERIA

The 600,000 paranoid bunkers were built during the regime of Enver Hoxha, who ruled the country from 1944 to 1985.

The quotation on page 107 comes from Fatos Lubonja, *Piramidy z błota*.

MOLDOVA

The Georgian ruler is Stalin.

The Slaughter of Praga: in 1794, the Russian army under Suvorov captured Warsaw. Winning the battle, his troops, against orders, went on a rampage and killed 20,000 of the inhabitants of Praga, a district of the city.

Sheriff: a company that controls many businesses in Transnistria and is also involved in its politics. It has connections, political and personal, with President Igor Smirnov.

ON THE ROAD TO BABADAG

As a result of the Treaty of Trianon after World War I, the borders of Hungary were redrawn. Hungary lost ten cities and about a third of its inhabitants.

Jo napot means "hello".

Okęcie: the official checking passports is at the major Polish airport outside Warsaw.

"To sum up . . .": The quotation is from Mircea Eliade's "Romania: A Historical Sketch". A caution to the reader, for this quotation and for others in which the English is twice removed from the original language.

Eliade's Romanian was translated into Polish by Anna Kazmierczak, and from her Polish into this English. The stylistic-semantic drift inevitable in any literary translation is no doubt considerable here, having passed through two consecutive translators.

U lukomorya . . . is the opening of Pushkin's *Ruslan i Lyudmila*, a Russian classic, an epic poem in fairy-tale style.

The creator of *Hair* was Milos Forman. His Czech first name, Miloš, and the Polish poet-philosopher's last name, Miłosz, are close in sound.

"Dyzio the Dreamer" is a humorous poem for children by Julian Tuwim. Dyzio wishes the whole world were ice cream and cake.

"There was no shade . . .": A quotation from Miodrag Bulatović's "Red Rooster Flies Straight Up into the Sky". The Serbian original was translated into Polish by Maria Krukowska.

Bohdan Khmelnytsky was a Cossack leader; the seventeenth-century Khmelnytsky Uprising in Ukraine became emblematic in history of savage massacre (Poles and Jews were its victims). Jan Sobieski, a seventeenth-century king of Poland, was famous for a victory over the Ottoman Turks in the Battle of Vienna, which many believed saved Europe.

The Puszta: the Hungarian Plains, an emblem of Hungarian tradition and culture. The Hungarian word *puszta*, meaning "bare", "uninhabited", derives from the Slavic word for "empty" (e.g., in Polish, *pusty*).

"He stood on the edge. . .": the Kiš passage in Polish is Danuta Cirlic-Straszynska's translation from the Serbian.

"Wars were won . . ." and "Love is the key . . .": the Codreanu quotations come from the journal *Fronda* (6/1996), translated into Polish by Bogdan Koziel.

"They are coming!" and "Their faces, almost all bearded . . ." are from Peter Esterházy's *Transporters,* translated from the Hungarian into Polish by Elżbieta Sobolewska.